M000117093

EARTH TO TABLE BAKES

EARTH TO TABLE BAKES

Everyday Recipes for Baking
with Good Ingredients

Bettina Schormann and Erin Schiestel

PENGUIN

an imprint of Penguin Canada, a division of Penguin Random House Canada Limited

Canada • USA • UK • Ireland • Australia • New Zealand • India • South Africa • China

First published 2021

Copyright © 2021 by Bettina Schormann and Erin Schiestel

All rights reserved. Without limiting the rights under copyright reserved above, no part of this publication may be reproduced, stored in or introduced into a retrieval system, or transmitted in any form or by any means (electronic, mechanical, photocopying, recording or otherwise), without the prior written permission of both the copyright owner and the above publisher of this book.

www.penguinrandomhouse.ca

LIBRARY AND ARCHIVES CANADA CATALOGUING IN PUBLICATION

Title: Earth to table bakes : everyday recipes for baking with good ingredients / Bettina Schormann and Erin Schiestel.
Names: Schormann, Bettina, author. | Schiestel, Erin, author.
Identifiers: Canadiana (print) 20200406590 | Canadiana (ebook) 20200406604 |
ISBN 9780735239241 (hardcover) | ISBN 9780735239258 (EPUB)
Subjects: LCSH: Baking. | LCGFT: Cookbooks.
Classification: LCC TX765 .S38 2021 | DDC 641.81/5—dc23

COVER AND BOOK DESIGN BY LISA JAGER
COVER AND INTERIOR PHOTOGRAPHY BY MAYA VISNYEI PHOTOGRAPHY
FOOD STYLING BY CLAIRE STUBBS
PROP STYLING BY CATHERINE DOHERTY

Printed and bound in China

10 9 8 7 6 5 4 3 2 1

Penguin
Random House
PENGUIN CANADA

To our moms and dads,
Dieter and Carolyn Schormann and
Peter and Mary Ellen Schiestel: we are
both strong women with a fierce work
ethic because of you. Thank you.

CONTENTS

Four Recipes for Each Season

JEFF CRUMP

BEFORE I MET BETTINA OR EVEN moved to Hamilton, Ontario, I was living in Berkeley, California, working at Chez Panisse, and learning from the world-famous Alice Waters. Waters is the founder of the Slow Food movement, and she is legitimately an inspiration. Her vision and execution are flawless, and in the time I spent at Chez Panisse I adopted many of her values. The ideals of the Slow Food movement are very common sense. Their aim is to engage the general public to care more about the food they eat and to consider where it comes from. Although the ideas of "slow food" and "eating local" had been taken up by a handful of chefs in Canada at the time, they had not yet piqued the interest of the general public, so I was inspired to bring Waters's ideas and her Slow Food values back to Ontario with me.

I met Bettina in 2001 on my very first day as the new chef of the Ancaster Mill in Ancaster, Ontario. I was a young, hotshot chef, full of ideas and energy, and I had decided that Ancaster was going to be my home—a place to plant roots and develop a career I could be proud of. I was going to need a strong team at the Mill, but I had no idea who would be on that team. The Hamilton-area restaurant world was new to me, and I had no idea if there would be any talent to work with or if anyone would even care about how I wanted to change the food scene.

Then I ran into Bettina—literally. She was working in a very tiny pastry area with two other women. Everyone was working with their heads down, but I insisted on handing Bettina my card. She kind of brushed me off, bringing some of my worries to the surface when she said, "Thanks. I have a hundred and fifty cheesecakes to make. Can we talk later?" We did not hit it off.

When Bettina finally sat down to talk with me, I discovered that she had her own ideas. They were similar to mine but not exactly the same. She was a cook who could really hold her own in the kitchen. I knew she could and would do the work that needed to be done at the Ancaster Mill, but she was never going to say "yes, chef" or jump to attention when I entered the kitchen. She had her own opinions about what was best. It was hard to tell if we would be able to work together, or if she was always going to work to her own beat. I was concerned.

Then, the conversation took a turn. Bettina started to ask more about Slow Food. She seemed to be interested in the academic aspects of Slow Food, and we talked about Slow Food's University of Gastronomic Sciences in Bra, Italy. It turned out she was interested in food security and the idea of eating local, despite not having heard much about these topics before. I had captured her attention. As she told me more about her first few years spent working in commercial kitchens where the environments were quite toxic, I felt lucky in that moment to be able to offer her something different: an approach to food that would satisfy her intellectual interests and also be focused on locality and flavour. She was in.

In the years that followed, Bettina's entire approach to food changed, and I am proud to say that I influenced that change. She continued to head up an extremely productive pastry team, making bread, à la carte desserts, and an impressive Sunday brunch spread of pies and cakes. People simply could not resist them! She began to find ways to incorporate more fresh and local ingredients into her baking and intuitively adjusted her approach with the shifting seasons.

Over our many years together, Bettina has shown me how to work smarter and helped me to develop a dream team in our kitchen. We have forged a strong connection based on similar values: mutual respect and work ethic. As a team, Bettina and I have been working together for more than eighteen years, and I believe we will continue to do so for the rest of our lives.

In contrast to Bettina, Erin entered our lives in 2004, quiet as a mouse—and seemingly out of nowhere. At the time, she was a sixteen-year-old high school co-op student working in the salad section of our kitchen. Even though she was a star when it came to making appetizers and shared plates, she always had an eye on the pastry section.

I like to think that Bettina became the best pastry chef in the country with me at the Ancaster Mill. Erin, I know for sure, arrived as a legit prodigy. Within months of working together, Bettina and Erin were making puff pastry daily from scratch, baking pristine loaves of bread in a tired old convection oven, churning fresh butter for the dining room, and pumping out a thousand individual apple tarts each week. Their knowledge and skill blew past anything I could have shown them so quickly, and before long I found myself heading to the pastry section of the kitchen just to eat and talk about music. When the pros are that good, you just get out of their way!

Today we all work closely to iron out all of the little details at our Earth to Table Restaurants. I count myself lucky to be part of a team that has Bettina and Erin in its ranks, and we are all lucky that they decided to focus their efforts to produce this gorgeous cookbook. Every time you pull a perfectly moist loaf out of the oven, cut a flavourful slice of pie, or enjoy a crunchy cookie with your tea, you have Bettina and Erin to thank for the many hours they've spent together perfecting these recipes—and for all of the passion they've put into them. My wish is that *Earth to Table Bakes* will end up in many professional kitchens and homes across the country: stained, dog-eared, and full of bookmarks and notes. Their recipes are already well-loved additions to my collection, and I'm so glad that you can now add them to yours as well.

Jeff Crump
Co-founder, Earth to Table: Bread Bar

INTRODUCTION BY

BETTINA SCHORMANN

ERIN AND I ARE PASSIONATE BAKERS. We both started out as line cooks, but once we got a taste of baking, we were hooked. We both love the rules, science, and structure of the baking world.

Our history is long—a lovely story that started sixteen years ago, in 2004. I had been the pastry chef at the Ancaster Mill in Ancaster, Ontario, for about four years before Erin came into my life. I didn't know it at the time, but she was the best thing that would ever happen to me.

When Erin joined the Ancaster Mill, she spent two years in the kitchen working as Garde Manger. In the hierarchy of a kitchen brigade, the Garde Manger is responsible for the preparation and execution of cold food like appetizers and hors d'oeuvres. As the Executive Pastry Chef at that time, I was aware of Erin's fierce work ethic and attention to detail but had no idea she wanted to make the switch to pastry. In fact, we passed over her twice in favour of other cooks who thought they wanted to be pastry chefs but quickly realized it was not for them once they actually rolled up their sleeves and got to work.

Two years into her time with us, Erin finally spoke up. I was more than happy to have her join the pastry team. I knew she was a hard worker, and despite not having a lot of pastry knowledge, she very quickly became my equal—if not better than me.

The six pastry chefs in our kitchen were responsible for bread service, dining room desserts, special event desserts, wedding desserts, wedding cakes, and the special little treats that customers would receive at the end of their meals known as *petits fours*. We worked in a tight 4- × 3-metre space and always had to navigate around each other. "Behind!" is a common commercial kitchen call that constantly rang through our tight space. Despite being first in and last to leave, we loved our jobs so much and there wasn't a lot of complaining. We would work with our music on and dance and sing as much as we could between production and execution. When you spend that much time with someone, you inevitably form a bond. Erin might not know it, but I consider her my best friend.

It was during these years that Erin and I started developing recipes that would end up in this book. The Frangipane Apple Tart (page 204) and the Classic Bread Bar Cheesecake with Rhubarb Compote (page 233) were staple special event desserts for us, and we would often

pump out hundreds of individual servings every week. The Citrus Currant Scones (page 73) were very popular for Sunday brunch, so by Saturday we'd have raw scones stockpiled in the freezer so that they could be freshly baked for our devoted brunch crowd. Even though we were a high-production kitchen, we were very fortunate to have embraced a seasonally changing menu as part of the restaurant's Slow Food philosophy. This meant we always had an excuse to feed our creative appetites: our Classic Bread Bar Cheesecake with Rhubarb Compote (page 233) became a Ricotta Cheesecake with Shortbread Crust and Stewed Strawberries (page 243) in the summer, and then an Acorn Squash Cheesecake with Almond Sablé Cookie Crust and Candied Pecans (page 255) in the fall. There was always a new flavour combination to look forward to.

In 2006, I won Pastry Chef of the Year for Ontario and was offered the opportunity to study in France. Walking the streets of Paris is a culinary school of its own. Shop after shop offered the most scrumptious-looking pastries. The dark crusted croissants and crusty baguettes were perfect. Not to mention all the charcuterie that lined the streets. While I was studying there, I learned many classic French techniques that I have been able to develop and modify for this book, including the ones used in the croissant recipes (pages 225, 236, 247, 259, 275) and the recipe for Blitz Puff Pastry (page 272), which is used as the base for many of our tarts. While I was eating at the best bakeries in the world, I was developing a palate for the kind of food I wanted to produce with Erin.

Shortly after I returned from France, I spent two weeks in New York City working in some of the best restaurants there. On the first day, I was at Jean-Georges with James Beard Award winner Johnny Iuzzini, followed by two days at Per Se, owned by the famous Thomas Keller. I then spent the remaining time at Craft, the James Beard Award–winning restaurant owned by Chef Tom Colicchio. It was there that I had the pleasure of working with Pastry Chef Karen DeMasco. Karen herself is a James Beard Award winner, and I was able to pick her brain for a full week. Her work ethic and hands-on approach were inspirational and have definitely influenced the way I work. She taught me the benefits of making as much as possible from scratch, and not cutting corners just because it's easier. These lessons furthered my attention to detail and took our kitchen to the next level. In this book, the Blueberry Apple Streusel Muffins (page 85) are a version of Karen's recipe for Apple Cider Muffins, which she shared with me fourteen years ago. We still make these muffins every day at the restaurant because they are just that good!

In the blink of an eye, Erin and I had been working together at the Ancaster Mill for eight years. I loved my job, but one day I woke up and realized that there was a chance I might miss out on some of the finer things in life, such as getting married and having kids, if I continued to work the way I had been. I switched to part-time hours and started selling my baking at farmers markets instead. My setup was really simple—I would make only the coveted muffins, fresh fruit pies, and bread. It was while working at the farmers market that I cracked the code on the perfect Sweet Pie Dough (page 270) and developed my favourite Crumble Topping (page 284), which I would use on pies and all kinds of other desserts. I also realized how much people appreciate seasonal baking and how satisfying it was to be an entrepreneur.

The market stall was very successful, and I was thinking it might be time to start selling my goodies out of a brick-and-mortar business. At the same time, Jeff Crump, who was then Executive Chef at the Ancaster Mill, was also thinking that he wanted to open his own place—one where he could sell pizza and burgers. It took a third party to inform us that bread and pizza are actually the same thing and require the same equipment for production, and once we'd had our "aha" moment, Jeff and I took our newfound insight to Aaron, the owner of the Ancaster Mill, who quickly agreed to collaborate on a new restaurant. Jeff would be the Chef, I would be the Baker/Pastry Chef, and Aaron would offer his business expertise. Together, the three of us opened Earth to Table: Bread Bar in Hamilton, Ontario, on August 17, 2010.

Not long after we were up and running, I was surprised and blessed by a pregnancy. This is when Erin came back into my life. She seamlessly stepped into the Head Baker/Pastry Chef position at Bread Bar. Erin continued to work as Head Baker when I returned to work as a manger—a position that offered more flexibility. Eventually, she went on to head up production at our second location in Guelph, Ontario, in February 2015. Since writing this book, we've opened a third location, also in Hamilton. Erin is the Executive Baker/Pastry Chef for all three and is succeeding in so many ways.

The moment I realized what I was getting into when I decided to write this book, I understood that I could not do it by myself. I also understood that Erin had become a world-class pastry chef, so I asked her to join me in this adventure of writing *Earth to Table Bakes*. True to her nature, her contributions have been both wonderful and delicious. This book really is the accumulation of the many years that Erin and I have been working together and learning from each other. Erin has included some of the best doughnut, cake, and croissant recipes she's developed over the years, and I've written up my favourite recipes for cookies, tarts, and savoury treats. Together, we filled in the rest of the gaps. Erin and I have always been a team that works flawlessly together, and we hope you'll enjoy the fruits of our special relationship that emerge in the pages of this book. Our biggest hope is that these recipes create magical moments and memories in your kitchen, just as they have for us over the years.

HOW TO USE THIS BOOK

IN *EARTH TO TABLE BAKES*, WE bring our philosophy of using locally sourced, high-quality ingredients to some of our favourite sweet and savoury baking recipes. Six chapters that range from Cookies to Bars and Squares to Scones, Muffins, and Biscuits to Loaves and Cakes to Doughnuts, Puffs, and Other Yeasted Goods (including meringues!) to Pies and Tarts (both sweet and savoury!) will satisfy all of your everyday baking needs.

The section that follows those chapters, Four Recipes for Each Season, is subdivided into Spring, Summer, Fall, and Winter and offers a quartet of recipes that highlight the bounty each season has to offer. We've included recipes for a seasonal croissant, quiche, pudding, and cheesecake in each one. While we encourage you to use fresh and local ingredients as much as possible throughout the book, the recipes in these sections feature seasonal ingredients and flavours as the star. This was our way of incorporating the Earth to Table philosophy while still offering many other delightful recipes for you to enjoy.

The final section of the book, Staples, includes the component recipes you will see used over and over again in this book. They are often so delicious and versatile that they are used in a variety of ways in many different main recipes.

Alongside many of our recipes, you will find that we've added a Kitchen Tip or two. This is where we offer kitchen hacks, ideas for substitutions, notes on ingredients, and other tricks that will help to ensure success with a particular recipe. They can be used alongside the section that follows, Baking Like a Pro, which provides more general tips and techniques for getting the most out of your baking, as well as the Ingredients and Tools and Equipment sections, which will guide you toward setting yourself up for success and help to ensure you get the perfect bake every time you turn on the oven.

In this book, we do not use—and do not recommend that you use—gluten-free flours. Leaving gluten-free flours out of our recipes is a decision we made at Bread Bar after much taste-testing and experimentation, and one that is not always popular. Here, we stick to that decision because these recipes simply will not turn out the way they should if you make substitutions. Having said that, you will find a few gluten-free recipes in this book because they are gluten-free by design. Two examples are Coconut Lover Fantasy Squares (page 51) and Flourless Chocolate Nemesis Cake (page 121), which are made with gluten-free flour, or no flour at all. Both are delicious, which is not always the case in our experience with gluten-free baking. If a recipe in this book is gluten-free, we will let you know.

BAKING LIKE A PRO

COMPARED TO BAKING IN A COMMERCIAL kitchen, baking at home can be tricky. In a commercial kitchen, all of the ingredients and tools are readily available: large bins of flour and sugar, flats of eggs, cases of butter, baking sheets, cake pans—you name it. And there are always multiple mixers at the ready. Sometimes you even get a personal dishwasher! It's complete luxury. Baking at home is very different. You need to wash your own dishes, make sure you have all of the ingredients before you start baking, and see if you even have the right pan to use. When we bake at home, we face these challenges too, but over the years we've found that there are some tips and techniques you can use regardless of where you're baking.

TIPS FOR BAKING SUCCESS

Read the whole recipe. As you prepare to make a recipe, create a pantry list of what you already have. Make sure you have enough on hand to complete the recipe and that the ingredients are the best ones on offer. If you settle for "this will do" or "close enough," we can almost guarantee that you will not be satisfied with the end result. The same is true for tools and equipment: if you don't have what you need and proceed with a recipe anyway, you might have a bad baking experience and be less likely to try that recipe again.

Good ingredients matter. Buy the best quality chocolate or the freshest produce you can find. That doesn't always mean buying the most expensive stuff. Many of the best ingredients are local ones, which travel a shorter distance from producer to consumer and are often less expensive as a result. Any effort you put in to sourcing high-quality ingredients will only add to the mouthwatering textures and flavours of whatever you're baking.

Use a timer! But only as a reminder that you have something in the oven or on the stove. Every oven is a little different, so ultimately you want to use visual cues and touch or movement tests to confirm doneness. However, if you forget that you were baking altogether, your cake or tart or scone will be ruined before you even get the chance to consider whether it's ready.

Consider investing in a quality oven thermometer. Ovens can vary in temperature, and the actual temperature inside the oven compared to the readout may be way off. Placing an oven thermometer directly in the oven will help you determine the actual temperature of your oven so you can be sure you're giving your baked goods the precise heat they need for a successful bake.

You don't always need to sift. Don't feel that you must sift the dry ingredients used in a recipe unless you're specifically instructed to do so. We stopped sifting years ago—in fact, outside of cooking school, I'm not sure we ever sifted. If you need to add air to a batter, it's much easier to add it by creaming the fat (butter, shortening, or vegetable oil) with the sugar than by sifting the flour. It's true that cocoa powder, cake flour, and icing sugar can get particularly clumpy, but you can break them up by simply whisking them in a bowl while they're still dry.

ESSENTIAL BAKING TECHNIQUES

Laminating dough This is a technique used to make flaky pastries such as croissants, Danishes, and puff pastry. These doughs are made up of many layers of fat sandwiched between layers of dough, which puffs up as a result of yeast added to the dough in yeasted laminated products (such as croissants, pages 225, 236, 247, 259, 275) or simply the steam created by the butter layers heating up during baking (as in Blitz Puff Pastry, page 272). Yeasted or not, the layering and folding of dough and butter is a delicate process and needs to be done with care to ensure a puffy, flaky final product. Laminating dough can be intimidating for a home baker, but with planning, patience, and practice this technique can be mastered by anyone! Creating beautiful, golden brown croissants or a flaky, buttery tart crust is incredibly rewarding, and we encourage you to try it. For step-by-step instructions and photos, see the recipe for Plain Croissants (page 275).

Crumb coating Adding a thin layer of frosting to the exterior of your cakes before adding a thicker, final coat of frosting creates a crumb coat. Chilling the crumb coat thoroughly before continuing with the final coat will ensure that any stray crumbs stay trapped and prevent them from appearing on the surface of the final coat of frosting, which will give your cake a clean, professional look. Chocolate crumbs in that beautiful white buttercream? No, thank you! If you're making a layer cake, adding a crumb coat will also help to fill any gaps between the cake layers, providing a solid surface on which to smooth the final coat of icing.

TIPS FOR CRUMB COATING SUCCESS

• Once you've filled a cake, place it in the fridge for at least 15 to 20 minutes to chill, or until it's firm, before adding the crumb coat. This will ensure that the layers don't wobble around while you're working. A stable, solid cake is much easier to frost.

- Separate a small amount of buttercream from the batch and use it to crumb coat the cake. This will prevent you from introducing crumbs into the frosting you'll use for the final, perfect coat. You can add more to the bowl as needed.
- The crumb coat does not have to be entirely smooth, but do make sure to fill any gaps between the cake layers before moving on to the final coat.
- The crumb coat needs to set before you move on to the final coat. Transfer the cake to the refrigerator to chill for 15 to 20 minutes, or until it's firm to the touch.

Tempering Tempering refers to slowly adding a hot liquid to an egg mixture—for example, when making custards like the one for Coconut Dream Pie (page 187). Whisking an egg mixture while very slowly ladling in a hot liquid will gently bring up the temperature of the eggs to the same temperature as the hot liquid, ensuring that they don't scramble. If that happens, there's nothing to do but start over.

Creating a double boiler Cooking delicate ingredients like chocolate or eggs in a double boiler allows you to cook them in a gentle way. You may also hear it referred to as a *bain-marie* in professional kitchens. You can purchase a double boiler, but there's no need to because you can easily make one at home.

To make a double boiler, place a medium heatproof bowl (stainless steel or glass) over a medium saucepan of simmering water, making sure that the bottom of the bowl does not come into direct contact with the water beneath it. Unlike direct heat, which could scorch or ruin your recipe, the steam from the boiling water will warm the heatproof bowl and bring up the temperature of the ingredients slowly.

Blind baking For the pie recipes in this book, it's common to bake the pie shell for a period of time on its own, without any filling. This is called blind baking. To blind bake a pie shell, crumple a piece of parchment paper into a ball. Spread it back out and lay it into the bottom and up the sides of the unbaked pie dough. Fill it with dried beans, chickpeas, or rice. Placing some weight on the dough will keep the empty shell from puffing up while it bakes. Ceramic pie weights made specifically for this purpose are available, but they can be quite pricey. Dried beans or rice work just as well, and you can use the same beans to blind bake pie shells in the future, too. Simply store them in an airtight container at room temperature until next time. Once you've finished blind baking the pie crust, you can remove the weights and parchment paper and continue with the recipe.

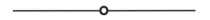

INGREDIENTS

WE HAVE A PASSION FOR GOOD INGREDIENTS—and not just when it comes to fruits and vegetables. Anything that's prepared locally and is fresh is going to make whatever you're baking taste even better, so why not put a little extra time and energy into sourcing some locally made butter or hunting down some dark chocolate made with simple, high-quality ingredients? Read on for our suggestions on stocking your fridge and pantry with the best quality staples for all your baking adventures.

BUTTER

Butter and baking go together like bacon and eggs or wine and cheese. In most cases, you can't have one without the other. When it comes to baking, there is nothing like the flavour and texture of butter, which makes it nearly impossible to swap it out for other fats in most recipes. You know the tender, melt-in-your-mouth feeling you get when you bite into some of your favourite baked goods? That's because of butter: its melting point is just below body temperature, which means it begins to melt as soon as you put it in your mouth. Butter also prevents tough gluten strands from developing, which results in tender baked goods.

Salted butter really does not have a place in baking. Being able to control each ingredient in a recipe and knowing exactly how each ingredient reacts with the others is key to baking success. Each brand of salted butter has a different level of saltiness, and baked goods cannot be seasoned after they've been cooked. Adding salt separately will ensure that the flavour of your baked goods is not compromised. Always use unsalted butter with the recipes in this book.

SALT

You may know from your own cooking or baking that salt = flavour. However, salt is not necessarily added to recipes to make them taste salty. In fact, salt can be used to balance sweetness, amp up chocolate and coffee flavours, and even extend the shelf life of baked goods. Salt is also a factor in controlling the fermentation of yeast because it pulls moisture from other ingredients, thus slowing the fermentation process and ensuring even baking. Texturally, it strengthens the gluten structure, allowing salted baked goods to rise evenly in the oven without puffing up too quickly and then deflating.

In all of our recipes, we call for kosher salt. More specifically, we recommend Diamond Crystal kosher salt, which is readily available at most grocery stores. It has a cleaner taste than table salt because it does not contain non-caking additives or iodine. Iodized table salt has tinier, compact crystals that are heavier than Diamond Crystal kosher salt's larger, flakier crystals. This means there is more salt flavour in 1 teaspoon (5 mL) of table salt, for example, than in 1 teaspoon (5 mL) of Diamond Crystal kosher salt, which has flakes that are wider and pyramid-shaped instead of rounder and more dense as in some other kosher salts.

VANILLA AND OTHER EXTRACTS

Pure vanilla extract lends a subtle, sweet flavour to baked goods and can act as the star of the show in recipes for cakes, sugar cookies, and buttercream. It can also play a supporting role in the development of other flavours, such as chocolate, coffee, and fruit flavours. Vanilla substitutions just do not cut it. When you're at the grocery store, look for "pure vanilla extract." Artificial or imitation vanilla extract is concocted in a lab, and its flavour is very obviously inferior to the real stuff. Pure vanilla extract costs much more than imitation because of the time-consuming and labour-intensive growth and harvest of the crop (vanilla pods are harvested from climbing orchids!), but you won't regret using it.

There are about a hundred and fifty varieties of vanilla, but the most common are Madagascar bourbon and Tahitian. Pure vanilla comes in a few different forms, such as extract, vanilla beans with their seeds inside, vanilla paste, and vanilla powder. No matter the form, it will work well in your baked goods as long as it's pure. In this book, when we refer to "pure vanilla extract," we are always referring to Madagascar bourbon vanilla.

As for other extracts, such as almond or peppermint, we suggest using pure as well. There is almost no point in using imitation extracts, as they will impart an undesirable chemical flavour to your baked goods. We do not use extracts as an anchor to flavour recipes, but when used appropriately they can create important depth of flavour.

FLOUR

The recipes in this book call for different types of flours. Bread flour, all-purpose flour, cake flour, and whole wheat flour all serve a specific purpose and cannot be substituted. These flours have different protein contents, which translates to the level of gluten development they stimulate; the more protein in the flour, the more gluten will develop in the resulting dough. More gluten development gives rise to dough with more structure and stability, while less gluten development gives rise to dough that is tender and soft, without the addition of fat.

Cake flour has the lowest protein content and gives rise to the soft, tender crumb you want in baked goods like doughnuts (page 141). Bread flour, also known as hard flour, is high in protein. It creates the strong, elastic dough needed for croissants (pages 225, 236, 247, 259, 275) or baking bread. All-purpose flour is the most common flour, hence the name. It falls in the middle of the protein spectrum and works for most recipes.

Whereas bread, all-purpose, and cake flours come from grinding just a portion of the wheat grain, whole wheat flour is made from grinding the entire grain, also called a wheat berry. As a result, baked goods made using whole wheat flour have a bold, wholesome, and nutty flavour and texture that is rich in fibre and nutrients. Whole wheat flour usually is not the sole flour called for in a recipe and is most often used in combination with all-purpose or other flours, such as bread flour or cake flour, because the gluten content in whole wheat flour is much lower, resulting in less structure in baked goods.

CHOCOLATE

Being chocolate lovers, we are attracted to chocolatey desserts. Using high-quality ingredients matters, and chocolate is no exception. Premium chocolate can take a simple recipe for chocolate chip cookies to an entirely new level. By premium, we mean chocolate that has as few ingredients on its label as possible. There are no regulations for use of the word "premium" when it comes to chocolate, so do not let trigger words like "craft" or "small batch" on the packaging, or the store it is sold in, fool you. Your best bet is to read the list of ingredients. Chocolates labelled with cocoa beans, cocoa butter, sugar, and possibly milk are the best picks. Lower quality chocolate may have upwards of ten ingredients listed, including many preservatives, stabilizers, and artificial flavours.

Premium chocolate comes in many forms that lend themselves to different uses. Bars, blocks, wafers or callets, and chips are the most common. We use bars and callets most often in this book. Chocolate bars are great to keep on hand because you can easily chop them into whatever size you need, and they are great for melting or folding into cookie dough. Wafers or callets are small, disc-shaped chocolate pieces that do not contain stabilizers. They are perfect for making ganaches and glazes or in any recipe where chocolate needs to be melted. Chips are also small chocolate pieces that contain stabilizers in the form of fat so that they keep their shape when baked. Chocolate that contains stabilizers should not be used for melting since these stabilizers are intended to keep chips in chip-shape even when warm. Stirring chips together when melting often causes the chocolate to seize and become gritty and undesirable.

COCOA POWDER

There are two options when buying cocoa powder: natural and Dutch process. All of our recipes call for Dutch process cocoa powder. Natural cocoa powder is made from roasted cocoa beans, plain and simple. It is acidic and bitter with intense chocolate flavour. Dutch process cocoa powder, also known as alkalized cocoa powder, is treated to neutralize acidity. Because it is neutral, it does not react with baking soda and therefore is often paired with baking powder in recipes. It also has a deep, rich chocolate colour and a flavour that we like. Cocoa powder's floury texture works best in brownies, cakes, and doughnuts and can be used in buttercream. You can also use it in place of flour to coat the inside of baking and cake pans.

MILK AND ALTERNATIVES

Cow's milk contributes to the flavour, texture, and golden brown crust colour of baked goods because of its fat and sugar (lactose) content. We bake with whole (3.25%) cow's milk because of its higher fat content, which contributes to a richer mouthfeel in baked goods. It also activates gluten, dissolves sugars, and hydrates proteins and leavening agents. The milk in a rich brioche dough, for example, weakens gluten bonds, creating a tender bread compared to the leaner, chewier bread you would get without adding milk. Being a perishable product, properly stored fresh milk is important to the quality of baked goods, so make sure you keep it cold in an airtight container and also keep an eye on the best-before date!

Buttermilk is the secret ingredient in a lot of the recipes in this book. It adds an unmistakable flavour and texture to cakes and doughnuts. Buttermilk is made by converting the lactose in milk to lactic acid, giving rise to a tangy flavour. Buttermilk is not directly interchangeable with cow's milk in a recipe because of its acidity. You can make your own buttermilk by adding a little acid to cow's milk. The standard recipe for homemade buttermilk is to mix 1 cup (250 mL) of either whole (3.25%) or 2% milk with 1 tablespoon (15 mL) fresh lemon juice or white vinegar.

Heavy (35%) cream is used for its high fat content to create tender doughs. For example, cream used in scones (pages 74, 77) contributes to a super tender, cakey crumb.

Milk alternatives such as soy, almond, and oat milk are called for in some recipes, but not in this book. If you want to achieve good results, these milk alternatives are not interchangeable where a recipe calls for cow's milk. Milk alternatives contain many additives for shelf life, flavour, and texture, and these factors often work against the chemistry of baked goods. Canned coconut milk is the only milk alternative that makes an appearance in our recipes. Please be mindful that canned coconut milk is different from coconut beverage, which has many additives that will not contribute to the success of your baked goods.

MOLASSES

Molasses is a viscous byproduct of the sugar refining process. It is liquid at room temperature and is hydroscopic, meaning it pulls moisture from other ingredients and the air. Baked goods made with molasses will have a chewy, tender crumb.

In our recipes, we use fancy molasses. Molasses is made from boiling either sugar cane or sugar beet juice down to a syrup and removing the sugar crystals. The sugar crystals can be separated at different points in the refining process, resulting in different grades of molasses. Crystals removed early will result in sweeter molasses (fancy molasses), and crystals removed in the last stage will yield a more bitter and darker product (blackstrap molasses). Blackstrap molasses should be used only in recipes that strictly call for it. Buy unsulphured fancy molasses if you can—it tastes better because sulphur dioxide has not been added as a preservative.

EGGS

We encourage you to eat locally and seasonally as much as possible, so you might think that purchasing eggs from a local farm for your baked goods would be a good idea. Unfortunately, local eggs are usually not graded, meaning they are not given a size. In baking, the general rule is to use large eggs. We stick to this rule and specify large eggs for each recipe, just to make sure you don't forget! It's that important. Eggs are graded as peewee, small, medium, large, extra-large, and jumbo and range from 1½ to 2½ ounces (42 to 70 g). A large egg without shell is 1¾ ounces (50 g) or 3 tablespoons (45 mL). Eggs bought at a local farm may not be suitable for baking, but they are still the most delicious choice for breakfast.

BAKING POWDER AND BAKING SODA

It can be a little confusing to see both baking powder and baking soda called for in a recipe, but they each serve as leavening agents in different contexts. Baking soda works to leaven when there is a fair amount of acid in a recipe, and baking powder does the same when there is not. You use both when there is enough acid for the baking soda, but you still need the baking powder to help condition a batter and aid with smoothness and texture.

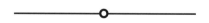

TOOLS AND EQUIPMENT

IF YOU'RE NEW TO BAKING, there are some essential tools you'll want to have on hand. These are some of our favourite and most used baking items.

MEASURING CUPS AND SPOONS

The cuter your measuring cups and spoons, the less accurate they will be. Look for measuring cups and spoons with a recognizable brand like KitchenAid or Cuisinart. You should also be mindful of the difference between dry and liquid measuring tools. Liquid measuring tools usually have a spout; accurately measure things like oil, yogurt, and water; and make it easy to pour them into a mixing bowl without spilling. Dry measuring tools accurately measure flour, nuts, and chocolate chips, for example, and can easily be levelled off with a flat edge.

MIXING BOWLS

Having a set of small, medium, and large mixing bowls is essential for baking. For recipes that do not require an electric stand mixer, purchase a set of glass, plastic, or stainless steel mixing bowls to serve all your baking needs.

STAND MIXER OR HAND MIXER

We almost exclusively use a stand mixer when baking. We find that it makes tasks like creaming, beating, and whisking easier while freeing up your hands to multitask. The interchangeable attachments and graduated speeds on a stand mixer can accomplish most tasks needed to make a variety of recipes. Having said that, a hand mixer will accomplish most of the methods in this book and is a perfect starting point if a stand mixer is not available to you.

WHISK

A heavy-duty whisk with a few sturdy loops is good for mixing and blending, whereas a whisk with many fine loops works well for aerating ingredients such as egg whites and cream.

SPATULAS

Like an extension of your own hand, a silicone spatula is irreplaceable for scraping down the bowl of a stand mixer or gently folding whipped cream or egg whites into a batter. An offset spatula, also called a pallete knife, makes appearances in our recipes as well. It has a long, flexible blade with a rounded end that bends up where it meets the handle. It is perfect for lifting cookies off a baking sheet, smoothing cake batter in a pan, and frosting cakes.

BAKING PANS

Baking sheets Do yourself a thousand favours and invest in at least two quality baking sheets. It is truly a shame to put a pretty quiche or dainty Florentine into the oven only to have a flimsy, cheap baking sheet warp and bend and ruin your hard work. Look for baking sheets that are heavy, which means they will distribute heat evenly, and have rims to trap spills.

Loaf pan In this book we use a 9- × 5-inch (2 L) metal loaf pan. Find a pan that is good quality to ensure even heat distribution and to prevent warping. Clean and dry meticulously to keep it in good condition.

Pie plate At the restaurant we use disposable 10-inch (25 cm) aluminum foil pie plates. They are good for home baking too: you can reuse them, and if you give a pie away, you don't have to worry about keeping track of who has your nice bakeware. You can always place a pie baked in an aluminum plate inside of a decorative plate when serving if you don't like the way the aluminum one looks. When we're not using aluminum pie plates, we favour glass ones because they are sturdy and bake pies evenly.

Doughnut pan A standard doughnut pan has six cavities and does not really have a substitute. If you are looking to make doughnuts, we suggest buying one or two. Two standard doughnut pans will fit beside each other in a standard oven.

SCALE

Most home cooks use volume measurements when baking, so we offer measurements in cups, teaspoons, and tablespoons (with their metric equivalents) for most ingredients. Scales do come in handy every once in a while, so you may want to keep your eyes open for a sale, but for the most part you will be safe without one when baking the recipes in this book.

PARCHMENT PAPER

Parchment paper is an unsung hero in a baker's kitchen. Most obviously, parchment paper eliminates sticking. Lining cake tins and baking sheets with it will help ensure that your baked goods slide off easily, and hanging an inch or two of parchment paper over the edge of a baking dish when you're making squares or bars can serve as a convenient way to lift the contents out of the dish once they've baked. But there are other ways parchment paper can help, too. Not all baking sheets and pans are created equal. Some distribute heat evenly, whereas others have hotter and cooler spots because of their material and construction. Lining your baking sheets creates a thin layer of air between the paper and the metal, helping to regulate heat distribution. Parchment paper also has a slightly rougher surface than a baking sheet, which helps control undesirable spreading of treats like cookies. And we cannot forget cleanup! Using parchment paper to create a barrier between a metal pan and a gooey, bubbling pie or crumble will prevent you spending hours scrubbing sugar off your pans!

ROLLING PIN

A rolling pin is a tool every baker should have. Your average hardwood pin with handles will do the job. Marble rolling pins are also available; marble stays cool to the touch and is good for rolling pie dough and scones that benefit from the butter in them remaining as cold as possible.

PASTRY BRUSH

Pastry brushes of varying sizes can be used to brush on egg washes, glazes, and cream. They can also be used to brush away excess flour when rolling out pie dough (pages 270, 271), Blitz Puff Pastry (page 272), and croissants (pages 225, 236, 247, 259, 275). We prefer natural bristle brushes to silicone because they do a better job of trapping and holding liquids.

To keep your brushes clean and fresh, hand wash them right after you're finished with them: run the brushes under hot water and scrub the bristles with dish detergent. Lay out brushes to dry completely, and make sure that there is no residual grease or food lodged where the bristles meet the handle. If your brush starts to shed excessively, it's time to replace it.

BENCH SCRAPER

Scrapers are priceless baking tools. A metal bench scraper is useful for dividing scone dough, making smooth edges on iced cakes, and scraping a work surface clean. A plastic scraper bends to the contours of a mixing bowl and will help you scrape out every last bit of batter or dough or pick up chopped nuts or chocolate off of a cutting board in one easy swipe.

KITCHEN TORCH

This is the tool you never knew you were missing! From torching the tops of Crème Brulée Pudding (page 241), to gently heating the bowl of a stand mixer to create the most fluffy Swiss Meringue Buttercream (page 280), to of course browning the cloud of meringue on top of Mile High Lemon Meringue Pie (page 189), we pull it out of the drawer often. Although it's not *necessary* for most of the recipes in this book, the more you bake, the more opportunities you will discover to use it.

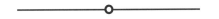

COOKIES

SUGAR COOKIES

There are a lot of recipes out there for sugar cookies, and this one is as classic as it gets. These are drop cookies rolled in sugar, and they pair perfectly with coffee or tea. No shaping, cutting, or icing is required—each cookie is just a delicious, tender, crispy bite to enjoy simply, on its own. **MAKES 24 COOKIES**

1. Preheat the oven to 360°F (185°C). Line 2 baking sheets with parchment paper.

2. In a medium bowl, whisk the flour, baking powder, salt, and baking soda. Set aside.

3. In a stand mixer fitted with the paddle attachment, mix the butter and 1½ cups (375 mL) of the sugar on medium-high speed until light and fluffy, about 3 to 5 minutes. Add the egg and vanilla. Mix well to combine. With the mixer on low speed, add the flour mixture and mix until combined. Add the sour cream and mix until smooth. If the dough becomes too stiff for the mixer, you may have to remove the bowl from the stand and finish mixing the dough with a spatula or wooden spoon.

4. Place the remaining ½ cup (125 mL) of sugar in a small bowl. For tea-size cookies, scoop portions of dough about 1½ tablespoons (22 mL) each. For larger cookies, scoop portions of dough up to 3 tablespoons (45 mL) each. Roll each portion into a ball and toss it in the sugar before placing it on a prepared baking sheet.

5. Bake tea-size cookies for 10 to 15 minutes and larger cookies for up to 25 minutes, until the edges of the cookies are just firm and the tops have not yet browned. Let cool slightly before transferring to a wire rack to cool completely.

6. Serve immediately or store in an airtight container at room temperature for up to 4 days.

2 cups (500 mL) all-purpose flour

1 teaspoon (5 mL) baking powder

1 teaspoon (5 mL) kosher salt

½ teaspoon (2 mL) baking soda

½ cup (125 mL) unsalted butter, room temperature

1½ cups (375 mL) + ½ cup (125 mL) granulated sugar, divided

1 large egg

1 teaspoon (5 mL) pure vanilla extract

¼ cup (60 mL) full-fat sour cream

KITCHEN TIP

• Once you have scooped the cookie dough and rolled it in sugar, you can freeze the raw dough. We do this all the time so we can pull out a couple of cookies at a time and bake them as needed. Simply arrange the dough balls on a baking sheet and place in the freezer until just frozen. Transfer them to a freezer bag or an airtight container and store in the freezer for up to 3 months.

WHITE CHOCOLATE MACADAMIA NUT COOKIES

This is a very straightforward cookie recipe, but you will notice a difference in taste depending on the quality of ingredients you use. At Bread Bar, we've emblazoned the phrase "good ingredients matter" on a wall at each of our locations because we believe in quality so much. You could easily purchase a package of white chocolate chips and your cookies would turn out fine, but if you source a delicious bar of Belgian white chocolate, your cookies will be even better. You might have to chop it into little pieces by hand, but the work will be worth it. **MAKES 18 TO 20 COOKIES**

¾ cup (175 mL) macadamia nuts

½ cup (125 mL) unsalted butter, room temperature

½ cup (125 mL) lightly packed brown sugar

⅓ cup (75 mL) granulated sugar

1 large egg

1 teaspoon (5 mL) kosher salt

½ teaspoon (2 mL) baking powder

½ teaspoon (2 mL) baking soda

½ teaspoon (2 mL) pure vanilla extract

1 cup (250 mL) all-purpose flour

¾ cup (175 mL) chopped good-quality white chocolate or white chocolate chips

1. Preheat the oven to 300°F (150°C).

2. Place the macadamia nuts on an unlined baking sheet and bake for 8 to 10 minutes, until toasted and brown. Let cool to room temperature. Increase the oven temperature to 360°F (185°C).

3. In a stand mixer fitted with the paddle attachment, cream the butter, brown sugar, and granulated sugar on medium speed. Scrape down the sides of the bowl and add the egg. Mix until combined. Add the salt, baking powder, baking soda, and vanilla. Scraping down the sides of the bowl as needed, mix until fluffy and smooth, about 5 minutes. Add the flour, white chocolate, and toasted macadamia nuts. Mix on low speed for about 1 minute. Remove the bowl from the stand and use a spatula to gently fold the batter to make sure the ingredients are well combined without knocking the air out of the dough. Some ingredients may get lost at the bottom of the bowl, so be sure to scrape them up.

4. Line the same baking sheet you used to toast the macadamia nuts with parchment paper. Roll the cookie dough into 1-inch (2.5 cm) balls, the equivalent of about 2 tablespoons (30 mL) of dough. Arrange the cookies on the prepared baking sheet about 2 inches (5 cm) apart. Bake for 15 to 20 minutes, turning the baking sheet after 10 minutes, until the cookies are golden brown. Let cool to room temperature.

5. Serve immediately or store in an airtight container at room temperature for up to 5 days.

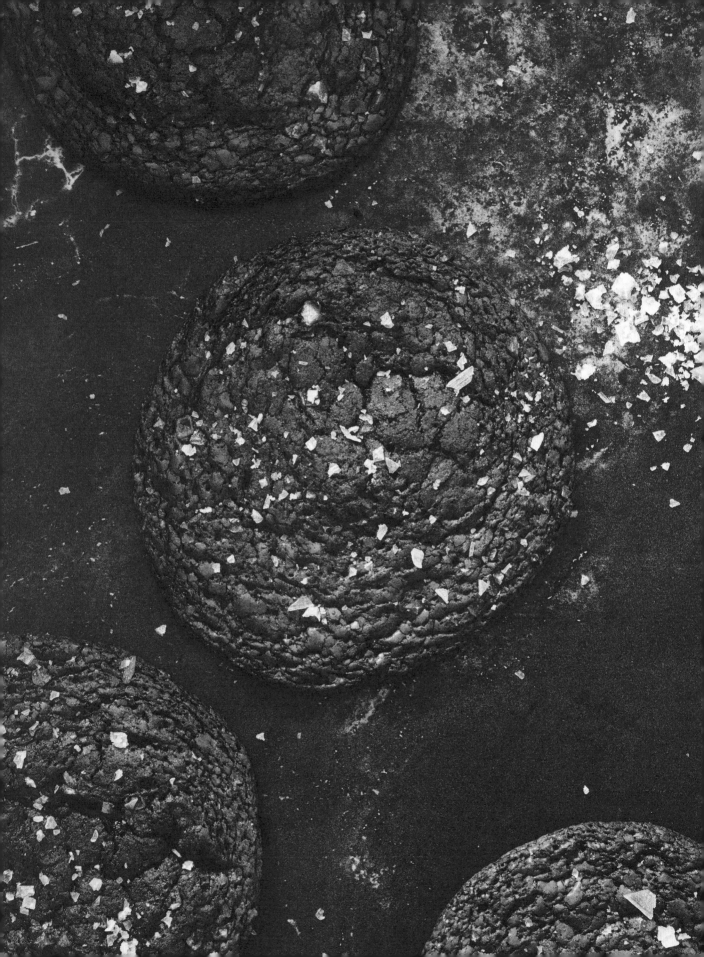

SALTED DARK CHOCOLATE RYE COOKIES

These cookies are an absolute treasure. They are rich, dense, and super chocolatey, and they use only rye flour, which makes them a friendlier option for those with gluten intolerances. Rye flour has much less gluten than wheat flour but does still have some gluten, so these cookies are not gluten free. The rye flour also contributes to their heavenly flavour. Before you begin baking, however, please note that the dough needs to chill in the fridge for at least six hours, or overnight, for the batter to be firm enough to scoop into cookies. Give yourself plenty of time! **MAKES 12 LARGE COOKIES**

1. In a small bowl, whisk the rye flour, baking powder, and kosher salt.

2. In a double boiler, or a large stainless steel bowl placed over a medium saucepan of simmering water, melt the chocolate and butter. Add the rye flour mixture and stir until well combined. Remove the bowl from the heat.

3. In a stand mixer fitted with the whisk attachment, whisk the eggs, sugar, and vanilla until the mixture is light and fluffy and has doubled in size, about 5 minutes.

4. Gently fold the egg mixture into the chocolate and rye flour mixture until combined. Cover the bowl with plastic wrap and chill in the fridge for at least 6 hours or overnight.

5. Preheat the oven to 360°F (185°C). Line 2 baking sheets with parchment paper.

6. Roll the cookie dough into 1-inch (2.5 cm) balls, the equivalent of about 2 tablespoons (30 mL) of dough. Arrange 6 cookies on each prepared baking sheet. Sprinkle each with a pinch of flaky sea salt. Bake for 12 to 15 minutes, until slightly puffed and the tops start to crack. Let cool to room temperature.

7. Serve immediately or store in an airtight container at room temperature for up to 4 days.

½ cup (125 mL) whole grain dark rye flour

½ teaspoon (2 mL) baking powder

½ teaspoon (2 mL) kosher salt

1 cup (250 mL) chopped good-quality dark chocolate

¼ cup (60 mL) unsalted butter

2 large eggs, room temperature

¾ cup (175 mL) lightly packed brown sugar

2 teaspoons (10 mL) pure vanilla extract

Flaky sea salt (we use Maldon), for garnish

SALTED TAHINI CHOCOLATE CHUNK COOKIES

In this recipe for chocolate chunk cookies, we substitute tahini for most of the butter we would normally use to deliver a delicious, nutty cookie that's a little bit healthier, too. **MAKES 18 TO 20 COOKIES**

HOMEMADE TAHINI (MAKES 1 CUP/250 ML)

1 cup (250 mL) unhulled sesame seeds

3 to 4 tablespoons (45 to 60 mL) extra-virgin olive oil

CHOCOLATE CHUNK COOKIES

½ cup (125 mL) Homemade Tahini or store-bought tahini, well stirred

¼ cup (60 mL) unsalted butter, room temperature

1 cup (125 mL) lightly packed brown sugar

1 large egg

1 large egg yolk

1 teaspoon (5 mL) pure vanilla extract

1 teaspoon (5 mL) baking soda

1 teaspoon (5 mL) baking powder

1 teaspoon (5 mL) kosher salt

2 cups (500 mL) chocolate chunks or chopped good-quality dark chocolate

1 cup (250 mL) all-purpose flour

Flaky sea salt (we use Maldon), for garnish

1. **MAKE THE HOMEMADE TAHINI** Place the sesame seeds in a wide, dry skillet over medium-low heat and toast for 5 to 7 minutes, stirring constantly, until they become fragrant and very brown but not burnt. Let cool to room temperature.

2. Place the sesame seeds in a food processor or a high-speed blender. Add 3 tablespoons (45 mL) of the olive oil. Blend for 2 to 3 minutes on high speed, scraping the bottom and sides of your equipment as needed. If the tahini is still very stiff, add the remaining 1 tablespoon (15 mL) of olive oil and blend for an additional minute, until the tahini reaches the consistency of natural peanut butter. Store leftover tahini, covered, in the refrigerator for up to 1 month. It may separate over time like a natural nut or seed butter does. If this happens, simply give it a good stir before using.

3. Preheat the oven to 360°F (185°C). Line 2 baking sheets with parchment paper.

4. **MAKE THE CHOCOLATE CHUNK COOKIES** In a stand mixer fitted with the paddle attachment, cream ½ cup (125 mL) of the Homemade Tahini, the butter, and sugar on medium speed until light and fluffy, about 1 minute. Add the egg, egg yolk, and vanilla. Mix on medium speed for 1 minute, then scrape down the sides of the bowl. Add the baking soda, baking powder, and salt. Mix until fluffy and smooth, about 5 minutes. Add the chocolate chunks and flour. Mix until combined, then remove the bowl from the stand.

5. Roll the cookie dough into 1-inch (2.5 cm) balls. Arrange the cookies on the prepared baking sheets about 2 inches (5 cm) apart. Sprinkle each with a pinch of flaky sea salt. Bake for 15 to 20 minutes, turning the baking sheets after 10 minutes, until the cookies are golden brown. Let cool completely.

6. Serve immediately or store in an airtight container at room temperature for up to 4 days.

PEANUT BUTTER COOKIES WITH MILK CHOCOLATE

Peanut butter cookies are a glorious treat on their own, but if you add milk chocolate, they become sublime. While plain peanut butter cookies tend to be on the dry side, the milk chocolate we use in this recipe helps keep the cookies super moist and creamy. **MAKES 18 TO 20 COOKIES**

1. Preheat the oven to 350°F (180°C). Line 2 baking sheets with parchment paper.

2. In a stand mixer fitted with the paddle attachment, cream the butter, granulated sugar, brown sugar, and peanut butter on medium speed until light and fluffy, about 2 minutes. Add the eggs and vanilla. Beat on high speed until smooth, about 3 minutes. Add the flour, baking powder, baking soda, and salt. Beat on low speed until just combined. Add the chocolate chips and mix until just combined. At this point, the dough should start to pull away from the sides of the bowl. Remove the bowl from the stand. Stir the batter with a spatula or wooden spoon to be sure the ingredients are well combined.

3. Roll the cookie dough into 1-inch (2.5 cm) balls, the equivalent of about 2 tablespoons (30 mL) of dough. Arrange the cookies on the prepared baking sheets about 2 inches (5 cm) apart. Bake for 15 to 20 minutes, turning the baking sheets after 10 minutes, until the edges of the cookies start to turn golden brown. Let cool completely.

4. Serve immediately or store in an airtight container at room temperature for up to 5 days.

1 cup (250 mL) unsalted butter, softened

¾ cup (175 mL) granulated sugar

¾ cup (175 mL) lightly packed brown sugar

½ cup (125 mL) creamy peanut butter

2 large eggs

1 teaspoon (5 mL) pure vanilla extract

2 cups (500 mL) all-purpose flour

1 tablespoon (15 mL) baking powder

1 teaspoon (5 mL) baking soda

1 teaspoon (5 mL) salt

¾ cup (175 mL) good-quality milk chocolate chips

FIVE SPICE GINGER MOLASSES COOKIES

These ginger cookies are the perfect combination of chewy and crisp. The rolling sugar adds sweetness and a slight crunch to the spicy, chewy middles. Be sure to cream the shortening and sugar for the suggested time. It needs to be very light and fluffy to ensure that the cookies spread the right amount and to ensure the perfect final texture. **MAKES 20 COOKIES**

1 cup (250 mL) vegetable shortening

1½ cups (375 mL) granulated sugar, divided

¼ cup (60 mL) fancy molasses

1 large egg

2 teaspoons (10 mL) baking soda

1 teaspoon (5 mL) cinnamon

1 teaspoon (5 mL) nutmeg

1 teaspoon (5 mL) kosher salt

½ teaspoon (2 mL) ground ginger

¼ teaspoon (1 mL) ground cloves

¼ teaspoon (1 mL) ground allspice

2½ cups (625 mL) all-purpose flour

1.   Preheat the oven to 350°F (180°C). Line 2 baking sheets with parchment paper.

2.   In a stand mixer fitted with the paddle attachment, beat the shortening, 1 cup (250 mL) of the sugar, and the molasses on high speed until light and fluffy, about 3 minutes. Reduce the speed to medium. Add the egg and increase the speed to high and mix for about 3 more minutes to increase the volume. Reduce the speed to medium. Add the baking soda, cinnamon, nutmeg, salt, ginger, cloves, and allspice. Mix to combine. Turn off the mixer and scrape down the sides of the bowl with a spatula. Add the flour and mix on low speed until just combined. Remove the bowl from the stand mixer. Stir the batter with a spatula or wooden spoon to be sure the ingredients are well combined.

3.   Place the remaining ½ cup (125 mL) of sugar in a medium bowl. Roll the cookie dough into 1-inch (2.5 cm) balls, the equivalent of about 2 tablespoons (30 mL) of dough. Drop each dough ball into the sugar and turn it to coat completely. Arrange the cookies on the prepared baking sheets about 2 inches (5 cm) apart.

4.   Bake for 15 to 20 minutes, turning the baking sheets after 10 minutes, until the edges of the cookies start to turn golden brown. Because these cookies are quite dark, determining when they are done can be tricky. In addition to the edges starting to brown, the cookies should be slightly puffed and the tops should be starting to crack. Let cool completely.

5.   Serve immediately or store in an airtight container at room temperature for up to 5 days.

TOASTED ALMOND SABLÉ COOKIES

These almond sablés are thin, crisp, and full of gusto. And, after you finish them with the egg wash and sanding sugar, they almost sparkle, too! Sablé cookies generally have little to no spread while baking, so you can place them close together on the baking sheet. We rolled out the dough and cut these cookies into a scalloped round, but you can cut them into any shape you like. **MAKES 24 COOKIES**

1. Preheat the oven to 350°F (180 °C).

2. Arrange the almonds in a single layer on an unlined baking sheet. Bake until they become fragrant and start to brown, about 12 minutes. Let cool completely. Chop the almonds. Reduce the oven temperature to 300°F (150°C).

3. In a medium bowl, combine the flour and salt. In a stand mixer fitted with the paddle attachment, cream the butter and brown sugar on medium speed until slightly fluffy, about 2 minutes. Add 2 of the egg yolks and the vanilla. Mix to combine. Add the flour mixture and mix on low speed until combined. Add the chopped almonds and mix until just combined.

4. Turn the dough out onto a lightly floured surface. Divide it in half and shape each half into a disc. Tightly wrap each disc in plastic wrap and chill in the fridge for 30 minutes.

5. Line 2 baking sheets with parchment paper. On a lightly floured surface, roll out the dough until it is about ⅛ inch (3 mm) thick. Using a 2-inch (5 cm) cutter, cut out cookies and place them on the prepared baking sheets. Dip the cookie cutter in flour before each cut to prevent it sticking to the dough.

6. In a small bowl, whisk the remaining 1 egg yolk with 1 tablespoon (15 mL) of water. Use a pastry brush to brush the top of each cookie with a thin layer of egg wash. Sprinkle evenly with the sanding sugar. Bake the cookies for 12 to 15 minutes, until golden. Let cool on a wire rack.

7. Serve immediately or store in an airtight container at room temperature for up to 1 week or in the freezer for up to 1 month.

½ cup (125 mL) whole raw almonds

2 cups (500 mL) all-purpose flour

1 teaspoon (5 mL) kosher salt

1 cup (250 mL) unsalted butter, room temperature

⅔ cup (150 mL) lightly packed brown sugar

3 large egg yolks, divided

1 teaspoon (5 mL) pure vanilla extract

½ cup (125 mL) sanding sugar, for garnish

KITCHEN TIP

- If you don't feel like chopping the almonds, you can always place them in a sealed freezer bag and smash them with a rolling pin until they're the right size—and if you're baking with kids, this method might be more fun!

OG GRAHAM CRACKERS

Have you ever tried a fresh baked graham cracker? Most of us tend to buy the premade version from the grocery store, but a fresh graham cracker is tasty on its own—and really is more like a cookie. As you work your way through this book, this recipe will come in handy. We refer to it in a wide range of recipes, so you might as well perfect it right now! **MAKES 32 COOKIES**

¾ cup (175 mL) all-purpose flour

½ cup (125 mL) whole wheat flour

¼ cup (60 mL) wheat germ

½ teaspoon (2 mL) kosher salt

½ teaspoon (2 mL) ground cinnamon

½ teaspoon (2 mL) baking soda

½ cup (125 mL) unsalted butter

½ cup (125 mL) lightly packed brown sugar

¼ cup (60 mL) heavy (35%) cream

1 tablespoon (15 mL) pure liquid honey

1. Preheat the oven to 350°F (180°C). Line 2 baking sheets with parchment paper.

2. In a medium bowl, whisk the all-purpose flour, whole wheat flour, wheat germ, salt, cinnamon, and baking soda.

3. In a stand mixer fitted with the paddle attachment, cream the butter, sugar, cream, and honey on medium speed for 1 minute. Scrape down the sides of the bowl. Mix on high speed for 2 to 3 minutes, until light and fluffy. Add the flour mixture and mix on low speed until well combined.

4. Turn the dough out onto a lightly floured surface. Roll the dough into a 12-inch (30 cm) square about ¼ inch (5 mm) thick. Using a ruler and a paring knife, cut the dough into 1½- × 3-inch (4 × 8 cm) rectangles. Transfer the cookies to the prepared baking sheets, evenly spacing 16 cookies on each baking sheet.

5. Bake for 15 minutes, turning the baking sheets about halfway through, until the cookies just start to brown. Let cool to room temperature.

6. Serve immediately or store in an airtight container at room temperature for up to 5 days.

KITCHEN TIP

• If you are preparing this recipe to make graham cracker crumbs to use in recipes like Classic Bread Bar Cheesecake with Rhubarb Compote (page 233), Lemon Zingers (page 49), or Banoffee Pie (page 193), there's no need to cut the dough into rectangles. Simply bake the whole 12-inch (30 cm) square after you roll out the dough. You may need to increase the baking time by about 5 minutes.

CHOCOLATE PEPPERMINT SANDWICH

The cookies used to make this cookie sandwich are chocolatey, wafer-thin, light, crispy, and delicious. The filling brings in peppermint flavour, but if you're not a fan of mint with your chocolate, simply omit the peppermint extract. You'll wind up with a cookie sandwich that tastes a lot like an Oreo instead! If you're like us and you can't get enough of these cookies, try using them in our recipes for Chocolate and Vanilla Brûlée Cheesecake (page 265) and Magic Bars (page 56) where they form a delicious cookie crust. **MAKES 24 COOKIE SANDWICHES**

1. MAKE THE CHOCOLATE COOKIE WAFERS In a stand mixer fitted with the paddle attachment, cream the granulated sugar, brown sugar, butter, and vanilla on medium speed until light and fluffy, about 2 minutes.

2. In a medium bowl, whisk the flour, cocoa powder, salt, and baking soda. Add the flour mixture to the butter mixture. Mix on low speed until just combined. Add the cream. Mix until just combined.

3. Using your hands, form the dough into two 5- × 2-inch (12 × 5 cm) logs. Tightly wrap each log in plastic wrap and place in the fridge for at least 1 hour or overnight.

4. Preheat the oven to 350°F (180°C). Line 2 baking sheets with parchment paper.

5. Remove the plastic wrap from the dough. Slice the dough logs into coins ⅛ inch (3 mm) thick. Arrange the cookies on the prepared baking sheets about 1 inch (2.5 cm) apart. Bake for 8 minutes. Turn the baking sheets and bake for an additional 2 minutes. The cookies are done when the tops are slightly cracked and look firm. Let cool completely.

6. MAKE THE PEPPERMINT FILLING In a stand mixer fitted with the paddle attachment, cream the icing sugar, butter, and peppermint (if using) on high speed until light and fluffy.

7. On a clean, flat surface, flip over half of the cookies. Spread about 2 tablespoons (30 mL) of filling on each of the cookies that you flipped over. Top with the remaining cookies.

8. Serve immediately or store in an airtight container at room temperature for up to 5 days or in the freezer for up to 3 months.

CHOCOLATE COOKIE WAFERS

¾ cup (175 mL) granulated sugar

½ cup (125 mL) lightly packed brown sugar

½ cup (125 mL) unsalted butter, softened

1 teaspoon (5 mL) pure vanilla extract

1 cup (250 mL) all-purpose flour

¾ cup (175 mL) cocoa powder

1 teaspoon (5 mL) kosher salt

½ teaspoon (2 mL) baking soda

¼ cup (60 mL) heavy (35%) cream

PEPPERMINT FILLING

3 cups (750 mL) icing sugar

½ cup (125 mL) unsalted butter, softened

1 teaspoon (5 mL) pure peppermint extract (optional)

ALMOND ANISE BISCOTTI

This classic biscotti pairs perfectly with a cup of coffee or tea. Dip the biscotti into the hot drink of your choice and, when you take a bite, let the licorice aroma from the aniseed and the nutty flavour of the almonds melt in your mouth. You might even find a few crumbs at the bottom of your cup for a delightful finish. Scoop up the little pieces with a spoon and enjoy every last bit. **MAKES 25 COOKIES**

1 cup (250 mL) raw almonds

3 cups (750 mL) all-purpose flour

1 tablespoon (15 mL) baking powder

1 teaspoon (5 mL) baking soda

1 teaspoon (5 mL) kosher salt

1½ cups (375 mL) granulated sugar

½ cup (125 mL) unsalted butter, melted

3 large eggs

1 tablespoon (15 mL) pure vanilla extract

2 teaspoons (10 mL) whole aniseed

1 large egg white

1. Preheat the oven to 375°F (190°C). Line a baking sheet with parchment paper.

2. Arrange the almonds in a single layer on an unlined baking sheet. Bake until they become fragrant and start to brown, about 12 minutes. Let cool completely. Chop the almonds. Reduce the oven temperature to 200°F (100°C).

3. In a medium bowl, mix the flour, baking powder, baking soda, and salt. In a large bowl, whisk the sugar, butter, eggs, vanilla, and aniseed. Add the flour mixture to the butter mixture. Use a spatula or wooden spoon to stir until well combined. Stir in the almonds.

4. Divide the dough in half. Using floured hands, shape each half into a 13- × 2-inch (33 × 5 cm) log. Transfer both logs to the prepared baking sheet, leaving some space between them. In a small bowl, whisk the egg white until foamy. Using a pastry brush, brush the egg white over the top and sides of each dough log. Bake for 30 minutes, until golden brown. Let cool completely on the baking sheet, about 25 minutes.

5. Transfer the logs to a clean cutting board. Using a serrated knife, cut the logs into ½-inch (1 cm) slices, on the diagonal. Arrange the slices on the same baking sheet you used to cook the dough logs. Bake for 8 minutes at 200°F (100°C). Turn the biscotti over. Bake for an additional 8 minutes, until just beginning to brown. Transfer the biscotti to a wire rack to cool.

6. Serve immediately or store in an airtight container at room temperature for up to 1 week.

CHOCOLATE TOFFEE SHORTBREAD

This recipe is our go-to for play dates, bake sales, and after-school treats. Not to mention a favourite for Christmas or any special event. The shortbread is classic and can be made without the chocolate and toffee bits, but they take this recipe to the next level, adding moisture and complementary flavours. If you use store-bought toffee bits to save time, read the product label before sending them to school with your child. Store-bought toffee usually includes a nut-based nougat. **MAKES 24 COOKIES**

1. Line a baking sheet with parchment paper.

2. MAKE THE TOFFEE BITS In a medium saucepan over high heat, combine the sugar, butter, water, corn syrup, and salt. Bring to a boil and cook until a candy thermometer reads 280°F (138°C). Stir once when the sugar comes up to temperature to even out the colour. Remove from the heat and carefully pour the toffee onto the prepared baking sheet. Let cool to room temperature. Break the toffee into large pieces. Place the pieces in a food processor and pulse them into bits.

3. Preheat the oven to 300°F (150°C). Line a baking sheet with parchment paper.

4. MAKE THE SHORTBREAD In a stand mixer fitted with the paddle attachment, mix the flour, cornstarch, icing sugar, and salt on low speed for 30 seconds. Add the butter, 2 to 3 tablespoons (30 to 45 mL) at a time, mixing until the dough is well combined and smooth. Add the chocolate and ½ cup (125 mL) of the toffee bits and mix until combined.

5. Transfer the shortbread dough to the prepared baking sheet. Either with wet hands or a rolling pin, press or roll out the dough until it covers most of the baking sheet. If using a rolling pin, cover the dough with a second sheet of parchment paper to prevent the dough sticking to the pin.

6. Bake for 20 minutes, or until the edges and tops start to turn a very light brown. Immediately after removing the shortbread from the oven, cut it into 1- × 2-inch (2.5 x 5 cm) rectangles, or any other shape you desire. Let cool completely before removing the shortbread from the baking sheet.

7. Serve immediately or store in an airtight container at room temperature for up to 5 days.

TOFFEE BITS
(MAKES 2 CUPS/500 ML)

¾ cup (175 mL) granulated sugar
½ cup (125 mL) unsalted butter
2 tablespoons (30 mL) water
1 tablespoon (15 mL) corn syrup
½ teaspoon (2 mL) kosher salt

SHORTBREAD

1 cup (250 mL) all-purpose flour
½ cup (125 mL) cornstarch
½ cup (125 mL) icing sugar
1 teaspoon (5 mL) kosher salt
¾ cup (175 mL) unsalted butter, softened
½ cup (125 mL) chopped good-quality dark chocolate
½ cup (125 mL) toffee bits

FLORENTINES

Florentines are delicate cookies, originally from Italy, that were quickly adopted by French cuisine. These lacy, crisp treats are probably the fanciest cookie in this book, but they are so easy to make, delicious, and sure to impress. **MAKES 24 COOKIES**

1½ cups (375 mL) sliced blanched almonds

3 tablespoons (45 mL) all-purpose flour

Zest of 1 orange

1 teaspoon (5 mL) kosher salt

¾ cup (175 mL) granulated sugar

¼ cup (60 mL) unsalted butter, cut into 1-inch (2.5 cm) cubes

2 tablespoons (30 mL) heavy (35%) cream

2 tablespoons (30 mL) corn syrup

½ teaspoon (2 mL) pure vanilla extract

½ cup (125 mL) coating chocolate

1. Preheat the oven to 350°F (180°C). Line 2 baking sheets with parchment paper.

2. In a food processor, pulse the almonds until they are finely chopped but not a paste. Transfer the almonds to a medium bowl. Add the flour, orange zest, and salt. Whisk to combine.

3. In a small saucepan over high heat, combine the sugar, butter, cream, and corn syrup. Bring to a boil and continue to cook for 1 minute. Remove from the heat and stir in the vanilla. Pour the sugar mixture into the almond and flour mixture and stir to combine. Let cool for 10 to 15 minutes, until the mixture is cool enough to handle.

4. Using your hands, roll 1-teaspoon (5 mL) portions of the dough into balls. Arrange 6 balls on each prepared baking sheet, leaving about 3 to 4 inches (8 to 10 cm) between the cookies, as they will spread. (You will need to bake the cookies in 2 batches.) Bake for 10 minutes, until the cookies are thin and an even golden-brown colour. Let cool.

5. While you're waiting for the cookies to cool, in a small bowl, heat the coating chocolate in a microwave oven in 15-second intervals, stirring between each interval, until melted and smooth. You can use the chocolate to garnish the cookies in a few different ways: (1) Hold a cookie vertically over the bowl and dip half of it in chocolate. (2) Hold a cookie horizontally over the bowl and dip just the bottom of it in chocolate. (3) Using a spoon or piping bag, drizzle the chocolate over the bottoms of the cookies in a zigzag pattern. Let the cookies rest until the chocolate is set.

6. Serve immediately or stack between pieces of parchment paper or wax paper and store in an airtight container at room temperature for up to 3 days.

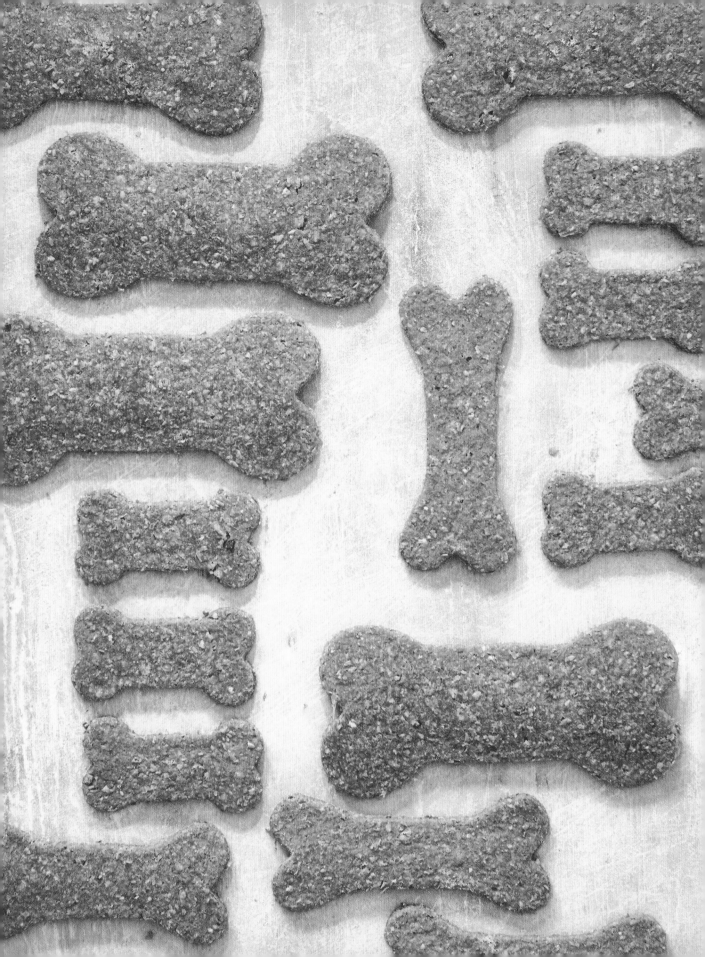

BRUCE AND CRICKET'S FAVOURITE PUPPY COOKIES

The downtown Hamilton location of Bread Bar is frequented by many dog owners. Walk by our storefront at any time of the day and you will see two or three patient pooches waiting outside. Being dog owners ourselves, we thought this recipe was important to include—dogs love baked goods too! Unless you have multiple dogs, fifty treats is a lot to feed a dog in two weeks, so we suggest freezing most of the batch and pulling treats out as needed. These dog biscuits are a great alternative to store-bought treats laden with additives and salt that just will not do for our best friends. **MAKES 50 PUPPY COOKIES**

1. Preheat the oven to 250°F (120°C). Line 2 baking sheets with parchment paper. Line a plate with paper towels.

2. In a large skillet over medium-high heat, cook the bacon for 10 minutes, until it turns a rich golden brown. Remove from the pan and let drain on the prepared plate.

3. Pour off all but about 2 tablespoons (30 mL) of the bacon fat from the pan. Add the chicken livers to the pan. Sauté over medium heat for 5 minutes, smashing them slightly with a wooden spoon until they break down into a paste.

4. Place the bacon and chicken livers in a food processor and process until smooth. Add the cornmeal and process until combined and a coarse mixture forms. Transfer the mixture to the bowl of a stand mixer fitted with the paddle attachment. Add the flour and peanut butter. Mix on medium speed to combine. Pour in the chicken stock and mix until everything comes together in a dough that feels moist to the touch.

5. Tip the dough out onto a well-floured surface and roll it out until ½ inch (1 cm) thick. Using a dog bone cookie cutter, or other fun doggy shapes, cut out cookies. Knead together the trimmings and cut out additional cookies to reduce waste. Arrange the cookies on the prepared baking sheets about 1 inch (2.5 cm) apart. They will not spread while baking, so they can be placed close together. Bake until the cookies are completely dry, about 3 hours. If they still feel a bit soft to the touch, bake for an additional 30 minutes. Let cool to room temperature.

6. Store in an airtight container at room temperature for up to 2 weeks or in the freezer for up to 3 months. Feed them to your dog frozen or at room temperature.

12 ounces (340 g) bacon, cut into 1-inch (2.5 cm) pieces
1 pound (450 g) chicken livers, cut into ½-inch (1 cm) pieces
¾ cup (175 mL) cornmeal
3 cups (750 mL) whole wheat flour
2 tablespoons (30 mL) natural peanut butter
1 cup (250 mL) low-sodium chicken stock

BARS
AND
SQUARES

GANACHE ICED BROWNIES

Using quality chocolate for this recipe is key to achieving the luscious chocolate flavour of your brownie dreams. Instead of adding an obvious coffee flavour, the addition of instant espresso powder to these brownies makes the chocolate flavour really shine. Feel free to bump it up by adding an additional teaspoon if a more intense coffee flavour suits your taste. **MAKES 18 BROWNIES**

1. Preheat the oven to 350°F (180°C). Line the bottom and sides of a 13- × 9-inch (3.5 L) baking dish with parchment paper, leaving a 1-inch (2.5 cm) overhang on all sides.

2. MAKE THE BROWNIES In a double boiler, or a large stainless steel bowl placed over a large saucepan of simmering water, combine the sugar, butter, cocoa powder, espresso powder, and salt. Cook, stirring occasionally, until the butter is completely melted and the mixture is smooth and glossy. Remove the bowl from the heat and let the mixture cool slightly, about 5 minutes.

3. Whisk the eggs into the chocolatey mixture one at a time. Add the vanilla and stir to combine. Fold in the flour and semisweet chocolate until no pockets of white flour remain. Transfer the batter to the prepared baking dish. Bake for 20 to 30 minutes, or until a cake tester comes out with a few moist crumbs. Let cool to room temperature in the baking dish.

4. MAKE THE GANACHE Place the semisweet chocolate and butter in a large bowl. In a small saucepan over medium heat, bring the cream just barely to a simmer. Pour the cream over the chocolate and butter. Let stand for 5 minutes, then stir with a spatula until combined and smooth. Spoon and swoosh the ganache over the brownies and place in the fridge for 1 to 2 hours to set.

5. Use the parchment paper overhang to lift the brownies out of the baking dish. Place them on a clean cutting board and pull the parchment paper away from the brownies. Run a knife under hot water for about 30 seconds to heat it up. Dry the knife with a clean kitchen towel. While the knife is still hot, cut the brownies into 18 squares, cleaning the knife after each cut. This will help create very clean, crisp cuts.

6. Serve immediately or store in an airtight container in the fridge for up to 4 days.

BROWNIES

2 cups (500 mL) granulated sugar

1 cup (250 mL) unsalted butter, cubed

1 cup (250 mL) dark cocoa powder

1 teaspoon (5 mL) instant espresso powder

1 teaspoon (5 mL) kosher salt

5 large eggs

2 teaspoons (10 mL) pure vanilla extract

¾ cup (175 mL) all-purpose flour

1 cup (250 mL) chopped semisweet chocolate

GANACHE

12 ounces (340 g) chopped semisweet chocolate

4 tablespoons (60 mL) unsalted butter, room temperature

2 cups (500 mL) heavy (35%) cream

LEMON ZINGERS

We call these "zingers" because the filling will make your lips pucker, unlike some other lemon bars that may fall flat on bright lemon flavour. Adding sweetened condensed milk to the filling makes these bars smooth and creamy—and they're especially perfect when you eat them right out of the fridge. Use our OG Graham Crackers recipe (page 32) for an entirely homemade crust or use store-bought graham cracker crumbs when time is of the essence. **MAKES 16 LEMON ZINGERS**

1. Preheat the oven to 375°F (190°C). Grease an 8-inch (2 L) square baking dish and line it with parchment paper, leaving a 1-inch (2.5 cm) overhang on all sides.

2. **MAKE THE GRAHAM CRUST** Place the graham cracker crumbs, butter, and sugar in a small bowl. Stir to combine. Firmly press the crumb mixture into the bottom of the prepared baking dish. Bake for 7 minutes. Remove from the oven and let cool. Reduce the oven temperature to 350°F (180°C).

3. **MAKE THE LEMON FILLING** In a medium bowl, whisk the condensed milk, egg yolks, lemon zest, and lemon juice until smooth. Pour over the crust. Bake for 25 minutes until the filling only jiggles slightly when the baking dish is touched. Let cool to room temperature, then transfer to the fridge to chill for at least 2 hours. Reduce the oven temperature to 200°F (100°C).

4. **MAKE THE CANDIED LEMON SLICES** Line a baking sheet with parchment paper. Using a mandoline or sharp knife, cut the lemon into 8 paper-thin slices. Discard the seeds and the rind ends of the lemon. In a medium saucepan, bring 1 cup (250 mL) of the sugar and the water to a rolling boil. Remove from the heat. Add the lemon slices and stir until softened, about 1 minute. Drain. Lay the poached lemon slices on the prepared baking sheet and sprinkle generously with the remaining ¼ cup (60 mL) of sugar. Bake until slightly crispy, about 45 minutes. Let cool completely, then cut each slice in half.

5. Use the parchment paper overhang to lift the zingers out of the baking dish. Place them on a clean cutting board and pull the parchment paper away from the bars. Run a knife under hot water for about 30 seconds to heat it up. Dry the knife with a

GRAHAM CRUST

1½ cups (375 mL) ground OG
  Graham Crackers (page 32) or
  store-bought graham cracker
  crumbs
6 tablespoons (90 mL) unsalted
  butter, melted
⅓ cup (75 mL) granulated sugar

LEMON FILLING

2 cans (14 ounces/414 mL each)
  sweetened condensed milk
10 large egg yolks
4 tablespoons (60 mL) lemon zest
1 cup (250 mL) + 2 tablespoons
  (30 mL) fresh lemon juice

CANDIED LEMON SLICES

1 large lemon
1 cup (250 mL) + ¼ cup (60 mL)
  granulated sugar, divided
1 cup (250 mL) water

recipe continues

clean kitchen towel. While the knife is still hot, cut the lemon zingers into 16 bars, cleaning the knife after each cut. This will help create very clean, crisp cuts. Top each bar with a candied lemon slice.

6. Serve immediately or store in an airtight container in the fridge for up to 1 week.

COCONUT LOVER FANTASY SQUARES

This recipe piles coconut on coconut on coconut and is deliciously gluten free without making any adjustments. Amid all that coconut, you'll find a delicious layer of mango between the cream filling and the whipped topping that makes these squares sing. Coconut has a versatile flavour that pairs well with many fruits like banana, pineapple, or even raspberries, so feel free to substitute an equal amount of your favourite fruit if you want to switch it up. **MAKES 18 SQUARES**

1. Preheat the oven to 325°F (160°C). Generously grease a 13- × 9-inch (3.5 L) baking dish.

2. **PREPARE THE TOASTED COCONUT** Arrange the coconut in an even layer on an unlined baking sheet. Toast for 12 minutes, stirring halfway. Let cool completely. This coconut will be divided to make the crust and the filling. Leave the oven on.

3. **MAKE THE CRUST** In a medium bowl, whisk the coconut flour, sugar, and salt. Add the creamed coconut, butter, and ½ cup (125 mL) of the Toasted Coconut. Using a spatula or your hands, stir until moist, coarse, and crumbly. Press the mixture into the bottom of the prepared baking dish. Bake until lightly browned, about 15 minutes. Let cool.

4. **MAKE THE COCONUT CREAM FILLING** In a medium saucepan over medium heat, whisk the coconut milk, sweetened condensed milk, cornstarch, and lime zest. Whisking constantly, bring to a boil and cook until thickened and glossy, about 6 minutes. Remove from the heat. Stir in the remaining 1 cup (250 mL) of the Toasted Coconut, the lime juice, vanilla, and coconut extract. Spread the filling evenly over the crust. Cover, placing plastic wrap directly on the surface of the filling to prevent a skin forming. Chill in the fridge for at least 3 hours.

5. One hour before serving, arrange the mango in an even layer over the filling.

6. **MAKE THE CREAM TOPPING** In a small heatproof glass or dish, stir together the gelatin and water until the gelatin blooms and the mixture becomes slightly solid, about 5 minutes. Warm in the microwave for about 20 seconds. The gelatin should be dissolved and just lukewarm. In a stand mixer fitted with the

TOASTED COCONUT

1½ cups (375 mL) sweetened coconut flakes or shredded coconut, divided

CRUST

1 cup (250 mL) coconut flour

2 tablespoons (30 mL) granulated sugar

1 teaspoon (5 mL) kosher salt

⅔ cup (150 mL) creamed coconut, melted

½ cup (125 mL) unsalted butter, softened

½ cup (125 mL) Toasted Coconut

COCONUT CREAM FILLING

1 can (14 ounces/400 mL) coconut milk

1 can (10 ounces/300 mL) sweetened condensed milk

3 tablespoons (45 mL) cornstarch

Zest of 1 lime

1 cup (250 mL) Toasted Coconut

¼ cup (60 mL) fresh lime juice

2 teaspoons (10 mL) pure vanilla extract

½ teaspoon (2 mL) pure coconut extract

2 mangoes, peeled and diced, or 4 cups (1 L) frozen mango chunks

recipe continues

CREAM TOPPING

1 tablespoon (15 mL) unflavoured
  gelatin powder

¼ cup (60 mL) cold water

2 cups (500 mL) heavy (35%) cream

3 tablespoons (45 mL) granulated
  sugar

1 teaspoon (5 mL) pure vanilla
  extract

½ teaspoon (2 mL) pure coconut
  extract

1 cup (250 mL) toasted coconut curls
  (optional)

whisk attachment, whisk the cream, sugar, vanilla, and coconut extract on high speed. Whisking continuously, add the gelatin in a slow stream. Continue whisking until the cream holds soft peaks. Cover the filling and mango with the topping and chill in the fridge for 1 hour before serving.

7. Run a knife under hot water for about 30 seconds to heat it up. Dry the knife with a clean kitchen towel. While the knife is still hot, cut the coconut squares into 18 squares, cleaning the knife after each cut. This will help create very clean, crisp cuts. Garnish each square with a few toasted coconut curls, if desired.

8. Serve immediately or cover with plastic wrap and store in the fridge for up to 4 days.

PEACH MELBA CRUMBLE SQUARES

Peach Melba, or the combination of peach and raspberry, is a true delight. Originally named in honour of Australian soprano Nellie Melba by French chef Auguste Escoffier in 1892, the flavour pairing works wonderfully with an oat crumble. Feel free to switch up the berries as you wish—blueberries and blackberries are also delicious with peaches. **MAKES 18 SQUARES**

1. Preheat the oven to 350°F (180°C). Lightly grease a 13- × 9-inch (3.5 L) baking dish and line it with parchment paper.

2. **MAKE THE WHOLE WHEAT CRUST** In a large bowl, whisk the all-purpose flour, whole wheat flour, brown sugar, and salt. Add the melted butter and vanilla. Using your hands, gently mix until the ingredients come together to form a dough. Pat the dough evenly into the bottom of the prepared baking dish. Bake for 20 minutes, until light golden brown. Let cool.

3. **MAKE THE PEACH MELBA FILLING** Place the peaches in a medium bowl. Add the sugar, cinnamon, vanilla, and flour. Toss gently to combine. Arrange the peaches in an even layer over the crust. Scatter the raspberries overtop. Sprinkle the Crumble Topping evenly over the peach and raspberry filling.

4. Bake for 30 to 40 minutes, until the topping is golden brown and the peaches and raspberries begin to release their juices and bubble slightly. Let cool to room temperature in the pan and cut into 18 squares with a sharp knife.

5. Store in an airtight container at room temperature for up to 2 days or in the fridge for up to 1 week.

WHOLE WHEAT CRUST

1 cup (250 mL) all-purpose flour

1 cup (250 mL) whole wheat flour

½ cup (125 mL) lightly packed brown sugar

1 teaspoon (5 mL) kosher salt

¾ cup (175 mL) unsalted butter, melted and cooled

2 teaspoons (10 mL) pure vanilla extract

PEACH MELBA FILLING

3 cups (750 mL) pitted and roughly chopped ripe peaches

¼ cup (60 mL) granulated sugar

½ teaspoon (2 mL) ground cinnamon

2 teaspoons (10 mL) pure vanilla extract

2 tablespoons (30 mL) all-purpose flour

1 cup (250 mL) fresh or frozen raspberries

3 cups (750 mL) Crumble Topping (page 284)

MAGIC BARS

Magic bars are layers of semisweet chocolate chips, shredded coconut, and chopped pecans held together with sweet, sticky condensed milk. This is a great recipe to get your kids involved in. There are a lot of layers to assemble, but kids love sprinkling the different ingredients over the base. These bars go by different names—Hello Dollies, Seven Layer Bars—but no matter the name, they are crowd-pleasers and an easy way to use up some odds and ends you might have in your pantry. **MAKES 15 BARS**

¾ cup (175 mL) lightly packed brown sugar

½ cup (125 mL) unsalted butter, softened

1 teaspoon (5 mL) pure vanilla extract

1 large egg

1 cup (250 mL) all-purpose flour

1 cup (250 mL) ground Chocolate Cookie Wafers (page 35)

½ teaspoon (2 mL) baking powder

¼ teaspoon (1 mL) kosher salt

1 cup (250 mL) semisweet chocolate chips

¾ cup (175 mL) sweetened shredded coconut

½ cup (125 mL) chopped pecans

8 ounces (235 mL) sweetened condensed milk

1. Preheat the oven to 325°F (160°C). Line a 9-inch (2.5 L) square baking pan with parchment paper, leaving a 1-inch (2.5 cm) overhang on all sides.

2. In a stand mixer fitted with the paddle attachment, cream the brown sugar and butter on medium speed until smooth. Add the vanilla and egg. Beat until combined, then scrape down the sides of the bowl. Add the flour, ground wafers, baking powder, and salt. With the mixer on low speed, beat until combined.

3. Press the chocolate dough into the bottom of the prepared baking pan. Bake for 10 minutes. Remove from the oven and spread the chocolate chips in an even layer on top of the crust. Repeat with the coconut and then with the pecans. Drizzle the condensed milk evenly overtop. Bake for 30 minutes, turning the pan halfway through, until set and light golden brown. Let cool for 30 minutes at room temperature. Transfer to the fridge to finish cooling.

4. Use the parchment paper overhang to lift the bars out of the baking dish. Place them on a clean cutting board and pull the parchment paper away from the bars. Using a sharp knife, cut into 15 bars.

5. Store in an airtight container in the fridge for up to 1 week.

KITCHEN TIPS

• You can substitute any variety of nuts for the pecans—just be sure to use an equal amount. Chopped walnuts, chopped almonds, and chopped hazelnuts all work well.

• The bars can be cut into any size—mini squares are great for a sweet treat in a packed lunch or as part of a larger platter of sweets served at a get-together; larger squares served with a scoop of ice cream make for an indulgent dessert.

NANAIMO BARS

A Canadian classic! Erin was in British Columbia for her thirtieth birthday and made a point to eat as many Nanaimo bars in Nanaimo, British Columbia—all in the name of research, of course—as she could. All of the recipes varied slightly, but she learned that the secret to the creamy, sweet filling is to use custard powder, which can be found at any grocery store. Erin may have had enough Nanaimo bars to last a lifetime on her trip to British Columbia, but she still can't resist a taste when we make these bars. They will leave you wanting more. **MAKES 24 BARS**

1. Line a 13- × 9-inch (3.5 L) baking dish with parchment paper, leaving a 1-inch (2.5 cm) overhang on all sides.

2. **MAKE THE CHOCOLATE COCONUT CRUST** In a double boiler, or a medium stainless steel bowl placed over a medium saucepan of simmering water, over medium-low heat, melt the butter. Whisk in the sugar and cocoa powder until dissolved. Remove from the heat. Add the eggs and whisk continuously for 3 minutes, until the mixture thickens and eventually becomes smooth. Using a wooden spoon, stir in the graham cracker crumbs, coconut, and almond flour until well combined. Press the mixture evenly into the bottom of the prepared baking dish.

3. **MAKE THE CUSTARD** In the bowl of a stand mixer fitted with the paddle attachment, add the butter and cream. Sift in the custard powder. Beat on medium-high speed until well combined, about 4 minutes. Add 1 cup (250 mL) of the icing sugar at a time, scraping down the sides of the bowl after each addition, until well combined. When all of the icing sugar is incorporated, beat until light and fluffy, about 2 minutes more.

4. Using an offset spatula or the back of a large spoon, spread the custard evenly over the crust in the baking dish. Chill in the fridge for 30 minutes.

5. **MAKE THE CHOCOLATE GLAZE** Clean the double boiler or stainless steel bowl you used to make the crust and prepare the double boiler again. Melt the chocolate chips and butter in the double boiler, stirring often to combine.

CHOCOLATE COCONUT CRUST

1 cup (250 mL) unsalted butter

½ cup (125 mL) granulated sugar

½ cup (125 mL) cocoa powder

2 large eggs, beaten

3 cups (750 mL) ground OG Graham Crackers (page 32) or store-bought graham cracker crumbs

1 cup (250 mL) sweetened shredded coconut

1 cup (250 mL) almond flour

CUSTARD

1 cup (250 mL) unsalted butter, softened

6 tablespoons (90 mL) heavy (35%) cream

¼ cup (60 mL) custard powder

4 cups (1 L) icing sugar

CHOCOLATE GLAZE

2 cups (500 mL) semisweet chocolate chips

2 tablespoons (30 mL) unsalted butter

recipe continues

6. Pour the glaze over the custard and spread it in an even layer. Refrigerate, uncovered, for 30 minutes. Cover loosely with plastic wrap and chill in the fridge overnight.

7. Use the parchment paper overhang to lift the bars out of the baking dish. Place them on a clean cutting board and pull the parchment paper away from the bars. Run a knife under hot water for about 30 seconds to heat it up. Dry the knife with a clean kitchen towel. While the knife is still hot, cut the bars into 24 squares, cleaning the knife after each cut. This will help create very clean, crisp cuts.

8. Store in an airtight container in the fridge for up to 2 weeks or in the freezer for up to 6 months.

S'MORES BARS

S'mores are a classic Canadian campfire treat. Toasted marshmallows and a piece of chocolate squished between two graham crackers leads to all sorts of melted deliciousness. In this recipe, we leave the campfire for the cottage, but we do invite you to make your own graham cracker base and homemade marshmallows. **MAKES 16 SQUARES**

1. Grease a baking sheet and dust it completely with a thin layer of icing sugar. Tap any loose icing sugar into a bowl to use for the top. Set aside.

2. Place ¾ cup (175 mL) cold water in the bowl of a stand mixer. Add the gelatin and stir once. Let the gelatin bloom for 10 minutes.

3. Meanwhile, in a medium saucepan over medium heat, combine the granulated sugar, corn syrup, and salt. Bring to a boil. Cook for about 5 minutes. The bubbles will be small and quick at first, but around the 5-minute mark, they will become quite large and begin to slow down.

4. Place the bowl with the gelatin on a stand mixer fitted with the whisk attachment. Mix on low speed. Carefully and slowly pour the syrup into the bowl. Once all of the syrup has been added, increase the speed to medium-high. Add the vanilla and mix for 7 to 10 minutes, until the mixture is light and fluffy. Using an oiled spatula, scrape the mixture onto the prepared baking sheet and spread it in an even layer. Dust the marshmallow evenly with the remaining icing sugar and chill in the fridge overnight, uncovered.

5. Using a sharp knife, cut the marshmallow into sixteen 1½- × 3-inch (4 × 8 cm) rectangles. These will be used to make the S'mores Bars. Cut any remaining marshmallow into squares, dust with icing sugar on all sides, and store in an airtight container at room temperature for up to 1 week.

6. Place the chocolate in a medium heatproof bowl. Heat it in a microwave oven in 15-second intervals, stirring between each interval, until melted, smooth, and shiny.

½ cup (125 mL) icing sugar, for dusting

¾ cup (175 mL) + ¼ cup (60 mL) cold water, divided

3 tablespoons (45 mL) unflavoured powdered gelatin (three ½-ounce/14 g packets)

2 cups (500 mL) granulated sugar

½ cup (125 mL) corn syrup

½ teaspoon (2 mL) kosher salt

1 tablespoon (15 mL) pure vanilla extract

1 cup (250 mL) good-quality milk chocolate

1 batch OG Graham Crackers (page 32)

recipe continues

7. Arrange 16 graham crackers on a clean baking sheet and top each with a marshmallow. Drizzle each marshmallow with melted chocolate and top with the remaining graham crackers while the chocolate is still melted.

8. S'mores Bars are best served immediately but will keep for the rest of the day. If you are not planning to enjoy the s'mores immediately, keep the crackers, marshmallows, and chocolate separate until ready to assemble.

KITCHEN TIP

• If you have a kitchen torch, you can torch the marshmallows before drizzling them with the chocolate to give you more of that campfire flavour.

WILD BLUEBERRY GINGER LATTICE BARS

This is a perfect dessert to showcase summer's wild blueberries. Its cooked berry filling is similar to that of a blueberry pie, but we prepare it in slab form with a classic shortbread crust. This makes it easy to cut into dessert-size portions or smaller bites. Serve it with vanilla ice cream and you cannot go wrong. **MAKES 12 BARS**

1. Preheat the oven to 350°F (180°C). Grease a 9-inch (2.5 L) square baking dish and line it with parchment paper, leaving a 1-inch (2.5 cm) overhang on all sides. Line a baking sheet with parchment paper.

2. **MAKE THE SHORTBREAD CRUST** Add the flour, butter, icing sugar, and salt to a food processor. Process for 1 to 2 minutes until a uniform dough forms. Press the dough evenly into the bottom of the prepared baking dish. Bake for 20 minutes, until light golden brown. Let cool.

3. **MAKE THE LATTICE TOP** In the bowl of a food processor, combine the cream cheese, butter, and icing sugar. Add the flour and pulse until the dough comes together in a soft ball. Turn the dough out onto a clean surface. Divide it in half, shaping each half into a square. Wrap each square tightly in plastic wrap and refrigerate for 1 hour.

4. On a well-floured surface, roll the dough to about ⅛ inch (3 mm) thick. Using a sharp knife, cut 12 strips of dough, each about ½ inch (1 cm) wide and at least 9 inches (23 cm) long.

5. Lay out half of the strips, parallel to one another with about a ½-inch (1 cm) space between them, on the prepared baking sheet. To create a lattice pattern, fold back every other strip halfway and lay one of the remaining strips perpendicular across the first set of strips. Unfold the folded strips over the perpendicular strip. Fold the parallel strips that are running underneath the perpendicular strip back over the perpendicular strip. Place a second perpendicular strip of dough beside the first one, leaving some space between the strips. Unfold the parallel strips over the second perpendicular strip. Repeat until the lattice is complete and you've used all of the strips. Place in the freezer for at least 30 minutes to stiffen.

SHORTBREAD CRUST

1½ cups (375 mL) all-purpose flour

¾ cup (175 mL) cold unsalted butter, cut into small cubes

½ cup (125 mL) icing sugar

½ teaspoon (2 mL) kosher salt

LATTICE TOP

8 ounces (225 g) plain cream cheese

½ cup (125 mL) unsalted butter, room temperature

½ cup (125 mL) icing sugar

2 cups (500 mL) all-purpose flour

1 large egg

Coarse sugar, for sprinkling

WILD BLUEBERRY GINGER FILLING

6 cups (1.5 L) fresh or frozen wild blueberries

1½ teaspoons (7 mL) fresh grated ginger

½ cup (125 mL) granulated sugar

2 tablespoons (30 mL) cornstarch

recipe continues

6. **MEANWHILE, MAKE THE WILD BLUEBERRY GINGER FILLING**
Place the blueberries and ginger in a medium saucepan. In a small bowl, whisk the sugar and cornstarch. Add it to the saucepan. Cook over low heat, until the blueberries release their juices and the mixture reduces by about half, about 30 minutes. You should wind up with about 2½ cups (625 mL) of filling. Pour the filling over the crust.

7. Remove the lattice from the freezer and trim away any edges that look like they will not fit into the dish on top of the filling. In a small bowl, whisk the egg with 1 tablespoon (15 mL) of water to make an egg wash. Using a pastry brush, brush the lattice with the egg wash. Sprinkle with coarse sugar. Carefully lift the lattice onto the filling.

8. Bake for 35 to 40 minutes, or until the lattice top is golden and the filling is bubbling. Let cool to room temperature. Cover and refrigerate for 1 hour to allow the filling to set.

9. Use the parchment paper overhang to lift the bars out of the baking dish. Place them on a clean cutting board and pull the parchment paper away from the bars. Using a sharp knife, cut into 12 bars.

10. Store in an airtight container in the fridge for up to 1 week.

OATMEAL CARAMELITAS

These decadent bars have a chewy, gooey caramel-chocolate filling nestled between an oatmeal crust. Making the caramel sauce yourself is a little more work than using store-bought, but oh-so worth it.

MAKES 12 BARS

1. **MAKE THE CARAMEL SAUCE** In a medium saucepan over high heat, bring the sugar, water, and corn syrup to a boil, whisking until the sugar is dissolved. Continue to boil, without stirring, for 5 to 10 minutes, until the mixture turns a dark amber colour and begins to smoke slightly. Immediately remove the saucepan from the heat. Be sure to keep a watchful eye—the colour change can happen quickly.

2. Very carefully and slowly, add the cream to the saucepan. The mixture will bubble up quite a bit. Carefully add the vanilla and salt. Whisk until the sauce is smooth and combined. Transfer the sauce to a glass jar or heatproof container with a tight-fitting lid. Let cool to room temperature, uncovered. The sauce will thicken considerably as it cools.

3. Preheat the oven to 350°F (180°C). Grease an 8-inch (2 L) square baking dish and line it with parchment paper, leaving a 1-inch (2.5 cm) overhang on all sides.

4. **MAKE THE OATMEAL CRUST** In a large bowl, whisk the flour, oats, brown sugar, baking soda, and salt.

5. Place the butter in a microwave-safe bowl and heat it in a microwave oven until melted. Stir in the vanilla. Pour the butter mixture over the flour mixture. Using a wooden spoon, stir until coarse crumbs form. Press half of the mixture evenly into the bottom of the prepared baking dish. This will form the crust. Bake for 10 minutes.

6. Sprinkle the milk chocolate chips in an even layer over the crust. Pour the caramel sauce evenly overtop. Sprinkle the flaky sea salt evenly over the caramel, then sprinkle the remaining oatmeal mixture on top. Bake for 16 to 20 minutes, until lightly golden. Let cool to room temperature. Cover loosely with plastic wrap and place in the fridge to chill for at least 1 hour.

CARAMEL SAUCE

1 cup (250 mL) granulated sugar
¼ cup (60 mL) water
1 teaspoon (5 mL) corn syrup
½ cup (125 mL) heavy (35%) cream
1 tablespoon (15 mL) pure vanilla extract
½ teaspoon (2 mL) kosher salt

OATMEAL CRUST

1 cup (250 mL) all-purpose flour
1 cup (250 mL) rolled oats
½ cup (125 mL) lightly packed brown sugar
½ teaspoon (2 mL) baking soda
¼ teaspoon (1 mL) kosher salt
10 tablespoons (150 mL) unsalted butter
1 teaspoon (5 mL) pure vanilla extract

1 cup (250 mL) milk chocolate chips
½ teaspoon (2 mL) flaky sea salt (we use Maldon), more to taste

recipe continues

7. Use the parchment paper overhang to lift the caramelitas out of the baking dish. Place them on a clean cutting board and pull the parchment paper away from the carmelitas. Using a sharp knife, cut into 12 bars.

8. Serve immediately or store in an airtight container in the fridge for up to 1 week.

SCONES,
MUFFINS,
AND BISCUITS

CITRUS CURRANT SCONES

We have been making different versions of this recipe for a very long time, but the pairing of citrus and currants is our original favourite. Rubbing the freshly grated citrus zest with the sugar amplifies the citrus punch by helping to release the oils in the zest. These scones taste amazing served with cold Whipped Clotted Cream (page 282). **MAKES 8 TO 10 SCONES**

1. Line a baking sheet with parchment paper.

2. Place the currants in a small bowl and cover them with hot water. Set aside.

3. In a large bowl, add the sugar, lemon zest, and orange zest. Rub the sugar and zest between your hands until fragrant. Add the flour, baking powder, baking soda, and salt. Whisk to combine. Using a box grater, grate the cold butter into the flour mixture and toss until it resembles coarse crumbs.

4. Drain the currants and pat them dry with a paper towel. Add the currants and buttermilk to the flour mixture. Using a wooden spoon, mix gently until the dough holds together.

5. Tip the dough out onto a well-floured work surface. Using your hands, pat the dough until it is about 1½ inches (4 cm) thick. Using a 3-inch (8 cm) round cutter, cut out circles. Gently gather the scraps together to cut as many circles as you can. If baking immediately, transfer the scones to the prepared baking sheet and place in the fridge to chill for 30 minutes. If baking at a later date, place the baking sheet in the freezer. Once the scones are frozen, transfer them to a zip-top bag. Scones can be kept in the freezer for up to 3 weeks.

6. Preheat the oven to 400°F (200°C).

7. Brush the top of each scone with melted butter. Sprinkle each with coarse sugar. Bake for 25 minutes, until the tops turn light brown. If baking from frozen, add about 10 minutes to the baking time. Let cool about 15 minutes before serving. Serve with butter and Whipped Clotted Cream.

8. Scones are best served on the day they are made but can be stored in an airtight container at room temperature for 1 more day.

¾ cup (175 mL) dried black currants
½ cup (125 mL) granulated sugar
1 teaspoon (5 mL) fresh grated
   lemon zest
1 teaspoon (5 mL) fresh grated
   orange zest
4¾ cups (1.2 L) all-purpose flour
1 tablespoon (15 mL) baking powder
¾ teaspoon (3 mL) baking soda
1¼ teaspoon (6 mL) kosher salt
1 cup + 1 tablespoon (265 mL) cold
   unsalted butter
2 cups (500 mL) buttermilk
3 tablespoons (45 mL) melted butter
Coarse sugar, for sprinkling

FOR SERVING

Unsalted butter
Whipped Clotted Cream (page 282)

KITCHEN TIP

- Using a box grater to grate cold butter into a dough is speedy and effective, and one of our favourite techniques. It cuts the butter into the perfect size to incorporate easily into dry ingredients and saves you from fussing with a pastry blender.

BOURBON PEACH CRUMBLE SCONES

Peach and bourbon is a flavour pairing that is sophisticated, and a little unexpected for scones, but these fuzzy fruits go perfectly with this southern spirit in just about any context. **MAKES 12 SCONES**

BOURBON PEACH COMPOTE

6 ripe peaches, peeled, pitted, and roughly chopped
1 cup (250 mL) lightly packed brown sugar
½ cup (125 mL) water
¼ cup (60 mL) unsalted butter
1 teaspoon (5 mL) ground cinnamon
2 tablespoons (30 mL) bourbon

SCONES

1 cup (250 mL) Bourbon Peach Compote
½ cup (125 mL) + 3 tablespoons (45 mL) heavy (35%) cream, divided
½ cup (125 mL) lightly packed brown sugar
¼ cup (60 mL) full-fat plain Greek yogurt
1 large egg
1 teaspoon (5 mL) pure vanilla extract
2½ cups (625 mL) all-purpose flour
2½ teaspoons (12 mL) baking powder
1½ teaspoons (7 mL) ground cinnamon
¼ teaspoon (1 mL) ground nutmeg
½ teaspoon (2 mL) kosher salt
¼ cup (60 mL) unsalted butter, frozen
½ batch Crumble Topping (page 284)

1. **MAKE THE BOURBON PEACH COMPOTE** In a medium saucepan over medium-low heat, combine the peaches, brown sugar, water, butter, and cinnamon. Cook for 10 minutes, stirring occasionally, until the butter melts and the mixture thickens. Add the bourbon and stir to combine. Remove the saucepan from the heat. Let cool.

2. Preheat the oven to 400°F (200°C). Line a baking sheet with parchment paper.

3. **MAKE THE SCONES** In a medium bowl, whisk 1 cup (250 mL) of the Bourbon Peach Compote, ½ cup (125 mL) of the cream, the brown sugar, yogurt, egg, and vanilla. Reserve any remaining compote for serving.

4. In a large bowl, whisk the flour, baking powder, cinnamon, nutmeg, and salt. Using a box grater, grate the butter into the dry ingredients and toss until the mixture resembles coarse crumbs.

5. Add the peach and cream mixture to the flour mixture. Using a wooden spoon, stir just until everything appears moistened. Use a ¼-cup (60 mL) measuring cup to drop scones 3 inches (8 cm) apart on the prepared baking sheet. Brush each scone with some of the remaining 3 tablespoons (45 mL) of cream, then sprinkle each with about 2 tablespoons (30 mL) of the Crumble Topping. Lightly press the crumble into the scone dough to ensure that it sticks. If baking the scones at a later date, place the baking sheet in the freezer. Once the scones are frozen, transfer them to a zip-top bag. Scones can be kept in the freezer for up to 3 weeks.

6. Bake for 20 to 25 minutes, or until lightly golden. If baking from frozen, bake for an additional 10 minutes. Let cool slightly. Serve the scones with a spoonful of the remaining compote on top. Scones are best served on the day they are made but can be stored in an airtight container at room temperature for 1 more day.

KITCHEN TIP

• Using a box grater to grate cold butter into a
dough is speedy and effective, and one of our
favourite techniques. It cuts the butter into the
perfect size to incorporate easily into dry
ingredients and saves you from fussing with a
pastry blender.

RASPBERRY RHUBARB SCONES

These scones are a serious Bread Bar cult favourite. The fruit options you can use really are limitless, but here we share the combination of raspberry and rhubarb because we love the sweet-tart balance it creates. The white chocolate the recipe calls for helps keep these scones extra moist. **MAKES 8 SCONES**

1. Line a baking sheet with parchment paper.

2. In a large bowl, combine the flour, sugar, baking powder, baking soda, and salt. Add the shortening and butter and use your hands to massage them into the flour mixture until it resembles coarse crumbs. Add the white chocolate and lightly toss to combine.

3. Add 1 cup (250 mL) of the cream and mix with your hands until just combined. Add the raspberries and rhubarb and continue mixing with your hands just until you have a soft, shaggy dough that stays together with no dry bits of flour on the bottom of the bowl. Make sure not to overwork the dough or the scones will be tough. Cover and chill for about 1 hour.

4. Tip the dough out onto a well-floured work surface. Roll out the dough into a rectangle about 1 inch (2.5 cm) thick. Cut the dough into 8 (3-inch/8 cm) squares. Place the scones on the prepared baking sheet, spacing them evenly. If baking immediately, chill in the fridge for 20 minutes. If baking at a later date, place the baking sheet in the freezer. Once the scones are frozen, transfer them to a zip-top bag. Scones can be kept in the freezer for up to 3 weeks.

5. Preheat the oven to 350°F (180°C).

6. Brush the top of each scone with the remaining ¼ cup (60 mL) of cream and sprinkle with a generous pinch of sugar. Bake for 20 minutes, turning the baking sheet halfway through, until the tops are golden brown. If baking from frozen, bake for an additional 10 minutes, turning the baking sheet halfway through. Transfer the scones to a wire rack and let cool.

7. Scones are best served on the day they are made but can be stored in an airtight container at room temperature for 1 more day.

4 cups (1 L) all-purpose flour

¾ cup (175 mL) granulated sugar, more for sprinkling

1 tablespoon (15 mL) baking powder

1 teaspoon (5 mL) baking soda

1 teaspoon (5 mL) kosher salt

⅔ cup (150 mL) vegetable shortening, cut into large pieces

⅔ cup (150 mL) unsalted butter, cut into large pieces, softened

1 cup (250 mL) white chocolate chips or shavings

1¼ cups (300 mL) heavy (35%) cream, divided

½ cup (125 mL) fresh or frozen raspberries

½ cup (125 mL) fresh or frozen rhubarb, sliced

PUMPKIN SCONES WITH GINGER GLAZE

Paired with a creamy flat white coffee, these pumpkin scones with their sweet glaze are a perfect quick breakfast or snack when the temperatures outside start to dip. Pumpkin purée keeps the scones moist, and buying it in a can is not cheating; the flesh from fresh pumpkins that you roast and purée yourself at home is typically too watery to bake with. Just be sure to buy pumpkin purée and not ready-made pie filling when you go to the grocery store. **MAKES 8 SCONES**

PUMPKIN SCONES

2 cups (500 mL) all-purpose flour

⅓ cup (75 mL) lightly packed brown sugar

1 tablespoon (15 mL) baking powder

1 teaspoon (5 mL) ground cinnamon

½ teaspoon (2 mL) kosher salt

½ teaspoon (2 mL) ground nutmeg

½ teaspoon (2 mL) ground cloves

¼ teaspoon (1 mL) ground ginger

½ cup (125 mL) cold unsalted butter

½ cup (125 mL) pumpkin purée

3 tablespoons (45 mL) whole (3.25%) milk

1 large egg

1 teaspoon (5 mL) pure vanilla extract

GINGER GLAZE

1 cup (250 mL) icing sugar

¼ cup (60 mL) candied ginger, finely chopped

1 tablespoon (15 mL) milk

1. Line a baking sheet with parchment paper.

2. **MAKE THE PUMPKIN SCONES** In a large bowl, whisk the flour, brown sugar, baking powder, cinnamon, salt, nutmeg, cloves, and ginger. Using a box grater, grate the cold butter into the dry ingredients and toss with your hands until the mixture resembles coarse crumbs.

3. In a medium bowl, whisk the pumpkin purée, milk, egg, and vanilla until smooth. Using a wooden spoon, stir the pumpkin mixture into the flour mixture until just combined, making sure not to overmix.

4. Tip the dough out onto a well-floured work surface and gently knead until everything is evenly combined. The dough will be sticky. Pat the dough into an 8-inch (20 cm) circle. Cut into 8 equal triangles. Arrange the scones on the prepared baking sheet, spacing them evenly. If baking immediately, chill in the fridge for 30 minutes. If baking at a later date, place the baking sheet in the freezer. Once the scones are frozen, transfer them to a zip-top bag. Scones can be kept in the freezer for up to 3 weeks.

5. Preheat the oven to 400°F (200°C).

6. Bake for 15 to 17 minutes, turning the baking sheet halfway through, until light golden brown. If baking from frozen, bake for an additional 10 minutes, turning the baking sheet halfway through. Let cool for 20 minutes before glazing.

7. **MAKE THE GINGER GLAZE** In a small bowl, whisk the icing sugar, candied ginger, and milk. Using a spoon, drizzle the glaze over each scone. Let set.

8. Scones are best served on the day they are made but can be stored in an airtight container at room temperature for 1 more day.

KITCHEN TIP

• Using a box grater to grate cold butter into a
dough is speedy and effective, and one of our
favourite techniques. It cuts the butter into the
perfect size to incorporate easily into dry
ingredients and saves you from fussing with a
pastry blender.

PEACH BROWN BETTY

A Brown Betty is often compared to a cobbler, crumble, or crisp, but it is actually a stand-alone. Whereas a crumble or crisp is topped with oats and a cobbler is topped with biscuits, the crunchy topping used in this recipe is made from bread crumbs. You can use store-bought bread crumbs, but for the ultimate Brown Betty, dry out two slices of 1-inch (2.5 cm) thick Brioche (page 278) in a 250°F (120°C) oven for ninety minutes, turning and flipping the bread once. Once it has cooled, you can pulse the brioche in a food processor to create coarsely ground crumbs. **SERVES 8**

1. Preheat the oven to 375°F (190°C). Grease a 9-inch (2.5 L) square baking dish.

2. Melt 2 tablespoons (30 mL) of the butter. In a medium bowl, combine the melted butter with the bread crumbs, granulated sugar, brown sugar, salt, and cinnamon.

3. In a large non-stick skillet over medium heat, melt the remaining 2 tablespoons (30 mL) of butter. Add the peaches and lemon juice. Cook for 12 to 15 minutes, until the peaches begin to caramelize. Remove the skillet from the heat and stir in half of the bread crumb mixture. Return the skillet to the heat and sauté the peaches with the bread crumb mixture until bubbly and fragrant, about 5 minutes. Transfer to the prepared baking dish. Top with the remaining bread crumb mixture.

4. Bake for 30 minutes, or until the topping is golden brown and the juices are bubbling. Let cool slightly before serving.

5. Wrap any leftovers tightly with plastic wrap and store in the fridge for up to 3 days.

4 tablespoons (60 mL) unsalted butter, divided
1 cup (250 mL) bread crumbs
¼ cup (60 mL) granulated sugar
¼ cup (60 mL) lightly packed brown sugar
1 teaspoon (5 mL) kosher salt
¼ teaspoon (1 mL) ground cinnamon
8 cups (2 L) pitted, peeled, and sliced ripe Freestone peaches (about 16 peaches) or frozen peaches
3 tablespoons (45 mL) fresh lemon juice

KITCHEN TIP

• Freestone peaches picked at the height of peach season will easily release their stones and peel without much trouble. However, frozen fruit is always a good option when fresh fruit is not available. Companies that sell frozen fruit purchase fruit at the peak of freshness and then flash freeze it, so you'll always get the best flavour.

LEMON RICOTTA MUFFINS

Ricotta cheese is wonderful when used in baking because it lends a fluffy, light crumb to recipes. Ricotta and lemon are a natural twosome: the bright zing of lemon complements the neutral, creamy cheese. In this recipe, a fragrant lemon sugar topping made by rubbing the oils from the zest into the sugar really makes the lemon flavour of these muffins sing. **MAKES 12 MUFFINS**

Zest of 1 lemon
1 cup (250 mL) granulated sugar
2 cups (500 mL) all-purpose flour
2 teaspoons (10 mL) baking powder
¼ teaspoon (1 mL) baking soda
½ teaspoon (2 mL) kosher salt
¾ cup (175 mL) full-fat ricotta cheese
¼ cup (60 mL) whole (3.25%) milk
2 large eggs
½ teaspoon (2 mL) pure vanilla
   extract
½ cup (125 mL) unsalted butter,
   melted and cooled

1. Preheat the oven to 350°F (180°C). Line a standard muffin tin with paper liners.

2. Place the lemon zest and sugar in a large bowl. Rub the two between your hands, working the sugar into the zest, until fragrant. Measure ¼ cup (60 mL) of the lemon sugar. Set aside to reserve for the muffin topping. Whisk the flour, baking powder, baking soda, and salt into the large bowl containing the remaining lemon sugar.

3. In a medium bowl, whisk the ricotta, milk, eggs, and vanilla. Add the melted butter and whisk until smooth. Gently stir the ricotta mixture into the flour mixture. The batter will be very thick.

4. Divide the batter evenly among the muffin liners, filling each about three-quarters full. Sprinkle the top of each muffin with some of the reserved lemon sugar. Bake for 25 to 30 minutes, until the tops are golden and a cake tester comes out clean. Let cool slightly in the tin, about 10 minutes. Tip the muffins out of the tin and place them on a wire rack to cool completely.

5. Muffins are best served on the day they are made but can be stored in an airtight container at room temperature for up to 1 week.

KITCHEN TIP

• When baking, always choose full-fat ricotta cheese. The desired texture of your baked goods cannot be reproduced by using "lite" or "low-fat" versions.

BLUEBERRY APPLE STREUSEL MUFFINS

One of Bread Bar's staple recipes is an apple cider muffin that visitors to the restaurant cannot get enough of. Here, we offer a version of that muffin with the delicious apple cider flavour, plus berries and a streusel topping to add some texture and interest. Baking the muffins for 10 minutes before adding the streusel will ensure that the topping does not sink into the dough and the tops of your muffins remain sweet and crumbly. **MAKES 12 MUFFINS**

1. Preheat the oven to 350°F (180°C). Line a standard muffin tin with paper liners.

2. **MAKE THE STREUSEL** In a small bowl, use a fork to combine the flour, sugar, and melted butter. Set aside.

3. **MAKE THE BLUEBERRY APPLE MUFFINS** In a stand mixer fitted with the whisk attachment, whisk the brown sugar, granulated sugar, canola oil, and eggs on medium speed until well combined, about 1 minute. Add the apple cider, sour cream, and vanilla and whisk on medium-low speed until combined. Add the flour, baking soda, cinnamon, and salt. Whisk until well combined. Using a silicone spatula, scrape down the sides of the bowl and whisk once more to ensure that all of the dry ingredients are well incorporated. Remove the bowl from the stand and fold in the blueberries.

4. Divide the batter evenly among the muffin liners, filling each about three-quarters full. Bake for 10 minutes. Remove from the oven and sprinkle 2 tablespoons (30 mL) of streusel over each muffin. Bake for an additional 15 minutes, until the muffins are puffed and the streusel is golden brown. Let cool slightly in the tin, about 10 minutes. Tip the muffins out of the tin and place them on a wire rack to cool completely.

5. Store in an airtight container at room temperature for up to 3 days.

STREUSEL

¾ cup (175 mL) all-purpose flour

⅔ cup (150 mL) granulated sugar

4 tablespoons (60 mL) unsalted butter, melted

BLUEBERRY APPLE MUFFINS

1¼ cups (300 mL) lightly packed brown sugar

1 cup (250 mL) granulated sugar

¾ cup (175 mL) canola oil

3 large eggs

1 cup (250 mL) apple cider

¾ cup (175 mL) full-fat sour cream

1 teaspoon (5 mL) pure vanilla extract

2¾ cups (675 mL) all-purpose flour

1½ teaspoons (7 mL) baking soda

1½ teaspoons (7 mL) cinnamon

½ teaspoon (2 mL) kosher salt

1½ cups (375 mL) fresh or frozen blueberries

OATMEAL MUFFINS STUFFED WITH WHISKY PEACHES

Oatmeal, whisky, and peaches make up one of Bettina's favourite flavour combinations. In our first cookbook, *Earth to Table Every Day*, we offered a whisky peach recipe to be served over ice cream. This time we fill these oatmeal muffins with whisky peaches for a delightful flavour explosion. But don't limit yourself to this flavour combination—oatmeal adds a mild toasty flavour that complements many other fruits as well, especially strawberries and apples. Substitute an equal amount of sweet apples such as Golden Delicious or Empire or even strawberries for the peaches if you want to make these muffins when peaches are out of season—or when you just want a change. **MAKES 12 MUFFINS**

WHISKY PEACHES

1 pound (450 g) fresh peeled and
   pitted Freestone peaches or frozen
   peaches, chopped
2 tablespoons (30 mL) fresh lemon
   juice
½ cup (125 mL) granulated sugar
1 tablespoon (15 mL) whisky

OATMEAL MUFFINS

1½ cups (375 mL) rolled oats, more
   for sprinkling
1 cup (250 mL) all-purpose flour
½ cup (125 mL) whole wheat flour
1½ teaspoons (7 mL) baking powder
1½ teaspoons (7 mL) baking soda
1 teaspoon (5 mL) kosher salt
2 large eggs
1½ cups (375 mL) unsweetened
   applesauce
¾ cup (175 mL) lightly packed brown
   sugar
½ cup (125 mL) full-fat sour cream
¼ cup (60 mL) canola oil
1 teaspoon (5 mL) pure vanilla extract
¼ cup (60 mL) Whisky Peaches

1. Preheat the oven to 350°F (180°C). Line a standard muffin tin with paper liners.

2. **MAKE THE WHISKY PEACHES** In a medium saucepan over medium heat, cook the peaches with the lemon juice, sugar, and whisky stirring constantly, until the mixture reaches a temperature of 216°F to 218°F (102°C to 103°C), making sure not to let the temperature exceed 218°F (103°C). Remove from the heat immediately. Let cool to room temperature.

3. **MAKE THE OATMEAL MUFFINS** In a medium bowl, combine the oats, all-purpose flour, whole wheat flour, baking powder, baking soda, and salt.

4. In a stand mixer fitted with the whisk attachment, whisk the eggs, applesauce, brown sugar, sour cream, canola oil, and vanilla. Add the wet ingredients to the dry ingredients and mix with a spatula until smooth.

5. Fill each muffin liner about one-third full of batter. Add about 1 teaspoon (5 mL) Whisky Peaches to each liner. Cover the filling with the remaining batter until each liner is three-quarters full. Sprinkle each muffin with oats. Bake for 20 minutes, until the tops are evenly browned and spring back when touched. Let cool slightly in the tin, about 10 minutes. Tip the muffins out of the tin and place them on a wire rack to cool completely.

6. Store in an airtight container in the fridge for up to 5 days.

KITCHEN TIP

• Make sure you don't wander off when making the whisky peaches. Peaches will burn at 220°F (104°C), so keep a close watch and make sure to pull them off the heat before they reach the danger zone.

POWER MUFFINS

In our previous cookbook, *Earth to Table Every Day*, we shared a recipe for vegan, gluten-free Power Cookies. Not all baked goods are created equal, though, and the deliciousness of that cookie was difficult to replicate in a muffin while maintaining its vegan, gluten-free status. This muffin uses flour and eggs, so it's not gluten free or vegan, but with so many different seeds and yogurt—and dried fruit, dates, and applesauce as the sweeteners—it's ultimately sugar free and full of all kinds of good things. These muffins will add a power punch to your morning—or any time of the day when you need it.

MAKES 12 MUFFINS

1. Preheat the oven to 475°F (240°C). Line a standard muffin tin with paper liners.

2. In a medium saucepan, combine the dates and water. Cook over high heat for about 10 minutes, until the dates are soft and about 2 tablespoons (30 mL) of water remain. Transfer the date mixture to a food processor or high-speed blender and process on high speed until a smooth paste forms. Set aside.

3. In a medium bowl, whisk the flour, baking powder, baking soda, cinnamon, salt, sunflower seeds, pumpkin seeds, hemp seeds, chia seeds, coconut, flaxseed, oats, and cranberries. Set aside.

4. In a stand mixer fitted with the whisk attachment, whisk the date paste, butter, vegetable oil, and eggs on high speed until light and fluffy, about 5 minutes. Fold the date and egg mixture into the flour mixture until combined. Fold in the yogurt and applesauce until smooth.

5. Divide the batter evenly among the muffin liners, filling each about three-quarters full. Bake for 5 minutes. Reduce the temperature to 375°F (190°C) and bake for an additional 12 to 15 minutes, making sure not to open the oven until the end of the second baking period. The muffins are ready when a wooden toothpick inserted into the centre comes out clean. Let cool slightly in the tin, about 10 minutes. Tip the muffins out of the tin and place them on a wire rack to cool completely.

6. Store in an airtight container at room temperature for 3 to 4 days.

½ cup (125 mL) pitted Medjool dates (about 15 dates)

1 cup (250 mL) water

2 cups (500 mL) all-purpose flour

2 teaspoons (10 mL) baking powder

1 teaspoon (5 mL) baking soda

1 teaspoon (5 mL) ground cinnamon

1 teaspoon (5 mL) kosher salt

¼ cup (60 mL) roasted sunflower seeds

¼ cup (60 mL) roasted pumpkin seeds

¼ cup (60 mL) hemp seeds

¼ cup (60 mL) chia seeds

¼ cup (60 mL) unsweetened shredded coconut

¼ cup (60 mL) ground flaxseed

½ cup (125 mL) rolled oats

¾ cup (175 mL) dried cranberries

½ cup (125 mL) unsalted butter, softened

1 cup (250 mL) vegetable oil

2 large eggs

1 cup (250 mL) full-fat plain Greek yogurt

½ cup (125 mL) unsweetened applesauce

GOAT CHEESE AND SPINACH BISCUITS

Chefs often keep notebooks filled with recipes that are barely legible and covered in grease stains from kitchens past. Flipping through one of these notebooks is always a trip down memory lane, and there are some recipes you just keep flipping to over and over again. This recipe is adapted from one found in an old notebook, and it is a keeper. The goat cheese can be switched out for an equal amount of feta, and the fresh spinach can be swapped out for an equal amount of chopped black olives or roasted red peppers for a completely different flavour profile. **MAKES 10 BISCUITS**

4 cups (1 L) all-purpose flour

3 tablespoons (45 mL) granulated sugar

2 tablespoons (30 mL) baking powder

1 teaspoon (5 mL) kosher salt

½ teaspoon (2 mL) fresh cracked black pepper

½ cup (125 mL) unsalted butter, frozen

4 large eggs

⅔ cup (150 mL) buttermilk, more for brushing

1 cup (250 mL) crumbled goat cheese

1 cup (250 mL) fresh baby spinach, roughly chopped

1. In a large bowl, whisk the flour, sugar, baking powder, salt, and pepper. Using a box grater, grate the frozen butter into the dry ingredients and toss with your hands until the mixture resembles coarse crumbs.

2. In a small bowl, whisk the eggs and buttermilk. Add the egg mixture to the flour mixture. Add the goat cheese and spinach. Using your hands, gently knead the dough until it just starts to hold together, being careful not to overmix.

3. Tip the dough out onto a well-floured work surface and continue to gently knead just until it forms a shaggy ball. Pat the dough into a disc about 1 inch (2.5 cm) thick. Cut the dough into 10 equal triangles. Line a baking sheet with parchment paper and arrange the biscuits on the prepared baking sheet. Brush the tops with buttermilk. Chill in the fridge for 30 minutes.

4. Meanwhile, preheat the oven to 325°F (160°C).

5. Bake for 20 minutes, turning the baking sheet halfway through, until golden brown. Let the biscuits cool slightly before transferring them to a wire rack to cool completely.

6. Biscuits are best served on the day they are made but can be stored in an airtight container at room temperature for 1 more day.

LOADED POTATO BISCUITS

These biscuits are similar to traditional biscuits but incorporate leftover mashed potatoes to help keep them tender and moist. With the addition of toppings you might find on a loaded baked potato, these biscuits are irresistible. They are also sturdy enough to hold the fillings for a breakfast sandwich—scrambled eggs and ham between a loaded potato biscuit will make you look forward to early mornings. **MAKES 8 BISCUITS**

1. In a medium bowl, whisk the flour, sugar, baking powder, and salt. Using a box grater, grate the frozen butter into the dry ingredients and toss with your hands until the the mixture resembles coarse crumbs. Using a wooden spoon, stir in the mashed potatoes, breaking them into chunks. Make a well in the mixture. Add the egg, water, and ⅓ cup (75 mL) of the milk. Add the scallions, cheddar, and bacon. Using your hands, gently knead to create a loose dough.

2. Tip the dough out onto a well-floured work surface and knead 6 to 8 times, until it holds together. Pat the dough into a disc about ¾ inch (2 cm) thick. Use a 3-inch (8 cm) round cutter to cut the dough into circles. Line a baking sheet with parchment paper and arrange the biscuits on the prepared baking sheet. Brush the tops with the remaining 2 tablespoons (30 mL) of milk. Chill in the fridge for 30 minutes.

3. Meanwhile, preheat the oven to 450°F (230°C).

4. Bake for 15 to 20 minutes, turning the baking sheet halfway through, until golden. Let the biscuits cool slightly before transferring them to a wire rack. If serving the biscuits as is, let cool to room temperature or serve warm. If making sandwiches with the biscuits, let cool completely. Use a serrated knife to slice the biscuits in half before stuffing them with your favourite fillings.

5. Biscuits are best served on the day they are made but can be stored in an airtight container at room temperature for 1 more day.

2½ cups (625 mL) all-purpose flour
¼ cup (60 mL) granulated sugar
2 tablespoons (30 mL) baking powder
1 teaspoon (5 mL) kosher salt
¼ cup (60 mL) unsalted butter, frozen
1½ cups (375 mL) leftover mashed
  potatoes
1 large egg, beaten
⅓ cup (75 mL) cold water
⅓ cup (75 mL) + 2 tablespoons
  (30 mL) whole (3.25%) milk, divided
2 scallions, chopped
½ cup (125 mL) shredded cheddar
  cheese
½ cup (125 mL) chopped cooked
  bacon

CHEDDAR JALAPEÑO BUTTERMILK BISCUITS

Bread Bar has been serving cheesy buttermilk biscuits with fried chicken every Friday for many years now. Jalapeños give these cheesy biscuits a slight zing. Eating soft, flaky biscuits alongside spicy foods helps turn down the heat in your mouth. They are a perfect accompaniment to soup, chili, and fried chicken. If you're not a fan of too much spice, enjoy them on their own smeared with a little butter.

MAKES 8 BISCUITS

2 cups (500 mL) all-purpose flour

1 tablespoon (15 mL) baking powder

2 teaspoons (10 mL) kosher salt

¾ cup (175 mL) cold unsalted butter, cubed

½ cup (125 mL) buttermilk

1 large egg

1 cup (250 mL) + ½ cup (125 mL) shredded sharp cheddar cheese, divided

2 jalapeño peppers, 1 cored and diced, 1 cored and thinly sliced

1 tablespoon (15 mL) flaky sea salt (we use Maldon)

1. In a stand mixer fitted with the paddle attachment, mix the flour, baking powder, and salt on low speed. Add the butter and mix until the butter is the size of peas.

2. Place the buttermilk and egg in a small bowl and beat lightly with a fork. With the mixer on low speed, quickly add the buttermilk mixture, 1 cup (250 mL) of the cheddar, and the diced jalapeño to the flour mixture. Mix on low speed until roughly combined.

3. Tip the dough out onto a well-floured work surface and lightly knead about 6 times. Roll the dough into a 10- × 5-inch (25 × 12 cm) rectangle. Using a sharp, floured knife, cut the dough into 8 equal rectangles. Line a baking sheet with parchment paper and arrange the biscuits on the prepared baking sheet, leaving about 2 inches (5 cm) between each biscuit. Chill in the fridge for 30 minutes.

4. Meanwhile, preheat the oven to 350°F (180°C).

5. Sprinkle the remaining ½ cup (125 mL) of cheddar evenly over the biscuits. Place 2 or 3 jalapeño slices on each one. Sprinkle each with flaky sea salt. Bake for 20 to 25 minutes, until the tops are brown and the biscuits are cooked through. Serve warm.

6. Biscuits are best served on the day they are made but can be stored in an airtight container at room temperature for 1 more day.

KITCHEN TIP

- If you prefer your biscuits to have less heat, be sure to remove all of the seeds and ribs from the jalapeños. If you like your biscuits extra spicy, add even more diced jalapeños to the batter, to taste!

LOAVES

AND

CAKES

ULTIMATE BANANA BREAD

This is quite possibly the easiest and most delicious banana bread we have ever made. We make this recipe all the time—and sometimes even bake it into muffins. If you want to make muffins, divide the batter evenly among the wells of a standard muffin tin, lined with paper liners, and reduce the baking time by half. Instead of one loaf, you'll wind up with about 12 muffins that make an easy-to-grab snack.

MAKES ONE 9- × 5-INCH (2 L) LOAF

1. Preheat the oven to 350°F (180°C). Grease and flour a 9- × 5-inch (2 L) loaf pan.

2. In a medium bowl, whisk the flour, salt, baking powder, and baking soda.

3. In a stand mixer fitted with the paddle attachment, mix the egg, butter, brown sugar, granulated sugar, and vanilla on medium speed for 5 minutes, until light and fluffy. Add the sour cream and mix for 30 seconds.

4. Add the flour mixture to the butter and sugar mixture. Mix on low speed until just combined. Add the overripe bananas and mix for 15 seconds. Remove the bowl from the stand and finish mixing with a spatula or wooden spoon, stirring and scraping the sides and bottom of the bowl until all ingredients are well combined. Transfer the batter to the prepared loaf pan.

5. Bake for 30 minutes. Cut the ripe banana in half lengthwise, following the curve of the banana. Remove the loaf from the oven and place the banana halves on top, cut side up. If you place the banana on the loaf any earlier, it will sink to the bottom. Return the loaf to the oven and bake for an additional 20 to 30 minutes, or until a wooden skewer inserted in the centre of the loaf comes out clean. Place the loaf pan on a wire rack and let cool in the pan for about 10 minutes. Turn the loaf out onto the wire rack to cool completely.

6. Store in an airtight container at room temperature for up to 4 days.

1 cup (250 mL) all-purpose flour

1 teaspoon (5 mL) kosher salt

½ teaspoon (2 mL) baking powder

½ teaspoon (2 mL) baking soda

1 large egg

½ cup (125 mL) unsalted butter, melted

½ cup (125 mL) lightly packed brown sugar

¼ cup (60 mL) granulated sugar

1 teaspoon (5 mL) pure vanilla extract

½ cup (125 mL) full-fat sour cream

2 overripe bananas

1 ripe banana

ZUCCHINI BREAD

This is a staple recipe in Bettina's house. It does not require any fancy equipment, and it's the only way she can get her six-year-old daughter to eat vegetables. She has to mask the undesirable taste and texture of zucchini with cinnamon, nutmeg, and ginger. Her partner, Tom, will always steal a slice before he goes to work, and the simplicity of the recipe means it's easy to always have a loaf available for snacking. **MAKES ONE 9- × 5-INCH (2 L) LOAF**

1 large or 2 small zucchinis

1 cup (250 mL) lightly packed brown sugar

2 tablespoons (30 mL) granulated sugar

⅔ cup (150 mL) vegetable oil

2 large eggs

2 teaspoons (10 mL) Madagascar vanilla

1½ cups (375 mL) all-purpose flour

1½ teaspoons (7 mL) ground cinnamon

¾ teaspoon (3 mL) ground nutmeg

½ teaspoon (2 mL) baking powder

½ teaspoon (2 mL) baking soda

¼ teaspoon (1 mL) ground ginger

1 teaspoon (5 mL) kosher salt

1. Preheat the oven to 360°F (185°C). Grease and flour a 9- × -5-inch (2 L) loaf pan.

2. Using a box grater, grate the zucchini to yield about 1½ cups (375 mL).

3. In a large bowl, whisk the brown sugar, granulated sugar, oil, eggs, and vanilla.

4. In a small bowl, whisk the flour, cinnamon, nutmeg, baking powder, baking soda, ginger, and salt.

5. Add the flour mixture to the egg mixture and stir to combine. Add the grated zucchini and stir until well combined.

6. Transfer the batter to the prepared loaf pan. Bake for 45 to 55 minutes, until a toothpick inserted in the centre of the loaf comes out clean and the loaf is nicely browned and peaking in the middle. Let cool in the pan for about 15 minutes, then turn the loaf out onto a wire rack to cool completely.

7. Store in an airtight container at room temperature for up to 5 days.

KITCHEN TIP

• You can easily add about 1 cup (250 mL) of chopped nuts or chocolate chips to this recipe when you add the zucchini without having to make any adjustments. Walnuts or pecans are tasty with zucchini and spices.

APRICOT AND PECAN LOAF

In this comforting loaf, the faint tartness of the smooth, sweet apricots works in perfect harmony with the buttery, astringent pecans—and both flavours are enhanced by the orange zest. Citrus is often used to highlight flavour, much like salt, and in this recipe it does wonders. When zesting the orange, make sure you zest only the thin outer skin. The white pith is bitter and not invited! To coax the most flavour out of the orange zest, we suggest mixing it with the granulated sugar in the stand mixer until it becomes fragrant. The skin of the orange has a bunch of oil, flavour, and fragrance that emerges when you beat the sugar with the zested rind. **MAKES ONE 9- × 5-INCH (2 L) LOAF**

1. Preheat the oven to 350°F (180°C). Grease and flour a 9- × 5-inch (2 L) loaf pan.

2. **MAKE THE APRICOT LOAF** In a stand mixer fitted with the paddle attachment, beat the sugar and orange zest on medium speed until the zest releases its oils and the mixture becomes fragrant, about 2 minutes. Add the all-purpose flour, whole wheat flour, baking powder, baking soda, and salt. Mix for 30 seconds, until combined.

3. In a medium bowl, whisk the oil, egg, and apple cider. Add the oil mixture to the flour mixture and mix on medium speed until just combined. Add the dried apricots. Mix until combined. Remove the bowl from the stand and finish mixing with a spatula or wooden spoon, stirring and scraping the sides and bottom of the bowl until all ingredients are well combined.

4. **MAKE THE PECAN TOPPING** In a small bowl, combine 2 teaspoons (10 mL) of the sugar, the water, and pecans. Toss until the pecans are evenly coated. Set aside.

5. Transfer the batter to the prepared loaf pan. Sprinkle the loaf evenly with the remaining 2 teaspoons (10 mL) of sugar and the Pecan Topping. Bake for 45 minutes, or until a wooden skewer inserted in the centre comes out clean. Let cool in the pan for about 10 minutes, then turn the loaf out onto a wire rack to cool completely.

6. Store in an airtight container at room temperature for up to 4 days or in the freezer for up to 3 months. If serving from frozen, bring the loaf to room temperature, then warm it in a 350°F (180°C) oven for 20 minutes to refresh it.

APRICOT LOAF

1 cup (250 mL) granulated sugar
2 teaspoons (10 mL) orange zest
1½ cups (375 mL) all-purpose flour
½ cup (125 mL) whole wheat flour
1½ teaspoons (7 mL) baking powder
½ teaspoon (2 mL) baking soda
1 teaspoon (5 mL) kosher salt
¼ cup (60 mL) canola oil
1 large egg
¾ cup (175 mL) apple cider
¾ cup (175 mL) dried apricots, chopped

PECAN TOPPING

4 teaspoons (20 mL) granulated sugar, divided
2 teaspoons (10 mL) water
¼ cup (60 mL) pecan pieces

ORANGE AND PISTACHIO LOAF

You are in for a treat when you taste this loaf. Fresh orange zest and juice make it light and sassy, while the pistachios add an earthy depth of flavour and a nice crunch. It's wonderfully moist and chock-full of mini chocolate chips, too. **MAKES ONE 9- × 5-INCH (2 L) LOAF**

¾ cup (175 mL) granulated sugar

¼ cup (60 mL) unsalted butter, softened

2 large eggs

1½ cups (375 mL) full-fat sour cream

2 tablespoons (30 mL) fresh orange juice

1 teaspoon (5 mL) fresh orange zest

3 cups (750 mL) all-purpose flour

1½ teaspoons (7 mL) baking powder

1 teaspoon (5 mL) baking soda

1 teaspoon (5 mL) kosher salt

1 cup (250 mL) good-quality mini chocolate chips

½ cup (125 mL) salted pistachio nuts, chopped

ORANGE GLAZE

½ cup (125 mL) icing sugar

3 tablespoons (45 mL) orange juice

1. Preheat the oven to 350°F (180°C). Grease and flour a 9- × 5-inch (2 L) loaf pan.

2. In a stand mixer fitted with the paddle attachment, cream the sugar and butter on medium speed. Add the eggs and mix until combined. Scrape down the sides of the bowl and mix again for about 2 minutes. Scrape down the sides of the bowl. Add the sour cream, orange juice, and orange zest. Mix, scraping down the sides of the bowl often, until light and creamy. Add the flour, baking powder, baking soda, and salt. Mix, scraping down sides of the bowl as needed, until just combined. Add the chocolate chips and pistachios. Mix until just combined.

3. Transfer the batter to the prepared loaf pan. Bake for 60 to 70 minutes, until a toothpick or wooden skewer inserted in the centre comes out clean. Let cool in the pan for about 10 minutes, then turn the loaf out onto a wire rack to cool completely.

4. **MAKE THE ORANGE GLAZE** In a small bowl, whisk the icing sugar and orange juice. Drizzle over the cooled loaf.

5. Store in an airtight container at room temperature for up to 4 days or in the freezer for up to 3 months. If serving from frozen, bring the loaf to room temperature, then warm it in a 350°F (180°C) oven for 20 minutes to refresh it.

CARROT CAKE SANDWICHES

These sandwiches are tender and have all of the familiar flavours of comforting carrot cake, but the cake-like batter is scooped and baked in cookie form before sandwiching velvety cream cheese frosting. Made for those who have a love affair with a generous frosting-to-cake ratio, these sandwiches are quick to mix up when that cream cheese craving hits. **MAKES 12 SANDWICHES**

1. Preheat the oven to 350°F (180°C). Line 3 baking sheets with parchment paper.

2. Spread the walnuts in an even layer on one of the prepared baking sheets. Toast in the oven for 10 minutes. Let cool, then finely chop the walnuts.

3. In a stand mixer fitted with the paddle attachment, mix the brown sugar, granulated sugar, and butter on medium speed until light and fluffy, 3 to 4 minutes. Add the eggs and vanilla. Beat until well combined.

4. In a large bowl, whisk the flour, baking soda, baking powder, cinnamon, nutmeg, ginger, and salt. Add the flour mixture to the butter mixture. Mix on low speed until just combined. Add the oats and carrots. Mix until combined. Chill the dough in the fridge until firm, at least 1 hour.

5. Scoop the dough onto the remaining prepared baking sheets in 2-tablespoon (30 mL) portions, leaving about 2 inches (5 cm) between each. Bake for 12 to 15 minutes, turning the pan halfway through, until golden brown. Transfer to a wire rack to cool to room temperature.

6. Place the chopped walnuts on a plate. Fill a pastry bag with the Cream Cheese Frosting and cut off the tip to create a 1-inch (2 cm) hole.

7. Flip over half of the mini carrot cakes. Pipe about 4 teaspoons (20 mL) of frosting in one big dollop directly in the middle of the cakes that are bottom side up. Place the remaining cakes on the frosting, bottom side down, to create a sandwich and press down slightly to squeeze the frosting to the edges of the cakes. Roll the edges of each sandwich in the chopped walnuts, pressing gently to make sure the walnuts stick to the frosting.

8. Store in an airtight container in the fridge for up to 3 days.

1 cup (250 mL) walnuts

1 cup (250 mL) lightly packed brown sugar

1 cup (250 mL) granulated sugar

1 cup (250 mL) unsalted butter, room temperature

2 large eggs, room temperature

1 teaspoon (5 mL) pure vanilla extract

2½ cups (625 mL) all-purpose flour

1 teaspoon (5 mL) baking soda

1 teaspoon (5 mL) baking powder

1 teaspoon (5 mL) ground cinnamon

½ teaspoon (2 mL) ground nutmeg

½ teaspoon (2 mL) ground ginger

¼ teaspoon (1 mL) kosher salt

2 cups (500 mL) rolled oats

1½ cups (375 mL) grated carrots

1 batch Cream Cheese Frosting (page 279)

KITCHEN TIP

- Try using heirloom carrots in this recipe to give your cookies an interesting colour variation!

CARROT CAKE ROLL

A fun twist on the crowd-pleasing favourite, this recipe elevates carrot cake to the level of an elegant dessert. Velvety cream cheese frosting rolled between layers of well-spiced cake ensures that the cake-to-frosting ratio is perfect in every bite. **SERVES 8 TO 10**

1. Preheat the oven to 375°F (190°C). Line a 15- × 10-inch (2 L) jelly roll pan with parchment paper, leaving an extra 1 inch (2.5 cm) of parchment paper sticking up on each long side of the pan.

2. **MAKE THE CARROT CAKE** In a medium bowl, whisk the flour, cinnamon, baking powder, ginger, salt, nutmeg, and cloves until combined.

3. In a large bowl, whisk the eggs and sugar for 1 minute, until thick. Add the carrots, oil, and vanilla. Whisk until combined. Use a silicone spatula to fold the flour mixture into the egg mixture until just combined.

4. Spread the batter evenly into the prepared jelly roll pan. Bake for 10 to 13 minutes, or until the top of the cake springs back when touched. Almost immediately after removing from the oven, while still quite warm, carefully use the overhanging parchment paper to lift the cake onto a clean flat surface. Starting at one of the short ends, slowly roll up the cake and parchment paper, until the whole cake has been rolled and forms a log. Transfer the cake roll to a wire rack and let cool to room temperature.

5. **MAKE THE ORANGE SPICE CREAM CHEESE FROSTING** While the cake is cooling, prepare 1 batch Cream Cheese Frosting. To the bowl of the stand mixer, add the orange zest and cinnamon. Mix on medium speed until combined.

6. Transfer the cake roll to a clean flat surface and carefully unroll it until it is flat again (it's okay if the ends curl up a bit). Spread the frosting evenly over the cake, leaving a ¾-inch (2 cm) border on all sides. Carefully roll the cake up, gently peeling away the parchment paper as you roll. Discard the parchment paper. Tightly wrap the cake roll in plastic wrap and chill in the fridge for at least 1 hour.

CARROT CAKE

1½ cups (375 mL) all-purpose flour

1 tablespoon (15 mL) ground cinnamon

2 teaspoons (10 mL) baking powder

1 teaspoon (5 mL) ground ginger

1 teaspoon (5 mL) kosher salt

½ teaspoon (2 mL) ground nutmeg

½ teaspoon (2 mL) ground cloves

6 large eggs

1 cup (250 mL) granulated sugar

4 cups (1 L) peeled and grated heirloom carrots

¼ cup (60 mL) canola oil

2 teaspoons (10 mL) pure vanilla extract

ORANGE SPICE CREAM CHEESE FROSTING

1 batch Cream Cheese Frosting (page 279)

Zest of 1 orange

½ teaspoon (2 mL) ground cinnamon

CANDIED WALNUTS

2 tablespoons (30 mL) lightly packed brown sugar

1 teaspoon (5 mL) kosher salt

1 teaspoon (5 mL) pure vanilla extract

½ teaspoon (2 mL) ground cinnamon

1 egg white

2 cups (500 mL) raw walnut halves

recipe continues

7. Preheat the oven to 300°F (150°C). Line a baking sheet with parchment paper.

8. MAKE THE CANDIED WALNUTS In a small bowl, whisk the brown sugar, salt, vanilla, cinnamon, and egg white. Add the walnuts and toss to coat evenly. Spread the walnuts in a single layer on the prepared baking sheet. Bake for 20 minutes. Remove the baking sheet from the oven to give the walnuts a stir. Bake for an additional 20 minutes. Stir the walnuts again as soon as you remove them from the oven to loosen them from the baking sheet. Let cool, then roughly chop the walnuts.

9. Unwrap the cake roll and slice it into discs. Place each disc on a plate and sprinkle it with candied walnuts.

10. Store any leftovers, wrapped tightly in plastic wrap, in the fridge for up to 3 days.

BIRTHDAY CELEBRATION CAKE

This has become a highly requested cake at Bread Bar—even for wedding cakes! Rainbow sprinkles are nostalgic and fun, but they're not meant to be a distraction: this cake is serious in the flavour department, too. The combination of buttermilk and the heavy dose of vanilla set this cake apart from boring vanilla birthday cakes. Even non–cake eaters will be asking for a second slice.

MAKES ONE 6-INCH (15 CM) ROUND LAYER CAKE

1. Preheat the oven to 350°F (180°C). Grease and flour three 6-inch (1 L) round cake pans. Line the bottom of each pan with parchment paper.

2. In a stand mixer fitted with the paddle attachment, cream the butter, granulated sugar, and brown sugar on medium-high speed for 3 minutes. Scrape down the sides of the bowl. Add the eggs and mix for 3 minutes, until very light and fluffy.

3. With the mixer on low speed, slowly drizzle in the buttermilk, oil, and 1 tablespoon (15 mL) of the vanilla. Increase the speed to medium-high. Mix until the batter doubles in volume and turns white, about 6 minutes. Reduce the speed to low. Add the flour, baking powder, and salt, mixing until just combined. Remove the bowl from the stand and use a silicone spatula to fold in ¾ cup (175 mL) of the sprinkles.

4. Divide the batter evenly among the prepared cake pans. Bake for 28 to 30 minutes, or until a cake tester inserted in the middle of the cakes comes out clean. Let cool in the pans for 20 minutes, then transfer the cakes to wire racks to cool to room temperature. Place the cakes in the fridge to chill for 1 hour.

5. Using a serrated knife, carefully trim the domed top off each cake to create a level surface. Trim away the outsides of the cake if they have turned dark during baking.

6. In a small bowl, stir together the milk and the remaining 1 teaspoon (5 mL) of vanilla. Brush the top of each cake with the mixture. This will keep the cake layers moist.

7. Transfer 1 cup (250 mL) of the buttercream to a small bowl and reserve it for piping a ring of frosting on the top of the cake. Place one layer of cake on a cake board or a flat plate. Place about

½ cup (125 mL) unsalted butter, softened

1¼ cups (300 mL) granulated sugar

¼ cup (60 mL) lightly packed brown sugar

3 large eggs

½ cup (125 mL) buttermilk

½ cup (125 mL) canola oil

1 tablespoon (15 mL) + 1 teaspoon (5 mL) pure vanilla extract, divided

1½ cups (375 mL) all-purpose flour

1 teaspoon (5 mL) baking powder

1 teaspoon (5 mL) kosher salt

¾ cup (175 mL) rainbow sprinkles or nonpareils + 1 tablespoon (15 mL), for garnish

1 cup (250 mL) whole (3.25%) milk

½ batch Swiss Meringue Buttercream (page 280)

recipe continues

½ cup (125 mL) of the buttercream on top. Using an offset spatula, spread the buttercream evenly over the top of the cake out toward and slightly off the edges. Repeat with the second and third layers, placing one on top of the other to create an even stack.

8.   Using the offset spatula, spread any excess buttercream down over the edges to start covering the sides of the cake. Keep adding more buttercream to your spatula to cover the sides of the cake in a thin layer of buttercream to create a "naked" cake as shown in the photo. It's important that all of the cake be covered with at least a small amount of buttercream to keep the exposed edges from drying out. Use the side of an offset spatula or bench scraper to add more frosting or to scrape as much frosting off as necessary to create your desired effect. Place the cake in the fridge to chill for at least 1 hour.

9.   Transfer the reserved 1 cup (250 mL) of buttercream to a piping bag fitted with a 1-inch (2.5 cm) star tip. Remove the cake from the fridge. Placing even pressure on the piping bag, create loops of frosting around the top edge of the cake. Finish off your masterpiece by sprinkling 1 tablespoon (15 mL) sprinkles over the piped detail. Return the cake to the fridge until it is time to serve.

10. To serve, remove the cake from the fridge and let stand at room temperature for about 1 hour. This will ensure optimal flavour and texture. To store, cut any leftover cake into slices and store them in an airtight container in the fridge for up to 1 week. If you want to freeze leftover cake, wrap slices separately (and tightly!) in plastic wrap and store them in the freezer for up to 3 months. Let thaw at room temperature before serving.

KITCHEN TIPS

- Make sure you don't wait too long before removing the cakes from their pans—they will be easier to remove if they're still a touch warm.
- Chilling the cake layers before stacking and frosting them will make assembling the cake much easier. Give yourself lots of time to make this recipe to ensure that you have time for this crucial step!

NATURALLY RED VELVET CAKE

The history of red velvet cake dates to the 1930s, when the owner of a suffering food dye company decided to release his own version of the Waldorf Astoria's red beet cake. Instead of using beets to colour the cake, he called for his own red food dye in an effort to bulk up sales. But it turns out that it is possible to get a red-hued chocolate cake without adding any dye—or beets—by using cocoa powder that is natural and non-alkalized. It can be found in most bulk food stores or online. While Dutch process cocoa will work in many recipes, non-alkalized is the way to go when making this red velvet cake. Non-alkalized cocoa powder is naturally a rusty, reddish colour, and although the resulting cake is not as vibrant as one made using red dye would be, we prefer to go the natural route. Read more about the difference between natural and Dutch process cocoa powder on page 10. With a little bit of food science, you can have a naturally red velvet cake—no food colouring required!

MAKES ONE 6-INCH (15 CM) ROUND LAYER CAKE

1. Preheat the oven to 325°F (160°C). Grease and flour three 6-inch (1 L) round cake pans. Line the bottom of each pan with parchment paper.

2. In a stand mixer fitted with the paddle attachment, cream the butter and brown sugar on high speed for 5 minutes. Reduce the speed to low. Add the eggs one at a time, scraping down the sides of the bowl after each addition. Increase the speed to medium-low and mix until combined, about 2 minutes.

3. In a large bowl, whisk the flour, cocoa powder, baking soda, and salt.

4. In a heatproof bowl, warm the buttermilk for 30 seconds in a microwave oven. Stir in the vanilla.

5. Sift one-third of the flour mixture into the butter and sugar mixture. Mix on low speed until combined. Turn off the mixer. Add one-third of the buttermilk mixture. Mix on low speed until combined. Turn off the mixer. Scrape down the sides of the bowl with a rubber spatula. Repeat the process until all of the flour mixture and all of the buttermilk mixture have been incorporated, making sure each addition is fully combined before adding the next.

¾ cup (175 mL) unsalted butter, softened

2¼ cups (550 mL) lightly packed brown sugar

3 large eggs

2¼ cups (550 mL) all-purpose flour

½ cup (125 mL) natural, non-alkalized cocoa powder

1½ teaspoons (7 mL) baking soda

¾ teaspoon (3 mL) kosher salt

1½ cups (375 mL) buttermilk

2 teaspoons (10 mL) pure vanilla extract

1 batch Cream Cheese Frosting (page 279)

1 cup (250 mL) fresh berries, such as strawberries, raspberries, and red currants, for garnish

recipe continues

6.   Divide the batter evenly among the prepared cake pans. Bake for 30 to 35 minutes or until a cake tester inserted in the middle of the cakes comes out clean. Let cool in the pans for 20 minutes. Run a sharp knife around the edges of the cakes to help release them from their pans, then transfer them to wire racks. Let cool to room temperature. Place the cakes in the fridge to chill for 1 hour.

7.   Using a serrated knife, carefully trim the domed top off each cake to create a level surface. Trim away the outsides of the cake if they have turned dark during baking.

8.   Place one layer of cake on a cake board or a flat plate. Place about ½ cup (125 mL) of the Cream Cheese Frosting on top. Using an offset spatula, spread the frosting evenly over the top of the cake. Repeat with the second and third layers, placing one on top of the others to create an even stack. To frost the cake in the "naked" style, stop here and let the beautiful, naturally red colour of the cake shine. If you prefer more frosting, spread additional frosting down over the sides to create a crumb coat (see Baking Like a Pro, page 5). Swoop and swirl more frosting over the sides of the cake to create a fluffy frosted look for the final coat. Pile the fresh berries generously on top to add to the red hue of the cake. Place the cake in the fridge to chill until you serve it.

9.   To serve, remove the cake from the fridge 1 hour before serving. To store, cut any leftover cake into slices and store them in an airtight container in the fridge for up to 1 week. If you want to freeze leftover cake, wrap slices separately (and tightly!) in plastic wrap and store them in the freezer for up to 3 months. Let thaw at room temperature before serving.

TRES LECHES CAKE

Spanish for "three milks," tres leches cake is a traditional dessert popular in Latin American culture. It is a light, airy cake soaked in a mixture of three milks, and it is so dreamy. Our introduction to tres leches cake was in the Mexican town of Tulum while on a much-needed vacation together. It was *amor* at first bite. Whipped cream or meringue on top is considered traditional. Here we have chosen meringue. It can be piped or swirled onto the cake to dramatic effect, making this cake perfect for a celebration. **MAKES ONE 8-INCH (20 CM) SQUARE CAKE**

1. Preheat the oven to 350°F (180°C). Grease and flour an 8-inch (2 L) square cake pan.

2. **MAKE THE VANILLA CAKE** In a stand mixer fitted with the paddle attachment, beat the egg yolks, sugar, and vanilla on medium-high speed until the mixture is smooth and has doubled in volume. Transfer the mixture to a medium bowl. Using a silicone spatula, fold in the flour, baking powder, and salt, being careful not to overmix.

3. In the clean bowl of a stand mixer fitted with the whisk attachment, whip the egg whites on high speed until stiff peaks form, about 4 to 5 minutes. Gently fold the whipped egg whites into the cake batter.

4. Transfer the batter to the prepared cake pan. Bake for 18 to 20 minutes, until light golden brown and a cake tester inserted in the middle comes out with a few moist crumbs. Remove from the oven and let cool to room temperature in the pan.

5. **MAKE THE THREE-MILK MIXTURE** In a medium bowl, stir together the sweetened condensed milk, evaporated milk, and whole milk to combine.

6. With the cake still in the pan, use a wooden skewer to create small holes all over the cake for the milk mixture to soak into. Pour the milk mixture over the cake, 1 cup (250 mL) at a time, allowing it to soak in. Cover and refrigerate for at least 2 hours, but preferably overnight, to give the cake a chance to completely absorb the milk mixture.

VANILLA CAKE

5 egg yolks
¾ cup (175 mL) granulated sugar
1 teaspoon (5 mL) pure vanilla extract
1 cup (250 mL) all-purpose flour
1 teaspoon (5 mL) baking powder
¼ teaspoon (1 mL) kosher salt
5 egg whites

THREE-MILK MIXTURE

1¾ cups (425 mL) sweetened condensed milk
1 can (12 ounces/350 mL) evaporated milk
½ cup (125 mL) whole (3.25%) milk

MERINGUE

4 large egg whites
½ cup (125 mL) granulated sugar

recipe continues

7. **MAKE THE MERINGUE** Place the egg whites and sugar in the stainless steel bowl of a stand mixer and place the bowl over a small saucepan of simmering water over low heat. Stirring constantly, cook until the sugar is dissolved. Return the bowl to the stand mixer fitted with the whisk attachment and beat on medium-high speed until stiff, glossy peaks form, about 8 minutes.

8. Transfer the meringue to a pastry bag and cut off the tip. Pipe the meringue onto the chilled cake in dollops of varying sizes. Use a small kitchen torch to lightly brown the meringue right before serving. To serve, use a hot, dry knife to cut the cake into squares.

9. Store any leftovers in an airtight container in the fridge for up to 4 days.

FLOURLESS CHOCOLATE NEMESIS CAKE

The decadence of this cake is indescribable, and it's also meant to be gluten free by design. That's our kind of gluten-free recipe! We've adapted this one from The River Café in London, England. The trick to the perfect bake is to place the cake pan in a water bath, which will help insulate this delicate cake from direct heat. **MAKES ONE 10-INCH (25 CM) ROUND CAKE**

1. Preheat the oven to 250°F (120°C). Grease a 10-inch (3 L) round cake pan and line the bottom with parchment paper. Find a roasting pan that the cake pan will fit inside. Line it with a clean kitchen towel.

2. In a stand mixer fitted with the whisk attachment, whisk the eggs and ½ cup (125 mL) of the sugar on high speed until the mixture has quadrupled in size, about 10 minutes.

3. In a double boiler, or a medium stainless steel bowl placed over a small saucepan of simmering water, melt the chocolate and butter, stirring occasionally to combine.

4. Place the remaining 1 cup (250 mL) of sugar in a small saucepan over medium heat. Add 1 tablespoon (15 mL) water and bring to a boil. Continue cooking until the sugar is completely dissolved. Carefully add the dissolved sugar to the melted chocolate and butter. Stir to combine.

5. With the mixer on low speed, slowly add the chocolate and sugar mixture to the egg mixture. Increase the speed slightly and mix until well combined.

6. Transfer the batter to the prepared cake pan. Knock the cake pan on the counter a couple of times to help release any excess air. Place the cake pan in the roasting pan. Fill the roasting pan with water so that it comes three-quarters of the way up the sides of the cake pan. Bake for 50 minutes, or until the cake starts to pull away from the sides of the pan. Let cool to room temperature in the water bath. (This might take up to 2 hours.)

7. Remove the cake from the water bath and invert it onto a serving plate. Serve with Chantilly Cream and fresh blackberries.

8. Store leftover cake, wrapped tightly in plastic wrap, in the fridge for up to 5 days.

5 large eggs

1½ cups (375 mL) granulated sugar, divided

12 ounces (340 g) good-quality dark chocolate, at least 60% cocoa content, chopped

1 cup (250 mL) unsalted butter, softened

Chantilly Cream (page 281)

1 cup (250 mL) fresh blackberries, for garnish

LEMON OLIVE OIL CRUMBLE CAKE

This cake is amazing! The extra-virgin olive oil lends a greenish hue to the crumb, and its fruity flavour pairs so well with the bright lemon flavour in the lemon simple syrup and the cake itself. Serve this cake with sweetened mascarpone cheese and fresh figs for an elegant dessert.

MAKES ONE 10-INCH (25 CM) ROUND CAKE

LEMON OLIVE OIL CAKE

4 large eggs

2½ cups (625 mL) granulated sugar

1½ cups (375 mL) extra-virgin olive oil

1½ cups (375 mL) 2% milk

Zest of 4 lemons

2¼ cups (550 mL) all-purpose flour

½ teaspoon (2 mL) baking powder

½ teaspoon (2 mL) baking soda

½ teaspoon (2 mL) kosher salt

1½ cups (375 mL) Crumble Topping
  (page 284)

LEMON SIMPLE SYRUP

½ cup (125 mL) granulated sugar

½ cup (125 mL) water

¼ cup (60 mL) fresh lemon juice

FOR SERVING

2 cups (500 mL) mascarpone cheese,
  room temperature

2 tablespoons (30 mL) icing sugar

4 to 6 fresh figs

KITCHEN TIP

- Substitute about 4 tablespoons (60 mL) orange or tangerine zest for the lemon zest in the cake and ¼ cup (60 mL) of the corresponding juice in the simple syrup if you want to switch up the citrus flavour.

1. Preheat the oven to 350°F (180°C). Grease and flour a 10-inch (3 L) round cake pan. Line the bottom with parchment paper.

2. **MAKE THE LEMON OLIVE OIL CAKE** In a medium bowl, whisk the eggs and sugar. Add the olive oil, milk, and lemon zest. Whisk to combine.

3. In a separate medium bowl, whisk the flour, baking powder, baking soda, and salt. Add the flour mixture to the olive oil mixture and stir just until smooth.

4. Transfer the batter to the prepared cake pan. Bake for 25 to 30 minutes. Carefully remove the cake from the oven and sprinkle the Crumble Topping evenly overtop. Bake for an additional 20 minutes, or until a cake tester inserted in the middle comes out clean.

5. **MAKE THE LEMON SIMPLE SYRUP** In a small saucepan over medium heat, combine the sugar and water. Bring to a boil without åstirring. Reduce the heat to low and continue to simmer for 2 minutes. Remove from the heat and let cool to room temperature. Stir in the lemon juice and set aside.

6. Remove the cake from the oven and let cool for 20 minutes in the pan. Run a sharp knife around the outside of the cake and turn it out onto a wire rack. Evenly drizzle the simple syrup overtop and let it soak in while the cake cools to room temperature.

7. Before serving, place the mascarpone and icing sugar in a small bowl and whisk until combined. Cut the figs into wedges. Serve the cake warm, with a dollop of the sweetened mascarpone and a few wedges of fig.

8. Store leftover cake, without the mascarpone or figs, in an airtight container in the fridge for up to 4 days, or wrap tightly in plastic wrap and store in the freezer for up to 1 month.

ANGEL FOOD CAKE

In the warmer months, we like to serve Angel Food Cake with macerated strawberries, blueberries, and fresh mint. Sometimes we make a Lemon Curd (page 177) with the leftover egg yolks from this recipe. You can dollop it over the cake slices and serve it with Chantilly Cream (page 281).

MAKES ONE 9-INCH (23 CM) CAKE

1. **MAKE THE MACERATED BERRIES** Place the mixed berries in a bowl. Add the sugar and vanilla and toss to coat evenly. Let rest at room temperature for at least 1 hour.

2. **MAKE THE ANGEL FOOD CAKE** Preheat the oven to 325°F (160°C). In a food processor, pulse the sugar until it becomes fine and powdery. Remove 1 cup (250 mL) and set aside. Add the flour and salt to the food processor. Pulse 10 times until the mixture is powdery and aerated.

3. In a stand mixer fitted with the whisk attachment, mix the egg whites and cream of tartar on low speed for about 1 minute, until foamy. Add the reserved 1 cup (250 mL) sugar. Increase the speed to medium-high and whip until soft peaks form, about 6 minutes.

4. Remove the bowl from the stand. Using a fine-mesh sieve, sift one-third of the flour mixture into the whipped egg white mixture. It is important to sift the flour mixture to keep the batter very light and airy. Using a silicone spatula, gently fold the flour mixture into the whipped egg white mixture, until combined. Repeat, adding the remaining flour mixture in two equal additions.

5. Transfer the batter to an ungreased 9-inch (3 L) tube pan. Bake for 40 to 45 minutes, turning the pan halfway through, until a cake tester inserted in the middle comes out clean. Flip the cake onto a wire rack to cool, leaving the pan on the cake. Let cool to room temperature.

6. Flip the pan back over and run a paring knife around the edges of the cake to release it from the pan. Serve with the macerated berries and Chantilly Cream, if desired.

7. Store leftover cake, without toppings, in an airtight container in the fridge for up to 5 days.

MACERATED BERRIES

4 cups (1 L) chopped fresh mixed berries (we like strawberries, raspberries, blueberries, and blackberries)

1 cup (500 mL) granulated sugar

1 teaspoon (5 mL) pure vanilla extract

ANGEL FOOD CAKE

1¾ cups (425 mL) granulated sugar

1 cup + 2 tablespoons (280 mL) all-purpose flour

¼ teaspoon (1 mL) kosher salt

12 large egg whites, room temperature

1½ teaspoons (7 mL) cream of tartar

1½ teaspoons (7 mL) pure vanilla extract

Chantilly Cream (page 281), for serving (optional)

KITCHEN TIP

- Because the cake is so delicate, we recommend using a serrated bread knife when cutting slices. The sawing motion required when using a bread knife will prevent the cake from being smushed down while cutting.

ESPRESSO BUNDT CAKE WITH
WHITE CHOCOLATE GANACHE

The humble Bundt cake—kicked up a notch! Chocolate and coffee are a sophisticated flavour pairing, and with a shiny glaze, this cake is really something to behold. In this recipe, the Bundt pan serves an important purpose: the hole in the middle gives the cake batter more pan to grab as it rises, preventing it from collapsing in the middle. The result: a perfect cake every time.

MAKES ONE 9-INCH (23 CM) BUNDT CAKE

ESPRESSO BUNDT CAKE

2½ cups (625 mL) all-purpose flour

½ cup (125 mL) Dutch process cocoa powder

2 teaspoons (10 mL) instant espresso powder

1 teaspoon (5 mL) baking soda

¾ teaspoon (3 mL) kosher salt

¾ cup (175 mL) full-fat sour cream

½ cup (125 mL) whole (3.25%) milk

1 cup (250 mL) unsalted butter, softened

1½ cups (375 mL) granulated sugar

4 large eggs

1½ teaspoons (7 mL) pure vanilla extract

WHITE CHOCOLATE GANACHE

2 cups (500 mL) chopped white chocolate

2 cups (500 mL) heavy (35%) cream

1 tablespoon (15 mL) instant espresso powder

KITCHEN TIP

• This cake is beautiful on its own, but to make it a real centrepiece, garnish it with shaved chocolate or chocolate-covered coffee beans for a bit of crunch.

1. Preheat the oven to 325°F (160°C). Grease a 9-inch (23 cm) Bundt pan and dust it with cocoa powder.

2. **MAKE THE ESPRESSO BUNDT CAKE** In a large bowl, whisk the flour, cocoa powder, espresso powder, baking soda, and salt. In a small bowl, combine the sour cream and milk.

3. In a stand mixer fitted with the paddle attachment, cream the butter and sugar on medium speed until fluffy. Scrape down the sides of the bowl. Add the eggs and vanilla. Beat until smooth.

4. Add half of the flour mixture and half of the milk mixture to the butter mixture. Mix on low speed until just combined. Turn off the mixer. Add the remaining flour mixture and milk mixture. Mix on low speed until just combined.

5. Spoon the batter into the prepared Bundt pan and spread it in an even layer. Bake for 45 to 50 minutes, until a cake tester inserted in the middle comes out clean. Let cool slightly in the pan, about 5 minutes. Carefully turn the cake out onto a plate to cool to room temperature.

6. **MAKE THE WHITE CHOCOLATE GANACHE** Place the white chocolate in a medium heatproof bowl. In a small saucepan over medium heat, bring the cream to a simmer. Whisk in the espresso powder. Immediately pour the hot cream over the white chocolate and whisk until completely smooth. Let cool to room temperature. Spoon it over the cake. Store any leftovers in an airtight container in the fridge for up to 1 week.

PLUM AND CARDAMOM COFFEE CAKE

The warm, earthy notes of cardamom complement summer's best plums in this simple and irresistible cake recipe. Plum and cardamom are a match made in heaven, so if you haven't experienced this combination before, it's time that you try it out. Any variety of plum can be used for this recipe—whatever your local store has at the height of stone fruit season will work beautifully.

MAKES ONE 8-INCH (20 CM) SQUARE CAKE

1. Cut the plums into ½-inch (1 cm) slices over a small bowl, collecting the juice. Set aside. Preheat the oven to 350°F (180°C). Grease an 8-inch (2 L) square cake pan and line the bottom with parchment paper.

2. In a large bowl, whisk the flour, sugar, cardamom, baking soda, baking powder, and salt. In a medium bowl, whisk the sour cream, butter, milk, egg, and vanilla. Add the butter mixture to the flour mixture. Stir until just combined.

3. Using a silicone spatula, fold in three-quarters of the sliced plums, being careful not to overmix. Transfer the batter to the prepared cake pan. Scatter the remaining plum slices on top, making sure to reserve the juice for the Plum Glaze.

4. Bake for 35 to 45 minutes, until golden brown and a cake tester inserted in the middle comes out clean. Let cool slightly, about 10 minutes. Run a thin knife around the edge of the pan and turn the cake out onto a plate.

5. MAKE THE PLUM GLAZE In a small bowl, whisk the icing sugar with the reserved plum juice. Add the milk and whisk until smooth. Drizzle over the cake before serving. Serve warm.

6. Store any leftovers in an airtight container at room temperature for up to 3 days.

8 whole medium ripe plums
2 cups (500 mL) all-purpose flour
¾ cup (175 mL) granulated sugar
1 tablespoon (15 mL) ground cardamom
1 teaspoon (5 mL) baking soda
1 teaspoon (5 mL) baking powder
½ teaspoon (2 mL) kosher salt
1¼ cups (300 mL) full-fat sour cream
½ cup (125 mL) unsalted butter, melted
¼ cup (60 mL) whole (3.25%) milk
1 large egg
1 teaspoon (5 mL) pure vanilla extract

PLUM GLAZE

1 cup (250 mL) icing sugar
Juice reserved from slicing plums
2 tablespoons (30 mL) whole (3.25%) milk

PINEAPPLE UPSIDE DOWN CAKE

When Erin was growing up, her mom would bake pineapple upside down cake and cover it in candles for Erin's birthday. Memories of our moms and grandmas baking are some of the best memories many of us have. We just had to include our version of this dessert here. **MAKES ONE 10-INCH (25 CM) ROUND CAKE**

POACHED PINEAPPLE AND SYRUP

1 pound (450 g) fresh pineapple, cored and thinly sliced lengthwise (about 1 medium pineapple)
1½ cups (375 mL) water
1½ cups (375 mL) granulated sugar

BUTTERMILK ALMOND CAKE

8 tablespoons (120 mL) unsalted butter, softened
1¼ cups (300 mL) granulated sugar
¼ cup (60 mL) lightly packed brown sugar
3 large eggs
½ cup (125 mL) buttermilk
½ cup (125 mL) canola oil
1 tablespoon (15 mL) pure vanilla extract
1 cup (250 mL) all-purpose flour
½ cup (125 mL) almond flour
1 teaspoon (5 mL) baking powder
1 teaspoon (5 mL) kosher salt
½ teaspoon (2 mL) ground nutmeg

1. Line a baking sheet with parchment paper.

2. **MAKE THE POACHED PINEAPPLE AND SYRUP** Place the pineapple, water, and sugar in a wide saucepan over medium-high heat. Bring to a boil. Reduce the heat to low and simmer for 15 minutes. Carefully remove the pineapple from the hot syrup and place it in a single layer on the prepared baking sheet. Let cool. Increase the heat to high and continue cooking the syrup until it reduces to about ¾ cup (175 mL). Let cool.

3. Preheat the oven to 350°F (180°C). Grease a 10-inch (3 L) round cake pan and line the bottom with parchment paper. Starting on the outside edge of the cake pan, create a ring of pineapple slices. Moving toward the middle of the cake pan, create slightly overlapping concentric circles with the pineapple. Carefully pour half of the cooled syrup overtop in an even layer. Reserve the remaining syrup.

4. **MAKE THE BUTTERMILK ALMOND CAKE** In a stand mixer fitted with the paddle attachment, cream the butter, granulated sugar, and brown sugar on medium-high speed for 3 minutes. Scrape down the sides of the bowl. Add the eggs and mix on medium-high speed for 3 minutes. Reduce the speed to low and slowly drizzle in the buttermilk, oil, and vanilla. Increase the speed to medium-high and mix until the batter doubles in volume and turns white, about 6 minutes. Reduce the speed to low and add the all-purpose flour, almond flour, baking powder, salt, and nutmeg. Mix until just combined.

5. Spoon the batter over the pineapple and smooth the top. Bake for 55 minutes, or until the top turns a deep golden brown and a cake tester inserted in the middle comes out clean. Let rest for 10 minutes in the pan. Invert the cake onto a plate. Serve warm with vanilla (or coconut!) ice cream and a drizzle of the remaining pineapple syrup. Store any leftovers in an airtight container in the fridge for up to 1 week.

KITCHEN TIP

• Cold cornbread can be quite dry and stiff. Make
sure you warm up the bread before enjoying any
leftovers.

CHEESY ROASTED RED PEPPER SKILLET CORNBREAD

This cornbread goes really well with barbecued steaks, baked potatoes, and coleslaw. You can even try baking the bread on the barbecue. Jeff Crump, the co-founder of Earth to Table, developed the recipe for JC's Original Hot Sauce, which is added to the cornbread batter. He suggests that you make your own hot sauce, but if you're tight on time, you can use your favourite store-bought sauce instead.

MAKES SIX 3-INCH (8 CM) ROUND LOAVES OR ONE 10-INCH (25 CM) ROUND LOAF

1. **MAKE JC'S ORIGINAL HOT SAUCE** In a large skillet, heat the oil until near the smoking point. Add the habanero, jalapeño, poblano, and red peppers and cook, stirring occasionally, until fork-tender and charred, about 15 minutes. Let cool.

2. Place the roasted peppers in a blender and add the rice vinegar, sugar, and salt. Purée on high speed for 3 minutes. Adjust the sweetness or seasoning to your taste.

3. Preheat the oven or a barbecue to 400°F (200°C). Grease 6 (3-inch/8 cm) cast iron pots or 1 (10-inch/25 cm) cast iron skillet.

4. **MAKE THE CORNBREAD** In a medium bowl, whisk the cornmeal, flour, sugar, salt, baking powder, and baking soda.

5. In a stand mixer fitted with the whisk attachment, mix the buttermilk, melted butter, and eggs on medium speed. Add the buttermilk mixture to the cornmeal mixture and stir until just combined. Fold in the Gouda, roasted red peppers, and hot sauce.

6. Divide the batter evenly among the prepared pots or place all of the batter in the prepared skillet. Bake or barbecue the small pots for 20 to 25 minutes or the large skillet for 40 to 45 minutes, until the edges are golden brown and the cornbread is firm to the touch when tapped in the middle. Let cool for 5 minutes.

7. Serve the smaller loaves of cornbread in their pots. Cut the large loaf of cornbread into 12 pie-shaped slices before serving.

8. Store leftover cornbread in an airtight container in the fridge for up to 5 days. Store leftover hot sauce in an airtight container in the fridge for up to 2 weeks.

JC'S ORIGINAL HOT SAUCE (MAKES 1 CUP/250 ML)

- 1½ teaspoons (7 mL) canola oil
- 2 habanero chilies, stemmed
- 3 jalapeño peppers, stemmed and halved lengthwise
- ½ poblano chili, chopped
- 2 sweet red peppers, halved and seeded
- ¾ cup (175 mL) unseasoned rice vinegar
- 2 teaspoons (10 mL) granulated sugar
- 1 teaspoon (5 mL) kosher salt

CORNBREAD

- 1½ cups (375 mL) cornmeal
- 1¼ cups (300 mL) all-purpose flour
- ⅓ cup (75 mL) granulated sugar
- 1 tablespoon (15 mL) kosher salt
- 2 teaspoons (10 mL) baking powder
- ½ teaspoon (2 mL) baking soda
- 1¾ cups (425 mL) buttermilk
- ¼ cup (60 mL) melted butter
- 2 large eggs
- 3 cups (750 mL) shredded Gouda or Monterey Jack cheese
- ½ cup (125 mL) chopped roasted red peppers
- ¼ cup (60 mL) JC's Original Hot Sauce or store-bought brand

SODA BREAD

Soda bread is a type of quick bread that uses baking soda instead of yeast as a leavening agent. This no-fuss recipe is perfect to bake while a big bowl of soup is cooking on the stove. It does not require any proofing time like a yeasted loaf of bread would, and it is so good for dunking and sopping up every last bit of broth at the bottom of your soup bowl. **MAKES ONE 9-INCH (23 CM) ROUND LOAF**

1¾ cups (425 mL) buttermilk

1 large egg

4¼ cups (1.1 L) all-purpose flour

3 tablespoons (45 mL) granulated sugar

1 teaspoon (5 mL) baking soda

1 teaspoon (5 mL) kosher salt

⅓ cup (75 mL) unsalted butter, frozen

KITCHEN TIP

• The colder the butter, the better. Cold butter contributes to the oven spring of the soda bread as the steam evaporates from the butter while baking.

1. Preheat the oven to 400°F (200°C). Place a 9-inch (23 cm) cast iron skillet in the oven to warm up as you make the dough.

2. In a medium bowl, whisk the buttermilk and egg. Set aside.

3. In a large bowl, whisk the flour, sugar, baking soda, and salt until combined. Using a box grater, grate the frozen butter into the dry ingredients and toss with your hands until the mixture resembles coarse crumbs. Add the buttermilk mixture to the flour mixture. Using your hands, gently work the dough until it comes together in a shaggy ball.

4. Tip the dough out onto a well-floured surface. Knead for about 30 seconds to ensure that all of the flour in the dough is moistened before you work it into a ball. Remove the hot skillet from the oven and place the dough in it. Using a sharp knife, slash the dough across its entire diameter twice to create a cross. This will help the loaf open up and will ensure that the bread bakes evenly.

5. Bake for 45 minutes, until golden brown. If the bread is browning quite heavily well before the 45-minute mark, loosely cover the loaf with aluminum foil for the remaining baking time. Transfer the loaf to a wire rack to cool before slicing.

6. Soda bread can be served warm, at room temperature, or toasted. Store in an airtight container at room temperature for up to 2 days, in the fridge for up to 1 week, or in the freezer for up to 3 months.

DOUGHNUTS, PUFFS, AND OTHER YEASTED GOODS

KITCHEN TIP

• The riper the banana, the better! A very ripe banana will keep your doughnuts moist and provide excellent banana flavour.

BANANA WALNUT CRUNCH DOUGHNUTS

Baked doughnuts are a super quick alternative to fried ones. They come together with just a whisk and are ready in a snap. This is a perfect recipe if you are trying to find a way to use that ripe banana in your freezer and are sick of making banana bread or muffins. The walnuts give the doughnuts some added texture, and what's a doughnut without a glaze? Pure maple syrup ties the banana and walnut flavours together well. **MAKES 12 DOUGHNUTS**

1. Preheat the oven to 350°F (180°C). Line 2 baking sheets with parchment paper and place a wire rack on one. Grease and flour 2 standard doughnut pans.

2. **MAKE THE BANANA WALNUT CRUNCH DOUGHNUTS** Spread the walnuts in an even layer on the prepared baking sheet without the wire rack. Toast in the oven for 10 minutes. Let cool to room temperature. Finely chop the nuts.

3. In a large bowl, whisk the flour, baking powder, salt, baking soda, nutmeg, and cinnamon until combined. In a medium bowl, whisk the bananas, eggs, brown sugar, oil, milk, and vanilla until thoroughly combined. Add the banana mixture and ½ cup (125 mL) of the chopped walnuts to the flour mixture. Using a wooden spoon, stir to combine, making sure not to overmix.

4. Spoon the batter into a large pastry bag and cut off the tip to create a ¾-inch (2 cm) hole. Pipe the batter into the wells of the prepared doughnut pans, filling each well to the top. Bake for 12 minutes, until the doughnuts are just cooked through. Let cool in the pans for 10 minutes, then transfer to the wire rack to cool completely.

5. **MAKE THE MAPLE GLAZE** In a small bowl, whisk the icing sugar, milk, and maple syrup until smooth. Dunk the top of each doughnut into the glaze. Let the glaze drip off into the bowl, then return the glazed doughnuts to the wire rack, glazed sides up, allowing the parchment-lined baking sheet to catch additional drips. Immediately sprinkle the doughnuts with the remaining ½ cup (125 mL) of walnuts and the banana chips. Let set for 20 minutes before serving.

6. Doughnuts are best served on the day they are made but can be stored in an airtight container at room temperature for 1 more day.

BANANA WALNUT CRUNCH DOUGHNUTS

1 cup (250 mL) raw walnuts

1¾ cups (425 mL) all-purpose flour

1½ teaspoons (7 mL) baking powder

¼ teaspoon (1 mL) kosher salt

¼ teaspoon (1 mL) baking soda

¼ teaspoon (1 mL) freshly ground nutmeg

¼ teaspoon (1 mL) ground cinnamon

1 cup (250 mL) mashed ripe bananas

2 large eggs

½ cup (125 mL) lightly packed brown sugar

¼ cup (60 mL) canola oil

2 tablespoons (30 mL) whole (3.25%) milk

1 teaspoon (5 mL) pure vanilla extract

½ cup (125 mL) banana chips, roughly chopped

MAPLE GLAZE

1 cup (250 mL) icing sugar

3 tablespoons (45 mL) whole (3.25%) milk

1 tablespoon (15 mL) pure maple syrup

SOUR CREAM GLAZED DOUGHNUTS

These cake-style glazed doughnuts are a cinch to make! They do not require heating litres of oil—3 inches (8 cm) of oil in the pan will do—and the addition of sour cream gives them great depth of flavour. Freshly grated nutmeg is far superior in flavour and aroma to ground and adds a hint of spice.

MAKES 12 TO 14 DOUGHNUTS

1. MAKE THE SOUR CREAM DOUGHNUTS In a large bowl, whisk the cake flour, baking powder, salt, and nutmeg.

2. In a stand mixer fitted with the paddle attachment, beat the sugar and butter on medium speed until sandy. One at a time, add the egg yolks, mixing until well combined. Add the vanilla and mix until combined. Add the flour mixture to the sugar mixture, mixing until just barely combined. Add the sour cream. Mix until just combined, to create a sticky dough. Cover the dough in the mixing bowl and chill in the fridge for 1 hour.

3. Line a baking sheet with parchment paper. Turn the dough out onto a well-floured work surface. Roll it out until it is ½ inch (1 cm) thick. Using a 4-inch (10 cm) round cutter and a 1-inch (2.5 cm) round cutter, cut the dough into rings. Dip the cutters in flour if the dough gets sticky and cutting becomes a challenge. Transfer the doughnuts to the prepared baking sheet and place them in the fridge to chill for 30 minutes.

4. Line a baking sheet with parchment paper and place a wire rack on top.

5. Fill a large skillet with 3 inches (8 cm) of canola oil and place it over medium-high heat. Using a candy thermometer to watch the temperature, bring the oil to 350°F (180°C). Shake any excess flour from the doughnuts and place a few in the skillet, frying in batches to prevent overcrowding. Fry for 1 to 2 minutes, then flip and fry for an additional 1 minute, until the doughnuts are light golden brown and cooked through. Carefully use a slotted spoon to remove the doughnuts from the oil and transfer them to the wire rack. Let cool for 5 minutes.

SOUR CREAM DOUGHNUTS

2⅓ cups (575 mL) cake flour

1½ teaspoons (7 mL) baking powder

1 teaspoon (5 mL) kosher salt

½ teaspoon (2 mL) fresh ground nutmeg

½ cup (125 mL) granulated sugar

2 tablespoons (30 mL) unsalted butter, room temperature

2 large egg yolks

½ teaspoon (2 mL) pure vanilla extract

⅓ cup (75 mL) full-fat sour cream

Canola oil, for frying

VANILLA GLAZE

3 cups (750 mL) icing sugar

1 teaspoon (5 mL) pure vanilla extract

⅓ cup (75 mL) hot water

¼ teaspoon (1 mL) kosher salt

recipe continues

6. **MAKE THE VANILLA GLAZE** In a medium bowl, whisk the icing sugar, vanilla, hot water, and salt to combine. Dunk each doughnut in the glaze, flipping it over in the bowl to coat both sides. Let the glaze drip off into the bowl, then return the glazed doughnuts to the wire rack, allowing the prepared baking sheet to catch additional drips. Let set for 20 minutes before serving.

7. Doughnuts are best served on the day they are made but can be stored in an airtight container at room temperature for 1 more day.

KITCHEN TIPS

- Cake flour is an important ingredient in this recipe. While all-purpose flour is good for most baking, it will not produce a doughnut with the soft and fluffy texture you definitely want.
- Scraps of dough can be re-rolled once before the dough gets too tough, but the remaining scraps can be fried as doughnut holes using the smallest round cutter. They will take about 1 minute to fry, about 30 seconds on each side.

PINEAPPLE FRITTERS

A tropical twist on a classic, these fritters are so bright and fruity, you won't even miss the apples. This is a brioche-style recipe, meaning the fritters are made from a rich, yeasted dough. It's easy to forget that brioche is a bread dough and needs to be mixed well, so make sure you don't cut corners at the mixing stage. If mixed correctly, the high fat content in the recipe offsets the well-developed gluten, resulting in a tender, rich dough when cooked. **MAKES 24 FRITTERS**

1. **MAKE THE FRITTERS** In a stand mixer fitted with the paddle attachment, combine the flour, sugar, and yeast. In a small bowl, whisk the warm water, eggs, egg yolk, and salt until well combined. With the mixer on low speed, add the egg mixture to the flour mixture. Increase the speed to medium and mix for 5 minutes, until well combined. Add the butter, one cube at a time, waiting until each cube is fully incorporated before adding the next one. Mix until the dough is smooth and well combined.

2. Remove the bowl from the stand. Lightly spray the dough with non-stick cooking spray. Cover with plastic wrap and let rest in the fridge overnight.

3. Line 3 baking sheets with parchment paper. Place a wire rack on top of one of the prepared baking sheets. Remove the dough from the fridge. Punch down the dough to release the air. Turn the dough out onto a well-floured surface. With floured hands, pat the dough out until it is about ½ inch (1 cm) thick. Spread the pineapple onto half of the dough and fold the other half overtop. Seal the edges.

4. Using your hands, flatten the dough again until it is about ½ inch (1 cm) thick. Using a knife, cut about twenty-four 2-inch (5 cm) squares. Use your hands to round each dough square into a ball. Arrange the round fritters on the 2 prepared baking sheets without the wire rack.

5. Heat the canola oil in a large saucepan over medium heat. Using a candy thermometer to watch the temperature, bring the oil to 350°F (180°C). Fry 2 or 3 fritters at a time for about 3 minutes on each side, until deep golden brown. The fritters will open up slightly because of the wet pineapple inside, so don't worry if they

FRITTERS

2⅓ cups (575 mL) all-purpose flour

3 tablespoons (45 mL) granulated sugar

1 tablespoon (15 mL) instant yeast

½ cup (125 mL) warm water

2 large eggs

1 large egg yolk

2 teaspoons (10 mL) kosher salt

1 cup (250 mL) unsalted butter, room temperature, cut into 1-inch (2.5 cm) cubes

Non-stick cooking spray

1 cup (250 mL) diced pineapple

1 to 2 quarts (1 to 2 L) canola oil, for frying

COCONUT GLAZE

2 cups (500 mL) icing sugar

½ cup (125 mL) sweetened shredded coconut

¼ cup (60 mL) coconut milk

1 teaspoon (5 mL) pure vanilla extract

¼ teaspoon (1 mL) ground nutmeg

recipe continues

change shape as they fry or if you lose a couple of pieces of pineapple along the way. Use a slotted spoon to remove the fritters from the oil and transfer them to the wire rack. Repeat with the remaining dough. Let the fritters cool to room temperature.

6.   MAKE THE COCONUT GLAZE In a large bowl, whisk the icing sugar, coconut, coconut milk, vanilla, and nutmeg until combined.

7.   Dunk each fritter in the glaze, turning to coat the whole surface. Let the glaze drip off into the bowl, then return the glazed fritters to the wire rack, allowing the prepared baking sheet to catch additional drips.

8.   Fritters are best served on the day they are made but can be stored in an airtight container at room temperature for 1 more day.

HONEY CRULLERS

Erin practically grew up in a Hamilton doughnut shop, so we just had to include a recipe for this doughnut shop favourite. Erin's dad would treat her and her siblings to hot chocolates and honey crullers many times a week when he met up with friends at his local spot. Crullers have a distinct airy texture that yeasted doughnuts do not. This recipe uses eggs as the leavening agent, resulting in an airy, open crumb. We finish these doughnuts by dunking them in a sweet honey glaze. It's a true classic for everyone to enjoy. **MAKES 16 DOUGHNUTS**

1. **MAKE THE CRULLERS** In a medium saucepan, bring the water, butter, icing sugar, nutmeg, and salt to a boil over medium heat. Add the flour and, using a wooden spoon, stir continuously over medium-low heat until combined and a film of flour forms on the inside of the pot. Remove from the heat.

2. Using a wooden spoon, stir the cooked dough for a minute, allowing it to cool slightly. Add the whole eggs one at a time, stirring each until well combined before adding the next. Add the egg whites. Stir until the mixture becomes smooth and glossy. It may not appear to come together at first, but the flour in the dough will absorb the eggs and egg whites to create a smooth paste. Transfer the dough to a pastry bag fitted with a 1-inch (2.5 cm) star tip.

3. Line a baking sheet with parchment paper and place a wire rack on top. Cut about sixteen 3-inch (8 cm) squares of parchment paper. Spray the top side of each square with non-stick cooking spray. Pipe a ring of dough onto each square.

4. Fill a large skillet with 3 inches (8 cm) of canola oil and place it over medium-high heat. Using a candy thermometer to watch the temperature, bring the oil to 375°F (190°C). Carefully place 2 to 3 crullers (with the paper squares) into the hot oil. When the paper separates from the crullers, use tongs to carefully pull the paper out of the oil. Fry for 2 to 3 minutes, then flip the crullers and fry the other side for an additional 1 minute, until light golden brown. Use a slotted spoon to remove the crullers from the oil and transfer them to the wire rack. Repeat until all of the dough has been fried. Let cool completely before glazing.

CRULLERS

1 cup (250 mL) water

6 tablespoons (90 mL) unsalted butter

2 tablespoons (30 mL) icing sugar

½ teaspoon (2 mL) ground nutmeg

¼ teaspoon (1 mL) kosher salt

1 cup (250 mL) all-purpose flour

3 large eggs

2 large egg whites

Non-stick cooking spray

1 to 2 quarts (1 to 2 L) canola oil, for frying

HONEY GLAZE

1½ cups (375 mL) icing sugar

3 tablespoons (45 mL) whole (3.25%) milk

2 tablespoons (30 mL) pure liquid honey

1 teaspoon (5 mL) fresh lemon juice

recipe continues

5. **MAKE THE HONEY GLAZE** In a medium bowl, whisk the icing sugar, milk, honey, and lemon juice until combined. Dunk each cruller in the glaze, flipping it over in the bowl to coat both sides. Let the glaze drip off into the bowl, then return the glazed crullers to the wire rack, allowing the prepared baking sheet to catch additional drips. For an extra-thick coating of glaze, let the first coat set for about 5 minutes, then dunk in the glaze again, repeating the process. Let set for 20 minutes before serving.

6. Crullers are best served on the day they are made but can be stored in an airtight container at room temperature for up to 3 days.

EARTH TO TABLE BAKES

BOSTON CREAM DOUGHNUTS

Boston cream doughnuts are an adaptation of Boston cream pie, which is traditionally a butter cake with a cream filling topped with a drippy chocolate glaze. What could be better than a handheld version? **MAKES 10 DOUGHNUTS**

1. **MAKE THE DOUGHNUTS** In a stand mixer fitted with the paddle attachment, combine the flour, sugar, and yeast on low speed. In a small bowl, whisk the eggs, egg yolk, water, and salt. With the mixer on low speed, add the egg mixture to the flour mixture. Increase the speed to medium and mix until well combined, about 5 minutes. Add the butter, one cube at a time, waiting until each cube is fully incorporated before adding the next one. Mix until the dough is smooth and well combined.

2. Remove the bowl from the stand. Lightly spray the surface of the dough with non-stick cooking spray. Cover the bowl with plastic wrap and let rest in the fridge overnight.

3. Line a baking sheet with parchment paper. Remove the dough from the fridge. Punch down the dough to release the air. Tip it out onto a well-floured work surface. With floured hands, pat the dough out until it is about ½ inch (1 cm) thick. Using a 2-inch (5 cm) round cutter, cut circles from the dough and place them on the prepared baking sheet. Cover with plastic wrap and let proof at room temperature for 1 hour.

4. Line a large plate with paper towels. Fill a large saucepan with the canola oil and place it over medium-high heat. Using a candy thermometer to watch the temperature, bring the oil to 350°F (180°C). Gently remove the doughnuts from the baking tray, taking care not to deflate them, and place them into the oil two at a time to avoid overcrowding the pot. Fry for 3 minutes on each side, until golden brown. Use a slotted spoon to remove the doughnuts from the oil and transfer them to the lined plate. Let cool to room temperature.

5. **MAKE THE VANILLA CREAM** In a medium saucepan, whisk the sugar, flour, cornstarch, and salt. Whisk in the eggs, cream, and vanilla. Cook over medium-low heat, stirring continuously, until

DOUGHNUTS

2⅓ cups (575 mL) all-purpose flour

3 tablespoons (45 mL) granulated sugar

1 tablespoon (15 mL) instant yeast

2 large eggs

1 large egg yolk

½ cup (125 mL) warm water

2 teaspoons (10 mL) kosher salt

1 cup (250 mL) unsalted butter, room temperature, cut into 1-inch (2.5 cm) cubes

Non-stick cooking spray

8 cups (2 L) canola oil, for frying

VANILLA CREAM

⅔ cup (150 mL) granulated sugar

2 tablespoons (30 mL) all-purpose flour

2 tablespoons (30 mL) cornstarch

½ teaspoon (2 mL) kosher salt

2 large eggs

2 cups (500 mL) heavy (35%) cream

½ vanilla bean, split and seeds scraped

2 tablespoons (30 mL) softened unsalted butter

CHOCOLATE GLAZE

1½ cups (375 mL) icing sugar

¼ cup (60 mL) cocoa powder

2 tablespoons (30 mL) whole (3.25%) milk

2 teaspoons (10 mL) pure vanilla extract

recipe continues

the mixture comes to a gentle boil. Remove from the heat. Add the butter. Whisk until melted and combined. Let cool to room temperature. Cover, placing plastic wrap directly on the surface of the vanilla cream to prevent a skin forming. Store in the fridge for up to 3 days. Just before using, whisk until smooth.

6. Line a baking sheet with parchment paper. Place a wire rack on the baking sheet. To fill the doughnuts, use a skewer to pierce the side of each doughnut. Press the skewer into the centre and gently wiggle the tip in a circular motion to create a small pocket inside the doughnut.

7. Fill a pastry bag with the vanilla cream. Cut off the tip to create a ½-inch (1 cm) opening. Holding a doughnut in your hand, insert the opening of the piping bag into the hole and fill the doughnut generously, until a small amount of filling spills out of the hole. You should feel the doughnut expand in your hand as you do this. Place the doughnut on the wire rack. Repeat until all of the doughnuts are filled with vanilla cream.

8. MAKE THE CHOCOLATE GLAZE In a medium bowl, whisk the icing sugar and cocoa powder. Add the milk and vanilla and whisk until the glaze is smooth and pourable. Dunk the top of each doughnut into the glaze. Let the glaze drip off into the bowl, then return the glazed doughnuts to the wire rack, glazed sides up, allowing the parchment-lined baking sheet to catch additional drips.

9. These doughnuts are best served on the day they are made but can be stored in an airtight container in the fridge for up to 2 days.

AFFOGATO WITH CHOCOLATE CHURROS

Affogato is the Italian word for "drowned." Here, ice cream is drowned in espresso and served with crunchy chocolate churros for dipping. **SERVES 4, ABOUT 2 CHURROS PER SERVING**

1. In a pie plate, stir the sugar and 2 tablespoons (30 mL) of cinnamon to combine. Set aside.

2. In a medium saucepan, bring the water, butter, icing sugar, ¼ teaspoon (1 mL) cinnamon, and salt to a boil over medium heat. Add the flour and cocoa powder. Using a wooden spoon, stir continuously over medium-low heat until combined and a film of flour forms on the inside of the pot. Remove from the heat.

3. Transfer the dough to a stand mixer fitted with the paddle attachment. Mix for 1 minute on low speed to quickly cool down the dough. Increase the speed to medium. Add 1 egg at a time, incorporating each egg completely before adding the next. Add the egg white. Mix until the dough becomes smooth and glossy. Transfer the dough to a pastry bag fitted with a 1-inch (2.5 cm) star tip. Line a large plate with paper towels.

4. Fill a large saucepan with 2 inches (5 cm) of canola oil and place it over medium-high heat. Using a candy thermometer to watch the temperature, bring the oil to 350°F (180°C). Pipe four or five 1½-inch (4 cm) lengths of churro dough directly into the hot oil, using scissors to snip them off when they are the right length. Work in batches to avoid overcrowding the pot. Cook for 2 to 3 minutes, turning the churros occasionally, until golden brown. Use a slotted spoon to remove the churros from the oil and transfer them to the lined plate to drain. Repeat until all of the dough has been fried. Let cool slightly.

5. While the churros are still warm, transfer them to the cinnamon sugar mixture and toss to coat. When ready to serve, scoop the ice cream into 4 small bowls or glasses. Pour the hot espresso overtop, dividing it evenly between each portion. Serve with warm churros.

6. These churros are best served on the day they are made but can be stored in an airtight container in the fridge for up to 2 days. Refresh leftover churros in a 350°F (180°C) oven for 5 minutes.

1 cup (250 mL) granulated sugar

2 tablespoons (30 mL) + ¼ teaspoon (1 mL) cinnamon, divided

½ cup (125 mL) water

3 tablespoons (45 mL) unsalted butter

1 tablespoon (15 mL) icing sugar

¼ teaspoon (1 mL) kosher salt

½ cup (125 mL) all-purpose flour

1 tablespoon (30 mL) Dutch process cocoa powder

2 large eggs

1 large egg white

1 to 2 quarts (1 to 2 L) canola oil, for frying

FOR SERVING

1 pint (500 mL) good-quality vanilla ice cream

1 cup (250 mL) hot espresso

KITCHEN TIP

- Switch up the flavour profile of this recipe by using a different flavour of ice cream. We like butterscotch ripple, coconut, or even coffee ice cream for a twist on the original.

STRAWBERRY GLAZED CHAI CAKE DOUGHNUTS

We love using berries at the height of their season, and chai tea is an unexpected but delicious flavour pairing with summer's best strawberries in these cakey doughnuts. **MAKES 6 DOUGHNUTS**

1. Preheat the oven to 350°F (180°C). Spray a standard doughnut pan with non-stick cooking spray. Line a baking sheet with parchment paper and place a wire rack on top.

2. **MAKE THE CHAI CAKE DOUGHNUTS** In a medium bowl, whisk the flour, sugar, cinnamon, baking powder, ginger, cardamom, allspice, salt, and baking soda. In a separate medium bowl, whisk the butter, egg, sour cream, milk, and vanilla until combined. Pour the butter mixture into the flour mixture and whisk until just combined, making sure not to overmix or the batter will become too thick.

3. Spoon the batter into a large pastry bag and cut off the tip. Pipe the batter into the wells of the prepared doughnut pan, filling each about three-quarters full. Bake for 9 to 10 minutes, or until the edges are lightly browned and the doughnuts spring back when poked lightly with a finger. Transfer the doughnuts to the wire rack. Let cool to room temperature.

4. **MAKE THE STRAWBERRY GLAZE** Place the strawberries in a food processor or a blender and purée until smooth. Strain the puréed strawberries through a fine-mesh sieve into a small bowl to eliminate any residual solids. Set aside. Place the white chocolate in a medium heatproof bowl. Heat it in a microwave oven in 15-second intervals, stirring between each interval, until melted and smooth. Add the icing sugar, vanilla, and strained strawberry purée. Stir to combine.

5. Dunk each doughnut in the glaze, flipping it over in the bowl to coat both sides. Let the glaze drip off into the bowl, then return the glazed doughnuts to the wire rack, allowing the prepared baking sheet to catch additional drips.

6. Doughnuts are best served on the day they are made but can be stored in an airtight container at room temperature for 1 more day.

Non-stick cooking spray

CHAI CAKE DOUGHNUTS

1 cup (250 mL) all-purpose flour

½ cup (125 mL) granulated sugar

2 teaspoons (10 mL) ground cinnamon

1 teaspoon (5 mL) baking powder

1 teaspoon (5 mL) ground ginger

1 teaspoon (5 mL) ground cardamom

½ teaspoon (2 mL) ground allspice

½ teaspoon (2 mL) kosher salt

¼ teaspoon (1 mL) baking soda

3 tablespoons (45 mL) unsalted butter, melted and slightly cooled

1 large egg

¼ cup (60 mL) full-fat sour cream

¼ cup (60 mL) whole (3.25%) milk

1 teaspoon (2 mL) pure vanilla extract

STRAWBERRY GLAZE

1 cup (250 mL) hulled and sliced strawberries, room temperature

6 ounces (170 g) white chocolate

½ cup (125 mL) icing sugar

¼ teaspoon (1 mL) pure vanilla extract

BOSTOCK

In the classic French pastry world, this dish would be known as *brioche aux amandes,* which sounds luxurious and wonderful. And this delightful breakfast or dessert is exactly that. It combines day-old brioche with simple syrup, jam, frangipane, and toasted almonds—all baked to perfection. The name "bostock" sounds so harsh, but don't be fooled, this dessert is delightful. **SERVES 8**

ALMOND FRANGIPANE

⅔ cup (150 mL) whole raw almonds

½ cup (125 mL) granulated sugar

½ cup (125 mL) unsalted butter, softened

1 large egg

2 tablespoons (30 mL) all-purpose flour

½ teaspoon (2 mL) kosher salt

½ teaspoon (2 mL) pure vanilla extract

VANILLA SIMPLE SYRUP

½ cup (125 mL) granulated sugar

½ cup (125 mL) water

½ vanilla bean, split and seeds scraped

1 loaf day-old Brioche (page 278) or store-bought

½ cup (125 mL) Raspberry Jam (page 285) or store-bought

½ cup (125 mL) sliced almonds

Icing sugar, for dusting

1. Preheat the oven to 350°F (180°C). Line a baking sheet with parchment paper.

2. **MAKE THE ALMOND FRANGIPANE** Arrange the almonds on an unlined baking sheet. Toast for 10 minutes. Let cool. Increase the oven temperature to 400°F (200°C). Line a baking sheet with parchment paper.

3. In a food processor, pulse the toasted almonds and sugar until finely ground. Add the butter, egg, flour, salt, and vanilla and process until smooth. Use a spatula to transfer the mixture to a small bowl.

4. **MAKE THE VANILLA SIMPLE SYRUP** In a small saucepan over high heat, combine the sugar, water, and vanilla. Bring to a boil. Cook the syrup for 2 to 3 minutes, stirring occasionally, until the sugar is dissolved. Remove from the heat and let cool.

5. To assemble the bostock, cut the brioche into 8 slices (about 1 inch/2.5 cm each), discarding the ends. Arrange the slices on the prepared baking sheet. Brush both sides of each slice with the vanilla simple syrup. Spread the top side of each slice with 1 tablespoon (15 mL) of the Raspberry Jam and 3 tablespoons (45 mL) of the almond frangipane. Sprinkle the sliced almonds overtop. Bake for 13 to 15 minutes, until the frangipane is puffed and the brioche is golden brown. Dust with icing sugar and serve immediately.

6. Store any leftovers in an airtight container in the fridge overnight. Before serving, refresh the bostock by heating it in a 350°F (180°C) oven for about 10 minutes.

CINNAMON ROLLS

This is a no-knead recipe and does not require a mixer. Folding the edges of the dough back over itself creates a dough that is very forgiving and perfect for anyone, but especially for beginners. The resulting texture is tender and perfectly melt-in-your-mouth. Here we use sour cream instead of the typical cream cheese in the glaze—you will love it! **MAKES 12 CINNAMON ROLLS**

1. **MAKE THE DOUGH** In a large bowl, whisk the flour, yeast, and salt. In a medium bowl, whisk the eggs, egg yolk, water, olive oil, and honey. Pour the egg mixture into the flour mixture. Using a silicone spatula, stir until a wet, sticky dough forms. Cover the bowl with plastic wrap and let stand at room temperature for 10 minutes.

2. Remove the plastic wrap from the bowl, but do not throw it out. Grab an outside edge of the dough, lift it up, and fold it over itself, pulling it to the centre of the dough mound. Turn the bowl 45 degrees and repeat folding and turning, making your way around the entire lump of dough, until you get back to where you started. You should have folded and turned the dough 8 times in all. Flip the dough mound over so that the folds and seams are on the bottom. Cover with the plastic wrap and let stand at room temperature for 30 minutes.

3. Repeat step 2 four more times. If you're worried about losing track of how many times you've folded the dough back on itself, make a mark on the plastic wrap each time before you let the dough stand for 30 minutes. The gluten will develop with each fold, and by the final fold the dough will be elastic with small pockets of air. Once you've folded the dough for the final time, cover it with plastic wrap and refrigerate for 16 to 24 hours—any longer and the dough may over-proof.

4. **MAKE THE CINNAMON FILLING** In a small bowl, stir together the sugar, cinnamon, and salt.

5. Grease a 13- × 9-inch (3.5 L) baking dish. Turn the dough out onto a lightly floured work surface. Roll it into an 18- × 12-inch (45 × 30 cm) rectangle. It should be about ½ inch (1 cm) thick. Brush the melted butter on top. Sprinkle the cinnamon sugar

DOUGH

4 cups (1 L) bread flour

1½ teaspoons (7 mL) instant yeast

2 teaspoons (10 mL) kosher salt

2 large eggs

1 large egg yolk

¾ cup (175 mL) water

⅓ cup (75 mL) extra-virgin olive oil

¼ cup (60 mL) pure liquid honey

CINNAMON FILLING

⅓ cup (75 mL) granulated sugar

2 tablespoons (30 mL) cinnamon

½ teaspoon (2 mL) kosher salt

6 tablespoons (90 mL) unsalted
  butter, melted

GLAZE

2 cups (500 mL) icing sugar

¼ cup (60 mL) full-fat sour cream

1 teaspoon (5 mL) pure vanilla
  extract

¼ teaspoon (1 mL) kosher salt

recipe continues

mixture evenly overtop. Starting from one of the long ends, tightly roll the dough into a log. Slice the log into 12 pieces, each about 1½ inches (4 cm) thick. Arrange the slices in the prepared baking dish. Cover with a clean kitchen towel and let the rolls rise at room temperature until puffed and almost doubled in size, about 2 hours.

6.   Position a rack in the middle of the oven. Preheat the oven to 350°F (180°C). Bake the rolls for 20 to 25 minutes, until golden and cooked through. Let cool for 20 minutes.

7.   MAKE THE GLAZE In a medium bowl, whisk the icing sugar, sour cream, vanilla, and salt. Drizzle the glaze over the warm cinnamon rolls and serve immediately.

8.   Store any leftovers in an airtight container at room temperature for 1 more day.

ENGLISH MUFFINS

Making English muffins at home is not terribly difficult, but you will need time and some patience. This recipe takes more than one day to complete. If you want fresh English muffins for Sunday morning, you need to start them on Saturday and then get up early on Sunday to finish them in time for breakfast. They may require a time investment, but the results will not disappoint. A fresh griddled and baked English muffin does not compare to anything you can buy in a store. **MAKES 12 ENGLISH MUFFINS**

1. In a medium bowl, combine the buttermilk, water, butter, and vegetable oil.

2. In a stand mixer fitted with the paddle attachment, mix the flour, yeast, sugar, and salt. With the mixer on low speed, add the buttermilk mixture and beat until a shaggy dough forms. Increase the speed to medium and beat until the dough is smooth and begins to pull away from the sides of the bowl but is still very wet and sticky, about 5 minutes.

3. Grease a medium bowl. Transfer the dough to the greased bowl and cover tightly with plastic wrap. Chill in the fridge overnight.

4. Line 2 baking sheets with parchment paper and dust generously with cornmeal. Turn the dough out onto a lightly floured work surface. Using a bench scraper, divide the dough into 12 equal pieces and roll each into a ball. Working with one ball at a time, shape each into a rough square. Pull the 4 corners into the centre of each ball to make rounds. Flip the balls onto the prepared baking sheets (6 per baking sheet), spacing them evenly, so that all of the seams are on the bottom. Sprinkle each ball with cornmeal and cover the baking sheet loosely with plastic wrap. Let stand at room temperature until the balls have doubled in size, about 1 hour.

5. Preheat the oven to 350°F (180°C).

6. Place a large skillet, preferably cast iron, over low heat. Carefully transfer 2 to 3 dough balls to the skillet. Keep the remaining dough covered. Cook for 5 to 7 minutes, until the bottoms are dark golden brown. Flip and cook the other side for another 5 to 7 minutes. Return the cooked English muffins to the baking sheets. Repeat until no dough balls remain.

1 cup (250 mL) buttermilk

1 cup (250 mL) water

¼ cup (60 mL) unsalted butter, melted

2 tablespoons (30 mL) canola oil, more for greasing

3½ cups (875 mL) all-purpose flour, more for dusting

1 tablespoon (15 mL) active dry yeast

1 tablespoon (15 mL) granulated sugar

2 teaspoons (10 mL) kosher salt

Cornmeal, for dusting

KITCHEN TIP

• Proofing the dough overnight will make it easier to handle and produces better flavour. If you're crunched for time, make sure you let the dough proof for at least 6 hours in the fridge.

recipe continues

7. Bake for 10 minutes, until the English muffins are firm to the touch. Let cool for 30 minutes before serving.

8. English muffins can be made 1 day ahead. Store in an airtight container at room temperature overnight and toast before serving.

EARTH TO TABLE BAKES

CRUMPETS

On weekend mornings, or sometimes even on weekdays, we like to whip up pancakes or waffles from scratch. So why not a crumpet? This recipe is dead easy and is just waiting for all those nooks and crannies to be filled with some Homemade Butter (page 283) or Whipped Clotted Cream (page 282) and Raspberry Jam (page 285). **MAKES 8 TO 10 CRUMPETS**

1. In a medium bowl, combine the flour, yeast, salt, and sugar. Add the warm water and stir until well combined. Cover with plastic wrap or a damp kitchen towel and let stand at room temperature for 1 hour, until the yeast is active and the batter is bubbly.

2. In a small bowl, dissolve the baking soda in the cold water. Add the baking soda mixture to the batter all at once and stir to combine. The mixture will be quite loose at this point and will almost seem stringy. Let stand for 30 minutes, until bubbly and active again.

3. In a lightly oiled 10-inch (25 cm) skillet over medium heat, place three 3-inch (8 cm) lightly oiled stainless steel cooking rings next to each other. Fill each ring with about ¼ cup (60 mL) of batter and cook for 15 minutes. The batter will start to bubble and form crevices that will set. Once they've set, use tongs to remove the rings. Flip the crumpets and cook for an additional 3 minutes to brown the tops. Transfer the crumpets to a plate. Repeat with the remaining batter.

4. Serve crumpets while they are still warm with Homemade Butter or Whipped Clotted Cream and Raspberry Jam.

5. Crumpets are best served on the day they are made but can be stored in an airtight container in the freezer for up to 3 months. Simply refresh them in a toaster before serving.

1½ cups (375 mL) all-purpose flour
2 teaspoons (10 mL) instant yeast
2 teaspoons (10 mL) kosher salt
½ teaspoon (2 mL) granulated sugar
1½ cups (375 mL) warm water
½ teaspoon (2 mL) baking soda
½ cup (125 mL) cold water

FOR SERVING

Homemade Butter (page 283)
Raspberry Jam (page 285)
Whipped Clotted Cream (page 282)

HOT CROSS BUNS

There is a lot of significance surrounding hot crossed buns and the Christian season of Lent. The dough is made with dairy, which is not allowed during Lent, and so they are enjoyed at the end of the season, with the cross representing the crucifixion of Jesus. This is a lot of weight for these little buns to carry. Let's take some weight off of these slightly sweet and spicy delights that are super easy and enjoyable to make and start enjoying them all year round. **MAKES 12 BUNS**

1. Preheat the oven to 350°F (180°C). Line a baking sheet with parchment paper.

2. In a small bowl, cover the raisins with boiling water and let stand for 10 minutes, until plump. Drain and pat dry with a kitchen towel.

3. In a stand mixer fitted with the dough hook, combine 2¾ cups (675 mL) of the flour, the sugar, orange zest, yeast, cinnamon, salt, ginger, nutmeg, and raisins on low speed. Slowly add the milk and mix until just combined. Add the butter and egg. Increase the speed to medium and mix until the dough is smooth and pulls away from the sides and bottom of the bowl, about 7 minutes. Transfer the dough to a lightly oiled medium bowl. Cover with plastic wrap and let stand at room temperature until the dough has doubled in size, about 1 hour.

4. Turn the dough out onto a lightly floured surface and divide it into 12 equal portions. Roll each portion into a ball and evenly space them on the prepared baking sheet. Cover again with plastic wrap and let stand for 1 hour at room temperature, until the buns double in size.

5. In a small bowl, combine the remaining ¼ cup (60 mL) of flour and the water and mix with a small spoon until smooth. Transfer the flour and water mixture to a piping bag and cut off the tip to create a ⅛-inch (3 mm) opening. Pipe a cross onto each bun.

6. Bake for 25 minutes, until the buns are evenly browned. Let cool to room temperature. Serve with Homemade Butter.

7. Store in an airtight container at room temperature for up to 2 days or in the freezer for up to 3 months.

1½ cups (375 mL) raisins

2¾ cups (675 mL) + ¼ cup (60 mL) all-purpose flour, divided

¼ cup (60 mL) granulated sugar

1 tablespoon (15 mL) fresh grated orange zest

1 tablespoon (15 mL) instant yeast

1 teaspoon (5 mL) ground cinnamon

1 teaspoon (5 mL) kosher salt

¼ teaspoon (1 mL) ground ginger

¼ teaspoon (1 mL) ground nutmeg

1 cup (250 mL) warm whole (3.25%) milk or 2% milk

2 tablespoons (30 mL) unsalted butter, softened

1 large egg

¼ cup (60 mL) water

Homemade Butter (page 283), for serving

KITCHEN TIPS

• We use raisins in this recipe, but you could substitute an equal amount of dried currants or dried cranberries if you prefer.

• Try using a plastic zip-top bag as a piping bag in a pinch. Simply place your filling in the bag and snip off the corner.

GARLIC KALE AND GOAT CHEESE SOUFFLÉ

Tangy goat cheese and garlicky kale come together in this delicious recipe that we think you should add to your brunch repertoire—a soufflé always impresses. Unlike a cake, which contains structural gluten to help maintain the rise, a soufflé is inflated with hot air, which means it will not stay puffed for very long after it is removed from the oven. Don't fret: it will remain delicious, even if it falls a bit before it gets to the table. For a real showstopper, plan to have it come out of the oven just as you are ready to serve it. **SERVES 2 TO 3**

1. Place the olive oil in a large skillet over medium heat. Add the garlic and sauté for 2 minutes, until it just begins to brown. Add the kale and toss to coat with the oil. Sauté for 3 to 5 minutes or until wilted. Remove from the heat and set aside.

2. Position a rack in the middle of the oven. Preheat the oven to 400°F (200°C). Grease a 6-cup (1.5 L) soufflé dish. Sprinkle it evenly with toasted bread crumbs, rotating the dish so the bread crumbs adhere to the greased dish.

3. In a medium saucepan over low heat, melt the butter. Using a wooden spoon, stir in the flour and cook, stirring constantly, for 2 minutes. Remove from the heat and whisk in the milk, ½ teaspoon (2 mL) of the salt, the nutmeg, and black pepper. Cook for 1 minute, whisking constantly, until smooth and thick. Remove from the heat and whisk in the egg yolks. Stir in the Parmesan, goat cheese, and kale. Transfer the mixture to a large mixing bowl.

4. In a stand mixer fitted with the whisk attachment, whisk the egg whites, cream of tartar, and the remaining ¼ teaspoon (1 mL) of salt on low speed for 1 minute. Increase the speed to medium and whisk for an additional 1 minute. Increase the speed to high and whisk until firm, glossy peaks form, about 4 minutes.

5. Transfer one-quarter of the egg whites to the bowl with the cheese and kale mixture and gently fold with a silicone spatula to combine. Gently fold in the rest of the egg whites.

2 tablespoons (30 mL) extra-virgin olive oil

1 tablespoon (15 mL) minced garlic

2 cups (500 mL) fresh baby kale, finely chopped

½ cup (125 mL) finely ground toasted bread crumbs or panko

3 tablespoons (45 mL) unsalted butter

5 tablespoons (75 mL) all-purpose flour

1 cup (250 mL) whole (3.25%) milk

½ teaspoon (2 mL) + ¼ teaspoon (1 mL) kosher salt, divided

¼ teaspoon (1 mL) nutmeg

¼ teaspoon (1 mL) black pepper

4 large egg yolks, room temperature

¼ cup (60 mL) finely grated Parmesan cheese

½ cup (125 mL) crumbled goat cheese

5 large egg whites, room temperature

½ teaspoon (2 mL) cream of tartar

recipe continues

6.   Transfer the mixture to the prepared soufflé dish. Reduce the oven temperature to 375°F (190°C) and immediately place the soufflé in the oven to bake for 30 to 35 minutes, without opening the oven door, until puffed and brown. Serve immediately. This soufflé does not keep well overnight.

KITCHEN TIP

• If you want to prepare some of this recipe in advance, complete steps 1 to 3 up to 2 hours ahead. Keep the mixture covered at room temperature until you're ready to proceed with whipping and folding in the egg whites just before baking.

CARAMEL CREAM PUFFS

The base of this recipe is choux paste, which sounds like it would be really challenging to make, but we assure you it is actually really hard to mess up. The key is to make the paste as smooth as possible before you pipe it onto the baking sheet. If piping the dough sounds intimidating, we are here to give you confidence: as long as you get the paste onto the baking sheet in some type of mound, it *will* puff, and before long you will have made a cream puff. The cream puffs have a crispy outside with a soft, rich dough. Filled with sweet cream, they are complete bliss in one bite. **MAKES 24 CREAM PUFFS**

1. Preheat the oven to 375°F (190°C). Line 2 baking sheets with parchment paper.

2. **MAKE THE CREAM PUFFS** In a medium saucepan over high heat, bring the water, butter, sugar, and salt to a boil. Immediately remove the saucepan from the heat. Add the flour all at once and stir with a wooden spoon until a dough ball forms. Place the saucepan over medium heat, stirring constantly, until a film forms on the bottom of the pot.

3. Transfer the dough to a stand mixer fitted with the paddle attachment. With the mixer on low speed, add the eggs one at a time, waiting until each egg is fully incorporated before adding the next. Mix until the mixture—called choux paste—is thick, smooth, and glossy.

4. Transfer the choux paste to a piping bag while it's still warm and cut off the tip. Pipe 2-inch (5 cm) circles of choux paste onto the prepared baking sheets. Bake for 25 minutes, turning the baking sheets halfway through, until golden brown all over. Be careful not to take them out of the oven too soon—if the cream puffs are undercooked, they will deflate and filling them will be a challenge. Let cool to room temperature.

5. **MAKE THE CARAMEL PASTRY CREAM** In a medium saucepan over high heat, bring the sugar, water, and lemon juice to a rolling boil. Cook over high heat until the mixture turns a deep reddish brown colour, about 20 minutes. Remove from the heat. Slowly and carefully stir in the butter and cream. The sugar is extremely hot, and the caramel will bubble up when you add the dairy. Carefully stir to combine. Remove 1 cup (250 mL) caramel from the saucepan and reserve, allowing it to cool completely, about

CREAM PUFFS

2 cups (500 mL) water
1 cup (250 mL) unsalted butter
¼ cup (60 mL) granulated sugar
2 teaspoons (5 mL) kosher salt
2⅔ cups (650 mL) all-purpose flour
12 large eggs

CARAMEL PASTRY CREAM

2 cups (500 mL) granulated sugar
1½ cups (375 mL) water
1 teaspoon (5 mL) fresh lemon juice
¼ cup (60 mL) unsalted butter, cubed
1 cup (250 mL) heavy (35%) cream
2 cups (500 mL) 2% milk
1 vanilla bean, split and seeds scraped
3 tablespoons (45 mL) cornstarch
3 large egg yolks
1 large egg
½ batch Stabilized Chantilly Cream (page 281)

MILK CHOCOLATE SAUCE

1 cup (250 mL) good-quality milk chocolate
1 cup (250 mL) heavy (35%) cream

recipe continues

1 hour. The caramel will become quite solid once it has cooled, but 1 minute in a microwave oven will make it pourable again.

6.   Place the saucepan with the remaining caramel sauce over medium heat. Add the milk and vanilla. Cook, stirring occasionally, until the mixture is smooth, about 5 minutes.

7.   In a small bowl, whisk the cornstarch, egg yolks, and egg until smooth. While whisking the caramel continuously, slowly add the egg mixture to it. Increase the temperature to high and bring to a boil. Remove from the heat immediately. Transfer the pastry cream to a medium bowl and cover, placing plastic wrap directly on the surface to prevent a skin forming. Let cool to room temperature, then transfer it to the fridge to chill for a few hours.

8.   MEANWHILE, MAKE THE MILK CHOCOLATE SAUCE Place the chocolate in a small bowl. In a small saucepan over medium heat, bring the cream to a boil. Remove from the heat and immediately pour the cream over the chocolate. Stir until smooth and combined.

9.   Place the chilled pastry cream in a large bowl. Fold the Stabilized Chantilly Cream into the pastry cream and mix until smooth. Transfer it to a piping bag and cut off the tip to create a ⅛-inch (3 mm) opening. Using a toothpick, poke a small hole in the bottom of each cream puff and use the holes to fill each one with pastry cream. Using a spoon, drizzle each cream puff with some of the reserved caramel and the chocolate sauce. These cream puffs do not keep well overnight.

KITCHEN TIP

• Once you pipe the choux paste onto the baking sheets, it can be frozen. Place the baking sheets in the freezer and, as soon as the dollops are frozen, transfer them to an airtight container or zip-top freezer bag and store for up to 3 months. When you want to make cream puffs, arrange the frozen dollops on a baking sheet and bake from frozen—just be sure to add about 5 minutes to the baking time.

GOUGÈRES

The base for this recipe is a choux paste, so the instructions for the Caramel Cream Puffs (page 171) apply—do not be intimidated! Once you make this recipe and realize how easy it is, you will be making gougères all the time because they are mouthwatering. The crispy, cheesy outside coupled with the puffy, creamy centres makes this recipe one of our favorites. We recommend using Gruyère cheese, but you can use any soft cheese you have on hand. **MAKES 8 TO 12 GOUGÈRES**

1. Preheat the oven to 375°F (190°C). Line a baking sheet with parchment paper.

2. In a medium saucepan over medium heat, cook the milk, butter, and salt until the butter is melted and the mixture just comes to a boil. Immediately reduce the heat to low and add the flour. Cook, stirring continuously, until the mixture is smooth and pulls away from the sides of the saucepan, about 3 minutes.

3. Transfer the mixture to a stand mixer fitted with paddle attachment. With the mixer on medium speed, add the eggs one at a time, waiting until each egg is fully incorporated before adding the next. Mix until the choux paste is smooth, thick, and glossy. Remove the bowl from the stand. Add ¾ cup (175 mL) of the Gruyère, the pepper, and thyme. Stir with a spatula or wooden spoon until combined.

4. Transfer the choux paste to a piping bag and cut off the tip to create a ½-inch (1 cm) opening. Pipe dollops about the size of a golf ball onto the prepared baking sheet. Sprinkle the dollops evenly with the remaining ½ cup (125 mL) of Gruyère. Bake for 20 to 25 minutes, turning the baking sheet after 10 minutes. Let cool.

5. Gougères are best served on the day they are made but can be stored in an airtight container at room temperature for 1 more day. If you do keep them overnight, be sure to refresh them by baking them in a 350°F (180°C) oven for about 5 minutes before serving.

1 cup (250 mL) 2% milk
½ cup (125 mL) unsalted butter
1 teaspoon (5 mL) kosher salt
1¼ cups (300 mL) all-purpose flour
6 large eggs
¾ cup (175 mL) + ½ cup (125 mL) shredded Gruyère cheese, divided
1 teaspoon (5 mL) fresh cracked black pepper
1 teaspoon (5 mL) chopped fresh thyme

KITCHEN TIP

- Once you pipe the choux paste onto the baking sheet, it can be frozen. Place the baking sheet in the freezer and, as soon as the dollops are frozen, transfer them to an airtight container or zip-top freezer bag and store for up to 3 months. When you want to make gougères, arrange the frozen dollops on a baking sheet and bake from frozen—just be sure to add about 5 minutes to the baking time.

LEMON CURD AND BLACKBERRY PAVLOVAS

The first rule of baking egg whites in this pavlova recipe is to make sure that zero yolk or oil of any kind makes it into your mixture. You're also aiming for zero humidity, so do your best to avoid making this recipe on a humid day. If you live in a humid summer climate, even a well air-conditioned home will not save the meringue from soaking up moisture in the air. The result: a meringue that will not crisp up and will be tacky to the touch and leaking egg whites. In this recipe, we top the pillow of crispy, sweet baked egg white with tart lemon curd and balance it out with mascarpone cream, then add blackberries to finish. We like blackberries because they tend to be a bit tart and help cut the sweetness of the meringue base, but an equal amount of any berry would work well here. This recipe is naturally gluten-free. **MAKES 6 PERSONAL PAVLOVAS**

1. Preheat the oven to 180°F (80°C). Line a baking sheet with parchment paper.

2. **MAKE THE MERINGUES** In a stand mixer fitted with the whisk attachment, whisk the egg whites on high speed until frothy. With the mixer still running, sprinkle in the sugar a little bit at a time, making sure it does not settle on the bottom of the bowl. Continue whisking until soft peaks form. Sprinkle in the cornstarch. Whisk to combine. Add the lemon juice all at once and whisk until the whites are firm and shiny, about 8 minutes.

3. Divide the egg white mixture into 6 evenly spaced dollops on the prepared baking sheet. Using the back of a spoon, gently spread out the mounds, making a well in the centre of each, until they are each about 4 inches (10 cm) in diameter. Take care to ensure that the meringue rounds remain separate. Bake for 2 hours, or until they easily come off the parchment paper. Turn off the oven and pull the door open about 1 inch (2.5 cm). Let set in the oven for 2 hours. It is important that they do not cool too quickly, or they will crack.

4. **MEANWHILE, MAKE THE LEMON CURD AND MASCARPONE CREAM** To make the lemon curd, in a medium saucepan, whisk the sugar, egg yolks, egg, and lemon zest until combined. Add the lemon juice and butter. Place the mixture over medium heat. Bring to a boil, stirring continuously and scraping down the

MERINGUES

3 large egg whites
¾ cup (175 mL) granulated sugar
1½ teaspoons (7 mL) cornstarch
1½ teaspoons (7 mL) fresh lemon juice

LEMON CURD

¼ cup (60 mL) granulated sugar
3 large egg yolks
1 large egg
Zest of 1 lemon
¼ cup (60 mL) fresh lemon juice
2 tablespoons (30 mL) unsalted butter

MASCARPONE CREAM

¼ cup (60 mL) mascarpone cheese, softened
1 tablespoon (15 mL) granulated sugar
½ cup (125 mL) heavy (35%) cream
½ teaspoon (2 mL) pure vanilla extract

½ pint (250 mL) fresh blackberries, or berries of choice

recipe continues

bottom and sides of the saucepan. Once the curd boils, remove from the heat immediately. Use a fine-mesh sieve to strain out the solids. Let cool.

5.   To make the mascarpone cream, rinse out and dry the bowl of the stand mixer. Using the whisk attachment, whisk the mascarpone and sugar until smooth and creamy. Add the cream and vanilla and whisk on high speed until soft peaks form.

6.   To serve, top each meringue equally with lemon curd, mascarpone cream, and blackberries.

7.   Store the meringues, without toppings, in an airtight container at room temperature for up to 1 week. Store the lemon curd and mascarpone cream in airtight containers in the fridge for up to 1 week.

KITCHEN TIP

• Whatever you do, make sure you do not put the meringues in the fridge. Refrigerators carry a lot of moisture and will very quickly melt them.

MERINGUE KISSES AND MUSHROOMS

This recipe was a surprise hit in Bettina's house. She made a meringue cake for Thanksgiving one year and had a bunch of leftover meringue, so decided to use it to make little meringue kisses. She put them in a bowl on the counter beside the beautiful cake and all of the kids couldn't get enough of the kisses—and ignored the cake. They also make a great gluten-free addition to any sweet table. We've added instructions for making meringue mushrooms here as well because they are just too cute! For the kisses, you will need to fit a piping bag with a star tip, and for the mushrooms, you will need a plain old round tip. **MAKES 30 TO 40 KISSES AND ABOUT 15 MUSHROOMS**

1. Preheat the oven to 180°F (80°C). Line 2 baking sheets with parchment paper.

2. In a stand mixer fitted with the paddle attachment, whisk the egg whites on high speed until foamy, about 3 minutes. Add the vanilla, cream of tartar, and salt. Whisk on high speed until the egg whites hold soft peaks, another 5 minutes. With the mixer running, gradually sprinkle in the sugar, making sure it does not settle on the bottom of the bowl. Continue whisking until all of the sugar has been added and stiff, shiny peaks form.

3. To make meringue kisses, fit a pastry bag with a ½-inch (1 cm) star tip and fill the bag halfway with meringue. To pipe the kisses, start with the tip softly touching a prepared baking sheet. Pipe a 1-inch (2.5 cm) round of meringue in a circle while pulling straight up. Repeat to make 30 to 40 kisses. It takes a bit of practice, but you will master this technique in no time. The first few might not be perfect, but you can still bake them. The shape is not all that important; each kiss will still be delicious.

4. To make meringue mushrooms, fit a pastry bag with a ½-inch (1 cm) round tip and fill the bag halfway with meringue. To pipe the mushroom caps, pipe round mounds, about 2 tablespoons (30 mL) each, making a quick circle with the piping tip but trying to finish on the side of the mushroom cap to avoid creating a peak. For the stems, pipe a little dollop of meringue and release pressure as you pull straight up. The resulting dollops should look like Hershey's Kisses.

½ cup (125 mL) egg whites, about 4 egg whites
1 teaspoon (5 mL) pure vanilla extract
¼ teaspoon (1 mL) cream of tartar
¼ teaspoon (1 mL) kosher salt
1 cup (250 mL) granulated sugar
1 tablespoon (15 mL) cocoa powder
½ cup (125 mL) coating chocolate

recipe continues

5. Bake the meringues for about 1 hour, or until they are very dry and easily come off the parchment paper. Let cool completely.

6. Dust the mushroom caps with cocoa powder using a small fine-mesh sieve. To assemble the mushrooms, place the coating chocolate in a heatproof bowl and melt it in a microwave oven in 15-second intervals, stirring between each interval, until smooth and shiny. Dip the bottom of a mushroom cap and the top of a mushroom stem in the chocolate. Press the caps and stems together and hold until the chocolate is set, about 30 seconds. Repeat with the remaining caps and stems.

7. Store in an airtight container at room temperature for up to 1 week.

KITCHEN TIP

- Whatever you do, make sure you do not put the meringues in the fridge. Refrigerators carry a lot of moisture and will very quickly melt them.

STRAWBERRY SMASH ETON MESS

This dessert is often said to have been created at Eton College in London, England, though you will find many storied versions of its more detailed history out there. All you need to know is that it is the perfect mix of creamy and crunchy, sweet and tart (though a little more on the sweet side). This dessert is also gluten free, so you can safely serve it to any intolerant friends or family without worry. **SERVES 6**

1. Preheat the oven to 180°F (80°C). Line a baking sheet with parchment paper.

2. **MAKE THE MERINGUE** In the stainless steel bowl of a stand mixer, combine the egg whites and sugar. Place the bowl above a medium saucepan of boiling water, making sure the bowl does not touch the water, to create a double boiler. Stir until the sugar is dissolved and the mixture is warm, about 5 minutes. Add the salt and cream of tartar. Stir to combine.

3. Place the bowl on a stand mixer fitted with the whisk attachment. Whisk on high speed until stiff, glossy peaks form and the meringue has nearly cooled to room temperature.

4. Using an offset spatula, transfer the meringue to the prepared baking sheet and spread it in a thin, even layer. Bake for 60 minutes. The meringue should still be white. Bake for an additional 15 to 30 minutes, or until the meringue is dry and crisp but still very white. Let cool to room temperature.

5. Break the meringue into 1-inch (2.5 cm) pieces. If you don't want to assemble the Eton Mess right away, store the meringue in an airtight container at room temperature for up to 1 week.

6. **MAKE THE STRAWBERRY SMASH** In a medium bowl, toss the strawberries, sugar, and vanilla to combine. Let stand for at least 30 minutes to macerate. Smash the strawberries with a fork until they become saucy. Cover and refrigerate for up to 3 hours.

7. Assemble the Eton Mess by creating layers of Chantilly Cream, strawberry smash, and meringue pieces in 6 clear 8-ounce (250 mL) glass jars. Repeat until there are 9 layers in each jar. Serve immediately. Once assembled, this dessert does not keep well overnight.

MERINGUE

3 large egg whites
¾ cup (175 mL) granulated sugar
½ teaspoon (2 mL) kosher salt
½ teaspoon (2 mL) cream of tartar

STRAWBERRY SMASH

4 cups (1 L) fresh summer strawberries, hulled and quartered
½ cup (125 mL) granulated sugar
½ vanilla bean, split and seeds scraped, or ½ teaspoon (2 mL) pure vanilla extract

½ batch Chantilly Cream (page 281)

PIES

AND

TARTS

COCONUT DREAM PIE

Easily Erin's favourite dessert of all time, this recipe has ultimate coconut flavour! The coconut milk and toasted coconut really make it a coconut lover's dream. Over the years, we have made many variations of this pie, and it is always a hit. **MAKES ONE 9-INCH (23 CM) PIE**

1. Preheat the oven to 350°F (180°C). Line a baking sheet with parchment paper.

2. On a lightly floured work surface, roll the Sweet Pie Dough into a 10-inch (25 cm) circle. Roll the dough around the rolling pin and unroll it over a 9-inch (23 cm) pie plate. Gently press the dough into the bottom and sides of the plate, folding any overhanging dough under itself along the lip. Crimp the edges and transfer to the fridge, uncovered, to chill for 20 minutes.

3. Crumple a piece of parchment paper into a ball. Spread it back out and lay it into the bottom and up the sides of the unbaked pie dough. Fill it with dried beans or lentils. Bake for 10 minutes. Remove the pie plate from the oven and carefully remove the dried beans by lifting the parchment paper out of the shell. Prick the half-baked shell a few times with a fork and return it to the oven to finish baking, another 5 to 8 minutes, until golden brown. Reduce the oven temperature to 325°F (160°C).

4. Sprinkle the coconut in an even layer on the prepared baking sheet. Bake for 3 minutes. Open the oven and gently stir the coconut with a wooden spoon. Continue baking for an additional 3 to 4 minutes, until golden brown. Let cool.

5. In a large saucepan over medium-high heat, bring the coconut milk, whole milk, and vanilla to a boil. Remove from the heat.

6. In a medium bowl, whisk the egg yolks and sugar until smooth. Add the cornstarch and salt. Whisk to combine. This mixture will be quite stiff.

7. Whisking the egg mixture continuously, very slowly pour the warm milk mixture into the bowl. This is called tempering (page 7) and it ensures that the warm milk does not cook and curdle the egg yolks. Continue whisking until you've poured in all of the milk and the mixture is smooth.

½ batch Sweet Pie Dough
(page 270)
1½ cups (375 mL) sweetened
shredded coconut
1¾ cups (425 mL) canned coconut
milk
1½ cups (375 mL) whole (3.25%) milk
½ vanilla bean, split and seeds
scraped
6 large egg yolks
1 cup (250 mL) granulated sugar
¼ cup (60 mL) cornstarch
1 teaspoon (5 mL) kosher salt
6 tablespoons (90 mL) cold unsalted
butter, cubed
¼ cup (60 mL) semisweet chocolate,
chopped
1 batch Chantilly Cream (page 281)

recipe continues

8. Transfer the mixture to the saucepan that contained the milk mixture. Cook on medium heat, stirring continuously, until bubbling, about 4 minutes. It is important that the mixture bubbles because this indicates that the cornstarch has been activated and the final pie filling will be nice and thick. Reduce the heat to low and cook for an additional 4 minutes, stirring occasionally. Remove from the heat and add 1 cup (250 mL) of the toasted coconut and the butter. Stir until the butter is melted and fully incorporated. Transfer the coconut cream to a medium bowl and cover, placing plastic wrap directly on the surface to prevent a skin forming. Chill in the fridge for 3 hours.

9. Place the chocolate in a heatproof bowl. Heat the chocolate in a microwave oven in 15-second intervals, stirring between each interval, until smooth. Use a pastry brush to brush the bottom and sides of the pie shell with the melted chocolate. This will create a barrier between the filling and the pie shell and will help keep the pie shell from getting soggy. Let the chocolate set for 10 minutes at room temperature. Pour the coconut cream into the chocolate-lined shell.

10. Dollop the Chantilly Cream onto the coconut cream. Garnish with the remaining ½ cup (125 mL) of toasted coconut. Place the pie in the fridge, uncovered, to chill for 1 hour before serving.

11. Store any leftovers, wrapped tightly in plastic wrap, in the fridge for up to 2 days.

KITCHEN TIPS

- Make sure you use canned coconut milk, and not coconut beverage from a carton, for this recipe. The beverage contains additives that will keep the pie filling from thickening.
- Ceramic pie weights can be purchased at a cake supply store, but dried beans, lentils, or chickpeas work just as well. Keep them in a container with a lid, as they can be used again whenever you need to blind bake a pie shell.

MILE HIGH LEMON MERINGUE PIE

In our version of lemon meringue pie, the lemon filling is baked in the pie shell instead of being cooked on the stovetop. This means that this pie slices beautifully and the filling will not ooze out when the slices are served. **MAKES ONE 9-INCH (23 CM) PIE**

1. Preheat the oven to 350°F (180°C). Line a baking sheet with parchment paper.

2. On a lightly floured work surface, roll the Sweet Pie Dough into a 10-inch (25 cm) circle. Roll the dough around the rolling pin and unroll it over a 9-inch (23 cm) pie plate. Gently press the dough into the bottom and sides of the plate, folding any overhanging dough under itself along the lip. Crimp the edges.

3. Crumple a piece of parchment paper into a ball. Spread it back out and lay it into the bottom and up the sides of the unbaked pie dough. Fill with dried beans or lentils. Bake for 10 minutes. Remove the pie plate from the oven and carefully remove the dried beans by lifting the parchment paper out of the shell. Prick the half-baked shell a few times with a fork and return it to the oven to finish baking, another 5 to 8 minutes, until golden brown. Reduce the temperature of the oven to 300°F (150°C).

4. **MAKE THE LEMON FILLING** In a medium bowl, combine the sugar and lemon zest. Rub the sugar and zest between your hands until fragrant. Add the flour and whisk to combine. Add the lemon juice and whisk until fully incorporated.

5. In a small bowl, whisk the eggs and salt. Add the egg mixture to the sugar mixture and whisk until smooth. Cover with plastic wrap and chill in the fridge for 2 hours.

6. Place the pie shell back in the oven. Pull out the oven rack the pie shell is on halfway and carefully pour the lemon filling into the pie shell. Filling the pie while it is in the oven is easier than trying to transfer it to the oven without spilling. Bake for 30 minutes, until the filling is set and the middle jiggles only slightly when you move the pie plate. Let cool to room temperature, then transfer to the fridge to chill for at least 1 hour.

½ batch Sweet Pie Dough (page 270)

LEMON FILLING

1 cup + 1 tablespoon (265 mL) granulated sugar

Zest of ½ lemon

¼ cup (60 mL) all-purpose flour

½ cup + 1 tablespoon (140 mL) fresh lemon juice (3 to 4 lemons)

3 large eggs

¼ teaspoon (1 mL) kosher salt

MERINGUE

8 large egg whites

1 cup (250 mL) granulated sugar

1 cup (250 mL) icing sugar

½ teaspoon (2 mL) kosher salt

½ teaspoon (2 mL) pure vanilla extract

recipe continues

7.   MAKE THE MERINGUE Place the egg whites and sugar in the stainless steel bowl of a stand mixer. Bring a small saucepan of water to a simmer over medium heat. Place the bowl on top. Whisk the egg whites and sugar until combined and the sugar is completely dissolved. Remove from the heat.

8.   Place the bowl on a stand mixer fitted with the whisk attachment and whisk on high speed until stiff peaks form, about 4 minutes. Add the icing sugar. Whisk on low speed until combined. Add the salt and vanilla and whisk until combined.

9.   Dollop the meringue onto the pie, swirling it with the back of a spoon to create many peaks and valleys. This will create a lot of surface area for browning. Using a small kitchen torch, thoroughly brown the meringue until deep golden brown. Slice in 6 portions and serve.

10. Store any leftovers in an airtight container in the fridge for up to 2 days.

KITCHEN TIP

• Ceramic pie weights can be purchased at a cake supply store, but dried beans, lentils, or chickpeas work just as well. Keep them in a container with a lid, as they can be used again whenever you need to blind bake a pie shell.

BANOFFEE PIE

This pie has all the components of a delicious dessert: crunchy graham crust, thick and sweet dulce de leche, fresh slices of banana, and fresh, billowy Chantilly Cream. You can even wow your guests by telling them you made the dulce de leche yourself! **MAKES ONE 9-INCH (23 CM) PIE**

1. **MAKE THE DULCE DE LECHE** Remove the paper wrappers from the cans of condensed milk. Place both cans on their sides in a large saucepan. Fill the saucepan with water, making sure the cans are completely submerged and there is at least 2 inches (5 cm) of water above them. Bring the water to a simmer over medium-high heat. Let simmer for 3 hours, checking the water level every 30 minutes to make sure it does not dip below the cans. Keep adding hot water as needed so that the cans are sufficiently covered. Using tongs, remove the cans from the saucepan and let cool to room temperature. Do not open the cans while they are warm, as the trapped steam could burn you.

2. Scoop the dulce de leche into a medium bowl and whisk until smooth. Cover with plastic wrap and store in the fridge until ready to use. Dulce de leche will keep for up to 2 weeks in the fridge when wrapped tightly. Leftovers are great for dipping fruit in or spooning over ice cream.

3. **MAKE THE GRAHAM CRACKER CRUST** In a medium bowl, stir the ground graham crackers, butter, and sugar to combine. Transfer the mixture to a 9-inch (23 cm) pie plate. Use the bottom of a measuring cup to press the mixture firmly into the bottom and all the way up the sides of the plate. Bake for 10 minutes. Let cool.

4. Spread 1¼ cups (300 mL) dulce de leche on the cooled crust. Arrange the banana slices on the dulce de leche, creating 2 layers of banana. Dollop the Chantilly Cream on the bananas. Place the pie in the fridge, uncovered, to chill for about 2 hours before slicing and serving.

5. Store any leftovers, wrapped tightly with plastic wrap, in the fridge for up to 2 days.

2 cans (10 ounces/300 mL each) sweetened condensed milk

1½ cups (375 mL) ground OG Graham Crackers (page 32) or store-bought graham cracker crumbs

5 tablespoons (75 mL) unsalted butter, melted

⅓ cup (75 mL) granulated sugar

2 large bananas, sliced crosswise about ½ inch (1 cm) thick

Chantilly Cream (page 281)

KITCHEN TIP

• Add chopped pecans, chocolate shavings, or toffee bits as a garnish for a bit of extra flavour.

RHUBARB CUSTARD PIE

Fresh rhubarb is one of those foods that indicates spring has finally arrived, but field rhubarb might not be available until well into May. We have been using hothouse rhubarb for a few years now, and although it might not be as hearty or as ruby red as the field variety, we love the soft pink stems that hothouse rhubarb offers—and we may love it even more because it allows us to enjoy this tart and creamy pie much earlier in the season. **MAKES ONE 9-INCH (23 CM) PIE**

½ batch Sweet Pie Dough (page 270)

4 cups (1 L) chopped rhubarb (½-inch/1 cm pieces)

1½ cups (375 mL) granulated sugar, divided

2 large eggs

⅓ cup (75 mL) all-purpose flour, more for dusting

¼ cup (60 mL) unsalted butter, melted

¼ cup (60 mL) heavy (35%) cream

KITCHEN TIP

• Ceramic pie weights can be purchased at a cake supply store, but dried beans, lentils, or chickpeas work just as well. Keep them in a container with a lid, as they can be used again whenever you need to blind bake a pie shell.

1. Preheat the oven to 375°F (190°C).

2. On a lightly floured work surface, roll the Sweet Pie Dough into an 11-inch (28 cm) circle, about ⅛ inch (3 mm) thick. Roll the dough around the rolling pin and unroll it over a 9-inch (23 cm) pie plate. Gently press the dough into the bottom and sides of the plate, folding any overhanging dough under itself along the lip. Crimp the edges and transfer to the fridge to chill for about 30 minutes.

3. Crumple a piece of parchment paper into a ball. Spread it back out and lay it into the bottom and up the sides of the unbaked pie dough. Fill it with dried beans or lentils. Bake for 25 to 30 minutes, or until golden brown. Remove the pie plate from the oven and carefully remove the dried beans by lifting the parchment paper out of the shell. Let cool to room temperature.

4. In a medium bowl, toss the rhubarb with ¼ cup (60 mL) of the sugar. Set aside. In a separate medium bowl, whisk the eggs, the remaining 1¼ cups (300 mL) of sugar, the flour, butter, and cream until smooth.

5. Arrange the rhubarb in an even layer on the bottom of the pie shell. Pour the egg mixture over the rhubarb. Bake for 1 hour, or until the top is puffed and golden in places and the middle jiggles only slightly when you move the pie plate. Let cool to room temperature, then transfer to the fridge to chill for at least 1 hour before serving.

6. Store any leftovers, covered in plastic wrap, in the fridge for up to 2 days.

HEAVENLY CHOCOLATE MINT CREAM PIE

The addition of peppermint extract gives a twist to this melt-in-your-mouth chocolate cream pie that makes for a great summertime dessert. **MAKES FOUR 3-INCH (8 CM) TARTS OR ONE 9-INCH (23 CM) PIE**

1. Preheat the oven to 375°F (190°C).

2. **MAKE THE CHOCOLATE COOKIE CRUST** To the bowl of a food processor, add the ground Chocolate Cookie Wafers, sugar, and butter. Pulse 4 or 5 times to combine. Divide the mixture evenly among four 3-inch (8 cm) tart pans with removeable bottoms. Press it firmly into the bottom and sides of each pan, using your fingers to make a crust about ¼ inch (5 mm) thick. If making a pie, use the same method of pinching and pressing the crumb mixture into a 9-inch (23 cm) pie plate. Bake for 10 minutes, until fragrant.

3. **MAKE THE CHOCOLATE MINT FILLING** In a medium saucepan, whisk the sugar, cornstarch, and salt. Add the egg yolks and milk. Whisk until smooth. Place the saucepan over medium heat. Cook, whisking continuously, until thick and bubbling, about 5 minutes. Reduce the heat to a simmer and let bubble gently for 1 minute. Remove from the heat.

4. Place the dark chocolate in a medium heatproof bowl. Pour the hot milk mixture overtop and whisk gently until the chocolate is melted and the mixture is smooth and glossy. Add the butter, vanilla, and peppermint. Stir until the butter is melted and the mixture is well combined. Pour the chocolate filling into a medium bowl and cover with plastic wrap. Chill in the fridge for at least 4 hours or overnight.

5. Dollop the Chantilly Cream into the crust, placing about ½ cup (125 mL) in each tart pan. Using an ice cream scoop, divide the filling evenly among the tart pans. Alternatively, spoon the filling into the tart pans first, or into the large crust if baking one large pie, and dollop the Chantilly Cream overtop. Let the pie chill, uncovered, for 1 hour. Before serving, garnish with fresh mint leaves.

6. Store any leftovers, wrapped tightly with plastic wrap, in the fridge for up to 2 days.

CHOCOLATE COOKIE CRUST

1½ cups (375 mL) ground Chocolate Cookie Wafers (page 35)

⅓ cup (75 mL) granulated sugar

4 tablespoons (60 mL) unsalted butter

CHOCOLATE MINT FILLING

⅔ cup (150 mL) granulated sugar

¼ cup (60 mL) cornstarch

½ teaspoon (2 mL) kosher salt

4 large egg yolks

3 cups (750 mL) whole (3.25%) milk

9 ounces (256 g) good-quality dark chocolate

2 tablespoons (30 mL) cold unsalted butter, cubed

1 teaspoon (5 mL) pure vanilla extract

1 teaspoon (5 mL) pure peppermint extract

Chantilly Cream (page 281)
Fresh mint leaves, for garnish

KITCHEN TIP

• To give this pie a festive twist that will make it perfect for winter, garnish it with crushed candy canes instead of fresh mint leaves.

CHOCOLATE PECAN PIE

This pecan pie is so decadent and rich. We make it often for markets, and it makes a perfect holiday dessert. Adding dark chocolate to the pie filling may be unexpected—some pecan pie lovers may be skeptical—but it works! Dark chocolate and pecans are a sophisticated pairing. This recipe will be sure to convert pecan pie purists. **MAKES ONE 9-INCH (23 CM) PIE**

½ batch Sweet Pie Dough (page 270)
4 ounces (115 g) semisweet chocolate, finely chopped
4 large eggs, lightly beaten
1½ cups (375 mL) corn syrup
½ cup (125 mL) granulated sugar
1 teaspoon (5 mL) pure vanilla extract
½ teaspoon (2 mL) kosher salt
½ teaspoon (2 mL) instant coffee
1 cup (250 mL) pecan halves

1. On a well-floured work surface, roll the Sweet Pie Dough into a 12-inch (30 cm) circle. Roll the dough around the rolling pin and unroll it over a 9-inch (23 cm) pie plate. Gently press the dough into the bottom and sides of the plate, folding any overhanging dough under itself along the lip. Crimp the edges and transfer to the fridge to chill for 20 minutes.

2. Preheat the oven to 350°F (180°C).

3. In a double boiler, or a medium stainless steel bowl placed over a small saucepan of simmering water, melt the chocolate, stirring occasionally, until smooth. Set aside.

4. In a medium bowl, use a wooden spoon to stir the eggs, corn syrup, sugar, vanilla, salt, and instant coffee to combine. Slowly add the melted chocolate and stir to combine.

5. Arrange the pecans in an even layer in the pie shell. Pour the filling overtop. Place the pie plate on a rimmed baking sheet to catch any drips. Bake for 50 to 60 minutes, turning the baking sheet at about the 25-minute mark, until just set. The filling should jiggle only slightly when you tap the pie plate. Transfer to a wire rack and let cool to room temperature. Wrap loosely in plastic wrap and transfer to the fridge to chill for at least 4 hours, or overnight, before serving.

6. Store any leftovers in an airtight container in the fridge for up to 2 days.

KITCHEN TIP

• Pecan halves or pecan pieces both work in this pie. Placing them in the empty pie shell first and covering them with the filling will ensure that the nuts do not burn in the oven.

PEACHES AND CREAM PIE

A twist on a traditional peach pie, this version incorporates dollops of crème fraîche that are baked with the fruit beneath a crumble topping. Serve with extra crème fraîche dolloped on top to take this recipe to new heights. **MAKES ONE 9-INCH (23 CM) PIE**

1. On a lightly floured work surface, roll the Sweet Pie Dough into a 12-inch (30 cm) circle. Roll the dough around the rolling pin and unroll it over a 9-inch (23 cm) pie plate. Gently press the dough into the bottom and sides of the plate. Trim the edges, leaving a 1-inch (2.5 cm) overhang. Fold the overhanging dough under itself along the lip. Crimp the edges and poke the bottom of the dough all over with a fork. Chill in the freezer for 30 minutes.

2. Preheat the oven to 350°F (180°C).

3. Place the peaches in a medium bowl. Sprinkle with the sugar, flour, and salt. Gently toss to evenly coat the peaches. Let stand for 15 minutes.

4. Sprinkle one-third of the Crumble Topping into the pie shell and dollop 2 tablespoons (30 mL) of the crème fraîche on top. Arrange the peaches on top, then dot with the remaining 3 tablespoons (45 mL) of crème fraîche. Sprinkle the remaining Crumble Topping in an even layer overtop. Bake for 50 minutes, until the peaches are bubbling and the crumble is golden brown. If you find that the edges of the pie dough are browning too quickly, cover them with foil and continue baking. Let cool for at least 15 minutes before serving. Serve warm or at room temperature.

5. Store any leftovers in an airtight container in the fridge for up to 2 days.

½ batch Sweet Pie Dough (page 270)
1½ pounds (675 g) ripe peaches, pitted and quartered
2 tablespoons (30 mL) granulated sugar
1 tablespoon (15 mL) all-purpose flour
½ teaspoon (2 mL) kosher salt
1 batch Crumble Topping (page 284)
5 tablespoons (75 mL) crème fraîche

PEAR TARTE TATIN

This upside-down pear tart with flaky crust is a show-stopping dessert. The recipe may look a little long, but if you read through it before baking, you will realize that it's totally doable—and as a bonus, anyone you serve it to will be so impressed. You'll be pretty dazzled with yourself, too. **SERVES 8**

1. Preheat the oven to 375°F (190°C).

2. On a lightly floured work surface, roll out the puff pastry and cut it into a 12-inch (30 cm) square, using a ruler as a guide. Store-bought puff pastry might not have to be completely rolled out, only lightly rolled to create a 12-inch (30 cm) square. Cut off the corners to create a circle 12 inches (30 cm) in diameter. Refrigerate until ready to use.

3. Place the pear wedges in a medium bowl. Add 2 tablespoons (30 mL) of the sugar, the salt, cinnamon, allspice, nutmeg, ginger, and cloves. Toss to coat evenly.

4. In a 10-inch (25 cm) ovenproof non-stick skillet, combine the remaining ¼ cup (60 mL) of sugar, the lemon juice, butter and water. Place the skillet over medium-high heat. Bring the mixture to a boil and cook, without stirring, until golden, about 5 to 7 minutes. Reduce the heat to medium-low. Arrange the pear wedges in a circle with the wide bottoms of the pears touching the edge of the skillet and the thinner tops of the pears coming together in the middle. It should look like pear sunshine. Cook without stirring for 10 to 12 minutes, until the pears start to soften but remain slightly crisp. Remove from the heat.

5. Drape the chilled puff pastry circle over the pears, tucking the edges under themselves so that the pastry does not hang over the sides of the skillet. Bake for 25 to 30 minutes, until the pastry is golden brown. Let cool in the skillet for 15 minutes.

6. Run a paring knife around the edge of the skillet and carefully invert the tart onto a serving plate. Serve warm with vanilla ice cream or Chantilly Cream.

7. Store any leftovers in an airtight container in the fridge for up to 2 days. Before serving, reheat in a 350°F (180°C) oven for 10 minutes.

1 pound (450 g) Blitz Puff Pastry (page 272) or store-bought puff pastry

3 ripe Bosc pears, peeled, cored, and cut into 18 equal wedges

2 tablespoons (30 mL) + ¼ cup (60 mL) granulated sugar, divided

1 teaspoon (5 mL) kosher salt

¼ teaspoon (1 mL) ground cinnamon

¼ teaspoon (1 mL) allspice

¼ teaspoon (1 mL) ground nutmeg

¼ teaspoon (1 mL) ground ginger

⅛ teaspoon (0.5 mL) ground cloves

1½ teaspoons (7 mL) fresh lemon juice or cider vinegar

2 tablespoons (30 mL) unsalted butter

2 tablespoons (30 mL) water

FOR SERVING

Good-quality vanilla ice cream or Chantilly Cream (page 281)

FRANGIPANE APPLE TART

This tart was on Ancaster Mill's wedding menu as a dessert option. Thank goodness it is a cinch to put together because we would make upwards of five hundred on most weekends during wedding season. Enjoy the marriage of apples, cinnamon, hazelnuts, and caramel in this luxurious dessert. **MAKES 8 TARTS**

HAZELNUT FRANGIPANE

½ cup (125 mL) unsalted butter, very soft
¼ cup (60 mL) ground hazelnuts
2 tablespoons (30 mL) icing sugar
2 tablespoons (30 mL) all-purpose flour
1 large egg

TARTS

1 teaspoon (5 mL) ground cinnamon
¼ cup (60 mL) granulated sugar
1 pound (450 g) Blitz Puff Pastry (page 272) or store-bought puff pastry
4 medium Empire or Golden Delicious apples (about 2 pounds/ 900 g)
3 tablespoons (45 mL) unsalted butter

FOR SERVING

1 batch Caramel Sauce (page 284)
Good-quality vanilla ice cream

1. MAKE THE HAZELNUT FRANGIPANE In a small bowl, use a silicone spatula to cream the butter, hazelnuts, icing sugar, flour, and egg until smooth. Set aside.

2. Preheat the oven to 375°F (190°C). Line a baking sheet with parchment paper.

3. MAKE THE TARTS In a small bowl, combine the cinnamon and sugar. Set aside.

4. Roll the puff pastry into a 22- × 12-inch (55 × 30 cm) rectangle. Use a 4-inch (10 cm) round cookie cutter to cut out 8 circles. Place the circles on the prepared baking sheet. Use a 3-inch (8 cm) round cookie cutter to score smaller circles inside the larger ones, making sure you don't cut all the way through the dough. Spread 1 tablespoon (15 mL) of frangipane to fill each of the smaller circles evenly.

5. Using an apple corer, remove the core from each apple. Slice the apples into rounds as thinly as possible and cut the slices in half. Layer about half an apple's worth of slices in the middle of each tart, on top of the frangipane, making sure to confine them within the smaller circles, until the apples stack about 1½ inches (4 cm) high. Place a small amount of butter on top of each tart, dividing it evenly among them. Sprinkle each with the cinnamon sugar mixture, dividing it evenly among the tarts. If you want to bake the tarts later, place the baking sheet in the freezer until the tarts are just frozen, then transfer them to a zip-top bag and freeze for up to 3 months.

6. Bake for 30 minutes, turning the baking sheet halfway through, until crispy and golden brown. If baking from frozen, bake for an additional 5 minutes. Serve with a drizzle of Caramel Sauce and vanilla ice cream.

7. Store any leftovers in an airtight container in the fridge for up to 2 days. Before serving, reheat in a 350°F (180°C) oven for 10 minutes.

PLUM HAND PIES

Have you ever longed for a way to enjoy a slice of pie on the go? This plum hand pie makes that possible. Sometimes you'll find hand pies at fast food restaurants, but they're usually full of stabilizers and syrups that detract from the flavour. This pocket of buttery, flaky pie crust is filled with juicy plums whose flavour is complemented by orange citrus and the complex spice of cardamom. When you take a bite, this pie will burst with fruit flavour—and it won't burn your mouth because we don't use any syrups (that's the stuff that burns). What could be better than making your own perfect capsuled pie? The only thing we can think of is eating it! **MAKES 12 HAND PIES**

1. Preheat the oven to 375°F (190°C). Line 2 baking sheets with parchment paper.

2. Place the plums in a medium bowl. Add the sugar, cornstarch, orange juice and zest, cardamom, and salt. Toss to coat evenly. Set aside.

3. On a lightly floured work surface, roll one disc of Sweet Pie Dough into a 16- × 11-inch (40 × 28 cm) rectangle. Using a ruler and a knife, trim it to 15- × 10-inches (38 × 25 cm). Use a pastry brush to sweep off any excess flour. Cut the dough into six 5-inch (12 cm) squares. Place 2 tablespoons (30 mL) of the plum mixture in the middle of each square. Using a pastry brush, brush the edges of one square with the egg. Immediately fold the dough in half, on the diagonal over the filling, pressing to seal. Repeat to seal the remaining squares.

4. Repeat step 3 with the second disc of Sweet Pie Dough.

5. Arrange the hand pies on the prepared baking sheets. Brush the top of each pie with the remaining egg and sprinkle with sanding sugar. Use a paring knife to poke a cross-shaped vent in the top of each pie. The vent will allow steam to escape. Bake for 25 to 30 minutes, until the crusts are golden brown and the filling is bubbling out of the vent. Let cool slightly. Serve warm.

6. These hand pies are best served on the day they are made but can be stored in an airtight container at room temperature for up to 2 days. Before serving, reheat in a 350°F (180°C) oven for 10 minutes.

2 cups (500 mL) pitted and diced (¼ inch/5 mm) plums

1 tablespoon (15 mL) granulated sugar

1 tablespoon (15 mL) cornstarch

2 teaspoons (10 mL) fresh orange juice

1 teaspoon (5 mL) fresh grated orange zest

1 teaspoon (5 mL) ground cardamom

½ teaspoon (2 mL) kosher salt

1 batch Sweet Pie Dough (page 270)

1 large egg, lightly beaten

Sanding sugar or raw sugar, for sprinkling

TOURTIÈRE

Tourtière is a classic French-Canadian dish. The beauty of this dish is that there is no official way of filling it. The Montreal version uses ground pork, whereas those in Saguenay–Lac-Saint-Jean slow cook a deep-dish shell, use different cuts of veal and beef, and add potatoes. The francophone population in Manitoba uses very different spices, including savory and celery salt, to flavour the meat, and the Acadian might add hare, chicken, or beef to the ground pork. This recipe will vary again if you are in Nova Scotia or New Brunswick, and here we add our take on the tourtière meat pie. Our meat is seasoned with four different spices, and we've added carrots, parsnips, and Worcestershire sauce. Neither of us is French Canadian, but we hope that the Québécois would be proud of this recipe.

MAKES ONE 9-INCH (23 CM) SAVOURY PIE

1. **MAKE THE TOURTIÈRE DOUGH** In a stand mixer fitted with the paddle attachment, combine the flour, parsley, thyme, salt, and pepper. With the mixer on low speed, add the shortening 1 tablespoon (15 mL) at a time, until all of the shortening has been added and the mixture is crumbly. Add the water and continue mixing on low speed until the dough comes together and becomes smooth, almost like a paste.

2. Transfer the dough to a lightly floured work surface. Lightly knead the dough, about 1 minute, until it pulls away from the floured surface. Divide it into 2 equal portions. Shape the dough into 2 discs and wrap tightly in plastic wrap. Place it in the fridge to chill for at least 1 hour. Use within 1 week or freeze for up to 3 weeks. If freezing, thaw the dough in the fridge the day before using it.

3. Preheat the oven to 425°F (220°C). Line a baking sheet with parchment paper.

4. On a lightly floured work surface, roll each disc into a 14-inch (35 cm) circle. Transfer one of the circles to a 10-inch (25 cm) pie plate. Gently press the dough into the bottom and sides of the plate, allowing any excess dough to hang over the edges. Transfer the pie plate and the remaining round of dough to the prepared baking sheet and chill in the fridge for at least 30 minutes.

TOURTIÈRE DOUGH

2 cups (500 mL) all-purpose flour

1 tablespoon (15 mL) chopped fresh parsley

1 teaspoon (5 mL) chopped fresh thyme

1 teaspoon (5 mL) kosher salt

½ teaspoon (2 mL) fresh cracked black pepper

1 cup (250 mL) vegetable shortening

⅓ cup (75 mL) cold water

TOURTIÈRE FILLING

2 tablespoons (30 mL) vegetable oil

1 medium carrot, peeled and grated

1 medium parsnip, peeled and grated

1 medium onion, diced

3 pounds (1.4 kg) ground beef and/ or pork and/or veal mix

2 cloves garlic, minced

½ cup (125 mL) rolled oats

1 teaspoon (5 mL) Worcestershire sauce

2 tablespoons (30 mL) kosher salt, divided

recipe continues

1 tablespoon (15 mL) ground
  cinnamon
1 teaspoon (5 mL) ground nutmeg
½ teaspoon (2 mL) allspice
½ teaspoon (2 mL) ground cloves

1 large egg, lightly beaten

5. MAKE THE TOURTIÈRE FILLING In a medium saucepan over medium heat, heat the vegetable oil. Add the carrot, parsnip, and onion. Cook until the carrot and parsnip are softened and the onion starts to brown, about 10 minutes.

6. In a large saucepan over medium heat, combine the ground meat, garlic, oats, Worcestershire sauce, salt, cinnamon, nutmeg, allspice, and cloves. Cook over medium heat, stirring occasionally, until the mixture boils. Reduce the heat to low and cook for 5 minutes, until the meat is cooked through. Let cool to room temperature.

7. Add the carrot mixture to the meat mixture. Stir to combine.

8. Spoon the filling into the chilled pie shell. Brush the dough resting on the lip of the pie plate with the egg. Place the dough round on top of the filling and press down on the lip of the pie plate to seal the pie. Using a small paring knife, cut a few slits in the top of the pie to create vents that will allow steam to escape. Trim and discard any excess dough. Crimp the edges of the pie. Bake for 35 minutes, until golden brown all over. Let cool for about 15 minutes before serving.

9. Store any leftovers, covered with plastic wrap, in the fridge for up to 5 days.

KITCHEN TIP

• This pie freezes well when it is unbaked. If you want to freeze the pie to bake later, wrap the whole thing tightly in plastic wrap and store it in the freezer for up to 3 months. If baking from frozen, add at least 30 minutes to the bake time.

RED ONION ALSATIAN TART

This is no ordinary tart. The deep-dish tart pan adds a grandeur that is truly impressive. You may think you have to be an onion lover to enjoy this one, but the long and slow cooking process of the onions adds sweetness and removes any astringency from them. Nutmeg rounds everything out by adding a warm, earthy flavour, and the result is just scrumptious. **MAKES ONE 10-INCH (25 CM) TART**

1. Preheat the oven to 400°F (200°C).

2. On a lightly floured work surface, roll the Savoury Pie Dough into a 16-inch (40 cm) circle. Roll the dough around the rolling pin and unroll it over a 10-inch (25 cm) round tart pan with 2-inch (5 cm) sides. Gently press the dough into the bottom and sides of the pan. Trim the excess dough hanging over the edge to ½ inch (1 cm). Fold the overhanging dough under itself along the lip. Lightly prick the bottom all over with a fork. Chill in the fridge for 30 minutes.

3. Crumple a piece of parchment paper into a ball. Spread it back out and lay it into the bottom and up the sides of the unbaked pie dough. Fill it with dried beans or lentils. Bake for 15 to 20 minutes, until the edges are golden. Remove the tart pan from the oven and carefully remove the dried beans by lifting the parchment paper out of the shell. Return the shell to the oven, baking for an additional 10 to 15 minutes, until golden all over. Let cool to room temperature. Keep the oven on.

4. Line a plate with paper towels. In a large non-stick skillet over medium heat, cook the bacon, stirring occasionally, until crisp, about 6 to 8 minutes. Transfer to the lined plate and let drain. Discard any extra fat sitting in the skillet. Return the skillet to the stove and melt the butter over medium heat. Add the onions and sprinkle with half of the salt and pepper. Cook, stirring occasionally, until just softened, about 2 minutes. Cover the skillet with a lid and continue to cook, stirring frequently, until the onions are soft and just starting to brown, about 20 minutes. Stir in the bacon. Remove from the heat and let cool for 10 minutes.

1 batch Savoury Pie Dough (page 271)
4 slices bacon, cut into ¼-inch
  (5 mm) pieces
¼ cup (60 mL) unsalted butter
2 pounds (900 g) red onions, halved
  lengthwise and thinly sliced
1 tablespoon (15 mL) kosher salt,
  divided
2 teaspoons (10 mL) fresh ground
  black pepper, divided
2 cups (500 mL) heavy (35%) cream
4 large eggs
½ teaspoon (2 mL) ground nutmeg

recipe continues

5.   In a medium bowl, whisk the cream, eggs, nutmeg, and the remaining salt and pepper. Stir in the onion mixture. Pour the filling into the tart shell, spreading the onions evenly. Bake for 25 to 30 minutes, until the filling is set. The filling should jiggle only slightly when the tart pan is tapped, and the top should be golden brown. Serve warm or at room temperature.

6.   Store any leftovers in an airtight container in the fridge for up to 2 days. Before serving, reheat in a 350°F (180°C) oven for 20 minutes.

KITCHEN TIP

• Ceramic pie weights can be purchased at a cake supply store, but dried beans, lentils, or chickpeas work just as well. Keep them in a container with a lid, as they can be used again whenever you need to blind bake a pie shell.

POTATO AND ONION TARTE TATIN

A classic tarte Tatin usually features apples or pears baked in a sweet upside-down tart. This savoury version of the classic is surprisingly simple to make and just as visually stunning as its sweet counterpart. With the addition of a hint of sweetness from the balsamic glaze, nothing gets lost in this take on the original. **MAKES 6 TARTS**

1. Preheat the oven to 425°F (220°C). Line a baking sheet with parchment paper. Dot six 5-inch (12 cm) pie plates with the butter cubes (3 cubes per plate).

2. On a lightly floured work surface, roll the puff pastry into a 16- × 11-inch (40 × 28 cm) rectangle. Using a cutter or a small plate as a guide, cut the pastry into six 6-inch (15 cm) rounds. Transfer the rounds to the prepared baking sheet and prick them all over with a fork. Chill in the fridge for 30 minutes, until firm.

3. Lay 2 or 3 onion rings in the bottom of each pie plate and sprinkle with half of the thyme, salt, and pepper. Arrange the potato slices in 2 layers on top so that they're slightly overlapping. They should completely cover the onion. Sprinkle with the remaining thyme, salt, and pepper. Place a puff pastry round on top of the potatoes in each pie plate. Bake for 20 minutes, until the pastry is golden brown.

4. **WHILE THE TARTS ARE BAKING, MAKE THE BALSAMIC GLAZE** In a small saucepan over high heat, bring the vinegar and sugar to a simmer. Cook until the mixture reduces to a syrup, about 4 minutes. Whisk in the butter, 1 tablespoon (15 mL) at a time, until melted and combined. Season with salt and pepper, to taste.

5. Invert the tarts onto serving plates and drizzle each with a spoonful of the balsamic glaze. Serve immediately. These tarts are best enjoyed warm.

6. Store any leftovers in an airtight container in the fridge for up to 2 days. Before serving, reheat in a 350°F (180°C) oven for 10 minutes.

3 tablespoons (45 mL) unsalted butter, cut into 18 cubes

1 pound (450 g) Blitz Puff Pastry (page 272) or store-bought puff pastry

1 medium yellow onion, peeled and sliced into ¼-inch (5 mm) thick rings

1 tablespoon (15 mL) chopped fresh thyme, divided

1 tablespoon (15 mL) kosher salt, divided

1 teaspoon (5 mL) fresh ground black pepper, divided

6 small new potatoes, sliced into ¼-inch (5 mm) thick rounds

BALSAMIC GLAZE

¼ cup (60 mL) balsamic vinegar

1 teaspoon (5 mL) granulated sugar

2 tablespoons (30 mL) unsalted butter, chilled

Salt and pepper

KITCHEN TIP

- If the balsamic glaze becomes too thick to pour over the tarts, a couple of seconds on the stovetop or in a microwave oven will warm it up and thin it out.

LEEK AND OLIVE TART WITH TWO CHEESES

This leek and olive tart is visually stunning and equally delicious. The brie cheese on top melts over the leeks, creating a creamy finish that is balanced by the salty Parmesan and olives. Make your own puff pastry if you have the time. It may seem daunting, but it will be far superior to anything you can purchase in a store. **MAKES ONE 9-INCH (23 CM) SQUARE TART**

3 large leeks, white and light green parts only

2 tablespoons (30 mL) extra-virgin olive oil

½ teaspoon (2 mL) kosher salt

½ pound (225 g) Blitz Puff Pastry (page 272) or store-bought puff pastry

1 large egg

1 tablespoon (15 mL) water

¼ cup (60 mL) pitted olives, chopped (see Kitchen Tip)

¼ cup (60 mL) fresh grated Parmesan cheese

1 teaspoon (5 mL) chopped fresh thyme

4 ounces (115 g) brie or camembert cheese, thinly sliced

1. Preheat the oven to 350°F (180°C). Line 2 baking sheets with parchment paper.

2. Cut the leeks in half, lengthwise, and place them on one of the prepared baking sheets, cut sides face up. Drizzle with the olive oil and sprinkle with the salt. Flip them over so the cut sides are face down. Bake for 25 to 30 minutes, until soft. Let cool to room temperature.

3. While the leeks are baking, roll the puff pastry into a 9-inch (23 cm) square. Transfer the dough to the second prepared baking sheet. Place it in the freezer until the leeks are cooked and cooled.

4. Create an egg wash by whisking the egg and water until combined. Remove the puff pastry from the freezer and brush the surface with the egg wash.

5. Arrange the leeks side by side on the puff pastry, cut sides face up. Evenly scatter the olives over the leeks. Sprinkle with the Parmesan and thyme. Arrange the brie over the tart, with half of the slices aligned on the left side and half aligned on the right in an alternating pattern. Bake for 25 to 30 minutes, until the pastry is golden brown and the bottom is crisp. Let cool slightly. Serve warm. This tart does not keep well overnight.

KITCHEN TIP

• Try to find a party mix of pitted olives. Adding a variety of olives will increase the flavour profile of the tart without any extra effort.

SPRING ONION AND ROASTED MUSHROOM TART

Spring onions, also known as scallions, are not often the star of a dish. They are usually added to balance out a recipe and improve the overall flavour. In this case, the spring onions are the star of the show. Coupled with roasted mushrooms lying on a pillow of creamy ricotta cheese and topped with cheddar, the spring onions shine on this exquisite canvas. **MAKES ONE 9- × -13-INCH (23 × 33 CM) TART**

1. Preheat the oven to 400°F (200°C). Grease a baking sheet.

2. In the bowl of a food processor, purée the ricotta until smooth, about 30 seconds. Add 1 egg yolk and 1 tablespoon (15 mL) of the olive oil. Pulse to combine. Transfer the mixture to a small bowl. Fold in the sour cream, ½ teaspoon (2 mL) of the salt and ¼ teaspoon (1 mL) of the pepper. Set aside.

3. In a large skillet over high heat, place the remaining 2 tablespoons (30 mL) of olive oil and the mushrooms. Add ½ teaspoon (2 mL) of the salt, ¼ teaspoon (1 mL) of the pepper, and 2 teaspoons (10 mL) of the thyme. Cook, stirring occasionally, until liquid has been released from the mushrooms and all of it has evaporated, about 10 minutes. Stir in 2 tablespoons (30 mL) of the butter and cook until the mushrooms are tender and slightly crisp, about 3 more minutes. Transfer to a bowl and let cool.

4. Cut the white parts of the onions into ½-inch (1 cm) slices on the diagonal. Slice enough of the green parts to measure 1 cup (250 mL). Discard the remaining green parts. In a medium skillet over low heat, melt the remaining 2 tablespoons (30 mL) of butter. Add the onions and the remaining 1 teaspoon (5 mL) of thyme, ½ teaspoon (2 mL) of salt, and ¼ teaspoon (1 mL) of pepper. Cook until soft and beginning to brown, about 2 minutes. Be sure not to stir the onions too much so they retain their shape. Remove from the heat and let cool in the skillet.

5. In a small bowl, whisk the remaining egg yolk with 1 tablespoon (15 mL) of water to make an egg wash. Set aside.

6. On a lightly floured work surface, roll the puff pastry into a 9- × -13-inch (23 × 33 cm) rectangle. Using a ruler and a paring knife, trim the dough to 8 × 12 inches (20 × 30 cm). Use a pastry brush to sweep off any excess flour. Transfer the dough to the

½ cup (125 mL) full-fat ricotta cheese

2 large egg yolks, divided

3 tablespoons (45 mL) extra-virgin olive oil, divided

¼ cup (60 mL) full-fat sour cream

1½ teaspoons (7 mL) kosher salt, divided

¾ teaspoon (3 mL) fresh ground black pepper, divided

1 pound (450 g) mixed mushrooms, such as button, shiitake, and cremini, chopped

1 tablespoon (15 mL) chopped fresh thyme, divided

¼ cup (60 mL) unsalted butter, divided

2 bunches spring onions, ends trimmed

1 pound (450 g) Blitz Puff Pastry (page 272) or store-bought puff pastry

4 ounces (115 g) aged cheddar, thinly sliced

recipe continues

greased baking sheet. Using a ruler and a paring knife, score the dough by running the knife around the perimeter of the pastry, ¼ inch (5 mm) from the edge, cutting only halfway through the dough. Use a pastry brush to cover the edges of the dough, outside the score mark, with the egg wash.

7. Spread the ricotta mixture evenly over the pastry, making sure to leave the border bare. Scatter half of the mushrooms over the ricotta. Lay the cheddar slices over the mushrooms. Gently combine the remaining mushrooms with the onions and scatter them over the cheese. Bake for 30 minutes, turning halfway through, until the cheese is bubbly and the crust is golden brown. Let cool for 10 minutes before serving. Serve warm with a side salad or bowl of soup.

8. Store any leftovers in an airtight container in the fridge for up to 2 days. Before serving, reheat in a 350°F (180°C) oven for 10 minutes.

FOUR RECIPES
FOR EACH SEASON

SPRING

STRAWBERRY RHUBARB JAM CROISSANTS

A quick way to jazz up a basic croissant recipe is to spread each triangle of croissant dough with something tasty before you roll it up. We have made many variations over the years, including painting hot sauce onto the dough with a pastry brush, spreading on a cinnamon bun–like filling, and even scattering sprinkles over the dough for a festive twist. Here, we incorporate two classic springtime flavours by adding strawberry rhubarb jam. **MAKES 18 CROISSANTS**

1. **MAKE THE STRAWBERRY RHUBARB JAM** Place the strawberries and rhubarb in a small bowl. Add the sugar and toss to coat evenly. Let stand for 30 to 45 minutes at room temperature to allow some of the juices to come out.

2. Transfer the mixture to a large saucepan and cook over medium heat, stirring continuously, until gently boiling. Reduce the heat to medium-low and cook until the mixture thickens, about 10 minutes, making sure to stir continuously so the jam does not burn. When the mixture is thick enough that it holds some of its shape as you run a spoon through it, remove the pan from the heat and let cool completely. Transfer to an airtight container and store in the fridge for up to 4 weeks.

3. **MAKE THE CROISSANTS** Follow steps 1 to 6 of the recipe for Plain Croissants.

4. Place a triangle of dough in front of you so that the base of the triangle is near your left hand and the pointed end is near your right hand. Use one hand to hold the triangle of dough down at the base end, about 2 inches (5 cm) from the edge, and use your other hand to very gently stretch out the point of the triangle to make it about 1 inch (2.5 cm) longer than it was to start. Spoon about 2 tablespoons (30 mL) of the Strawberry Rhubarb Jam onto the triangle. Using a pastry brush, spread the jam over the whole triangle of dough. Rotate the triangle so that the base is closest to you and the pointed end is pointing away from you. Starting at the base end, roll up the croissant. Some jam will squish out, which is okay. Place the croissant on the prepared baking sheet with the tip of the triangle on the bottom to help seal it shut. Repeat with the remaining dough triangles.

STRAWBERRY RHUBARB JAM
(MAKES ABOUT 2½ CUPS/625 ML)

3½ cups (875 mL) strawberries, hulled and cut into quarters
3½ cups (875 mL) rhubarb, cut into 1-inch (2.5 cm) pieces
1½ cups (375 mL) granulated sugar

CROISSANTS

1 batch Plain Croissants (page 275, steps 1 to 6)
4 egg yolks
½ cup (125 mL) heavy (35%) cream
Icing sugar, for garnish (optional)

recipe continues

If baking immediately, cover the croissants loosely with plastic wrap and let proof in a warm spot for 30 to 40 minutes, until the croissants are puffy and jiggly when you gently tap the baking sheet. If baking at a later date, place the baking sheet in the freezer immediately after rolling the croissants. Once they are frozen, transfer them to a zip-top bag. Croissants can be stored in the freezer for up to 1 week. Simply thaw in the fridge overnight and proceed with the recipe.

5. Preheat the oven to 375°F (190°C).

6. Prepare an egg wash. In a small bowl, whisk the egg yolks and cream. Using a pastry brush, gently brush each croissant with the egg wash, making sure to cover the whole surface in a thin layer. This will ensure a golden brown colour and a shiny top. Bake for 15 to 18 minutes, or until the croissants turn a light golden brown. Let cool and dust with icing sugar, if desired.

7. Croissants are best served on the day they are made but can be stored in an airtight container at room temperature for up to 3 days.

ASPARAGUS, LEEK, AND GRUYÈRE QUICHE

In Canada, spring is one of the most celebrated seasons, as most of us eagerly await the thaw after a long winter. Sometimes, however, the warmer weather doesn't arrive until after the first official day of spring has come and gone. Trying to eat seasonally generally suggests that you should wait until the first offerings of spring are ready for harvest, but if you've survived a Canadian winter, don't be afraid to push it a little and enjoy this delectable tart made from two delicious cold-weather vegetables, asparagus and leeks, before that day arrives. **SERVES 6 TO 8**

1. Preheat the oven to 350°F (180°C).

2. On a lightly floured work surface, roll the Savoury Pie Dough into an 18- × 9-inch (45 × 23 cm) rectangle. Roll the dough around the rolling pin and unroll it over a 14- × 4-inch (35 × 10 cm) tart pan with a removable bottom. Gently press the dough into the bottom and sides of the pan. Instead of trimming off any excess dough, fold it under itself to rest on the inside edge of the pan. Crimp the edges and transfer to the fridge to chill for at least 30 minutes.

3. Fill a large saucepan with 8 cups (2 L) water and 2 tablespoons (30 mL) of the salt. Bring to a boil. While you're waiting for the water to boil, prepare a large bowl of ice water. Once the water is boiling, add the asparagus and cook until tender, about 5 minutes. Using tongs, quickly transfer the asparagus to the ice water and submerge for 1 minute. Drain and refrigerate until completely cooled.

4. In a medium skillet over medium heat, melt the butter. Add the leek rounds and season with the remaining 1 teaspoon (5 mL) of salt and the pepper. Cook, without stirring, until the leeks are soft and starting to caramelize on one side, about 7 minutes. Using a spatula and trying to keep the leek rounds intact as much as possible, transfer them to a clean plate to cool.

5. In a medium bowl, whisk the eggs, half and half, and nutmeg.

6. Place the chilled tart shell on a rimmed baking sheet. Arrange the leeks, asparagus, and Gruyère in an even layer over the bottom of the shell. Pour the egg mixture on top. Bake for 50 to 60 minutes, until the filling is just set and jiggles only

½ batch Savoury Pie Dough
(page 271)

2 tablespoons (30 mL) + 1 teaspoon
(5 mL) kosher salt, divided

1 bunch asparagus, tough ends
removed

1 tablespoon (15 mL) unsalted butter

1 leek, white and light green parts
only, cut into rounds

½ teaspoon (2 mL) fresh cracked
black pepper

4 large eggs

1¼ cups (300 mL) half and half (10%)
cream

½ teaspoon (2 mL) ground nutmeg

1 cup (250 mL) shredded Gruyère
cheese

recipe continues

slightly in the middle when the pan is moved. Let cool for 15 minutes before serving.

7.   This quiche is best served on the day it is made, but leftovers can be stored in an airtight container in the fridge for up to 3 days. Before serving leftovers, reheat in a 350°F (180°C) oven for 10 minutes.

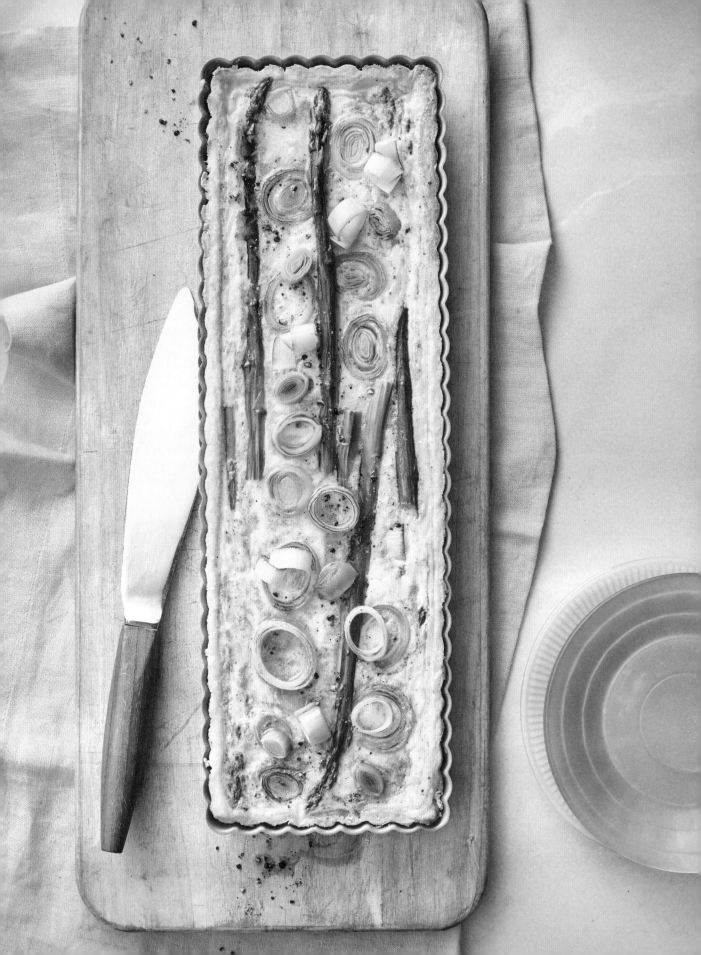

MAPLE PUDDING WITH BOURBON CREAM

In the spring, we always try to use as much maple flavour as we can. Sap is harvested from maple trees in the winter, and the syrup is produced shortly after, which means there's all kinds of fresh product available. Maple flavour pretty much goes with everything—savoury or sweet—so it's easy to incorporate. The bourbon whipped cream garnish on this maple pudding offers a nice toasty depth of flavour that cuts the sweetness of the pudding. And it's gluten-free, too! **SERVES 6 TO 8**

1. MAKE THE MAPLE PUDDING In a medium saucepan over medium heat, combine the milk, maple syrup, cream, salt, and vanilla. Cook until tiny bubbles just start to form on the surface, about 5 minutes.

2. In a small bowl, whisk the sugar and cornstarch to get rid of any lumps. Whisking the cream mixture continuously, sprinkle the cornstarch mixture into the warm cream mixture.

3. In a medium bowl, lightly whisk the egg yolks. Whisking continuously, slowly add about 1 cup (250 mL) of the cream mixture to the egg yolks to temper them. Pour the egg mixture into the warm cream and cook for 6 to 7 minutes, stirring constantly, until the pudding is the consistency of yogurt, about 6 to 7 minutes. Turn off the heat. Slowly stir in the butter.

4. Using a fine-mesh sieve, strain the pudding into a large bowl. Discard the vanilla pod. Cover, placing plastic wrap directly on the surface of the pudding to prevent a skin forming. Let cool to room temperature. Transfer to the fridge to chill until ready to serve.

5. MAKE THE BOURBON WHIPPED CREAM Just before serving, in a stand mixer fitted with the whisk attachment, combine the cream and sugar. Whisk on high speed until soft peaks form, about 5 minutes. Pour in the bourbon and whisk until stiff peaks form.

6. To serve, spoon the pudding into serving cups, top each with a dollop of bourbon cream, and garnish with Florentine pieces, if desired.

7. Store leftover pudding, covered tightly with plastic wrap and without garnishes, in the fridge for up to 3 days.

MAPLE PUDDING

2 cups (500 mL) 2% milk
1 cup (250 mL) pure maple syrup
1 cup (250 mL) heavy (35%) cream
1 teaspoon (5 mL) kosher salt
1 vanilla bean, split and seeds scraped
1 tablespoon (15 mL) granulated sugar
¼ cup (60 mL) cornstarch
2 large egg yolks
2 tablespoons (30 mL) unsalted butter, softened

BOURBON WHIPPED CREAM

1½ cups (375 mL) heavy (35%) cream
¼ cup (60 mL) granulated sugar
2 tablespoons (30 mL) bourbon

Florentines (page 40), for garnish (optional)

CLASSIC BREAD BAR CHEESECAKE WITH RHUBARB COMPOTE

Bettina picked up this recipe years ago when she was working in northern Manitoba as a cook for tree planting camps. All anybody ever wanted to eat was cheesecake, and because of this recipe, we eat a lot of it too. It's amazingly easy to make and is sure to impress. When we make this cake, we always use Lactantia cream cheese. We know the go-to cream cheese is usually Philadelphia brand, but we find we get better results with Lactantia. Just a heads-up. **MAKES ONE 10-INCH (25 CM) CHEESECAKE**

1. Preheat the oven to 250°F (120°C). Generously grease the sides of a 10-inch (3 L) springform pan.

2. **MAKE THE GRAHAM CRUST** In a medium bowl, combine the ground graham crackers, brown sugar, cinnamon, and salt. Add the butter and stir with a wooden spoon until the butter is fully incorporated. Transfer the mixture to the prepared springform pan and use your fingers or the bottom of a measuring cup to press it firmly into an even layer on the bottom of the pan.

3. **MAKE THE CREAM CHEESE FILLING** In a stand mixer fitted with the paddle attachment, mix the cream cheese and sugar on medium-high speed until smooth. Scrape down the sides of the bowl. Add the vanilla and mix until combined. Add the flour and mix on low speed until combined. Add the eggs and egg yolks and mix until fully incorporated. Add the milk and mix until just combined.

4. Pour the filling over the crust. Bake for 90 minutes, or until the centre of the cheesecake no longer looks wet and runny and jiggles only slightly when you move the pan.

5. Place the pan on a wire rack and run a thin knife around the cake. Release the cake from the pan, leaving the bottom of the springform pan beneath it. Let cool to room temperature, then transfer the cake to the fridge to chill for 3 hours.

6. **MAKE THE RHUBARB COMPOTE** In a small saucepan over low heat, combine the rhubarb and sugar. Once it starts to bubble, cook for about 10 minutes, mashing the rhubarb with the back of a spoon until it breaks down and the juices start to thicken.

GRAHAM CRUST

2 cups (500 mL) ground OG Graham Crackers (page 32) or store-bought graham cracker crumbs

½ cup (125 mL) lightly packed brown sugar

1 teaspoon (5 mL) cinnamon

1 teaspoon (5 mL) kosher salt

½ cup (125 mL) unsalted butter, melted

CREAM CHEESE FILLING

3 packages (8 ounces/225 g each) full-fat plain cream cheese, softened

2 cups (500 mL) granulated sugar

1 tablespoon (15 mL) pure vanilla extract

¼ cup (60 mL) all-purpose flour

4 large eggs

2 large egg yolks

½ cup (125 mL) whole (3.25%) milk

RHUBARB COMPOTE

2 cups (500 mL) chopped fresh rhubarb (about 4 large stalks)

½ cup (125 mL) granulated sugar

1 tablespoon (15 mL) fresh lemon juice

¼ teaspoon (1 mL) pure vanilla extract

recipe continues

Remove from the heat and stir in the lemon juice and vanilla. Transfer the mixture to a small airtight container and chill in the fridge for at least 1 hour. This will help thicken the juices even more. Store in an airtight container in the fridge for up to 1 week.

7.   To serve, generously spoon rhubarb compote over the cheesecake to create a stunning centrepiece or slice and serve each portion topped with a spoonful of compote.

8.   Store leftover cake in an airtight container in the fridge for up to 1 week.

SUMMER

BLUEBERRY CROISSANTS

A fun way to change up a basic croissant recipe is to flavour the roll-in butter. In the restaurant world, we refer to butter flavoured with additional ingredients as "compound butter." The ingredients you can add are limitless. Here we use cooked and strained fresh blueberries and lemon zest to make a flavourful compound butter and vibrant purple glaze that just screams summer. **MAKES ABOUT 18 CROISSANTS**

4 cups (1 L) fresh blueberries

1 tablespoon (15 mL) fresh grated lemon zest

2 tablespoons (30 mL) lightly packed brown sugar

3 cups (750 mL) icing sugar

1 teaspoon (5 mL) pure vanilla extract

1 batch Plain Croissants (page 275, steps 1 to 3 and 5 to 9)

1 pound (450 g) cold unsalted butter

2 tablespoons (30 mL) bread flour, divided

1. Place the blueberries, lemon zest, and brown sugar in a small saucepan and stir to combine. Cook over low heat for 8 to 10 minutes, until the blueberries have released their juices and start to bubble softly. Remove from the heat and let cool. Using a fine-mesh sieve, strain the blueberries over a medium bowl, pressing the solids firmly against the sieve with the back of a spoon to get out as much liquid as possible. Transfer the blueberry solids to a small bowl and chill in the fridge until completely cool. To the blueberry liquid, add the icing sugar and vanilla and whisk until smooth, creating a blueberry glaze. Cover with plastic wrap and set aside.

2. Prepare the croissant dough, following steps 1 to 3 of the recipe for Plain Croissants.

3. PREPARE THE ROLL-IN BUTTER Place the butter in a heatproof bowl and soften it in a microwave oven for about 15 seconds. Transfer the butter to a stand mixer fitted with the paddle attachment and beat on low speed until smooth, about 1 minute. Add the chilled blueberry solids and beat an additional 1 minute on low speed until combined. Do not overbeat or too much air will be incorporated into the blueberry butter. On a piece of parchment paper, spread the blueberry butter into a 6- × 10-inch (15 × 25 cm) rectangle. Sprinkle with 1 tablespoon (15 mL) of the flour and place another piece of parchment paper on top. The butter should be sandwiched between 2 pieces of parchment paper. Flip the sandwich over. Remove the piece of parchment paper on top. Sprinkle the butter evenly with the remaining 1 tablespoon (15 mL) of the flour. Wrap the butter in plastic wrap and chill in the fridge for 20 minutes. Make sure the roll-in butter is the same pliability as the chilled croissant dough before starting to laminate. If the butter and dough are different

temperatures, return them to the fridge until they are the same. The blueberries in the roll-in butter will make the dough a bit stickier than usual in the laminating process, so flour your work surface generously as you go.

4. Follow steps 5 to 9 of the recipe for Plain Croissants.

5. Bake the croissants for 15 to 18 minutes, or until they turn a deep golden brown. Let cool to room temperature, about 20 minutes.

6. Line a baking sheet with parchment paper and place a wire rack on top. Dunk the top of each croissant into the blueberry glaze and set them on the wire rack to allow any excess glaze to drip off.

7. Croissants are best served on the day they are made but can be stored in an airtight container at room temperature for up to 3 days.

HEIRLOOM TOMATO AND BURRATA QUICHE

Tomatoes picked at the peak of ripeness in the middle of summer are something we are all willing to wait for. They can be deliciously juicy and sweet as candy, and with the wide variety of heirloom tomatoes available today, the wait is even more worth it. However, even heirloom tomatoes can suffer from conventional farming. To be certain you are getting heirlooms with the full, rich, sweet flavour that will attack your taste buds, buy from someone who knows how to grow them, like a local farmer or an heirloom tomato stall at a market. Even the sweetest tomato has a bit of acidity, and the richness of the creamy burrata in this recipe cuts it perfectly. **SERVES 6 TO 8**

1. Preheat the oven to 375°F (190°C).

2. On a lightly floured work surface, roll the Savoury Pie Dough into a 16-inch (40 cm) circle. Using a pastry brush, sweep off any excess flour. Roll the dough around the rolling pin and unroll it over an 11-inch (28 cm) tart pan with a removable bottom. Gently press the dough into the bottom and sides of the pan and remove any excess dough with a paring knife. Transfer to the fridge to chill for at least 30 minutes.

3. In a stand mixer fitted with the whisk attachment, whisk the eggs, sour cream, milk, flour, thyme, salt, pepper, and nutmeg on low speed. Slowly increase the speed until combined.

4. Arrange the tomatoes and shredded mozzarella in the bottom of the chilled tart shell. Pour in the egg mixture, leaving about ¼-inch (5 mm) headspace between the egg mixture and the top of the tart shell. You may not need all of the egg mixture. Bake for 20 minutes, then reduce the temperature to 325°F (160°C) and bake for an additional 30 minutes, until the filling is just set and jiggles only slightly in the middle when the pan is moved. Let cool for at least 15 minutes before serving.

5. To serve, cut the quiche into 6 to 8 slices and divide them among plates. Cut the burrata into 6 to 8 slices and place a slice of the fresh cheese on each portion before serving.

6. Store any leftovers in an airtight container in the fridge for up to 2 days. Before serving leftovers, reheat in a 350°F (180°C) oven for 10 minutes.

½ batch Savoury Pie Dough (page 271)

5 large eggs

1 cup (250 mL) full-fat sour cream

1 cup (250 mL) whole (3.25%) milk

¼ cup (60 mL) all-purpose flour

1 tablespoon (15 mL) fresh thyme, finely chopped

1 teaspoon (5 mL) kosher salt

½ teaspoon (2 mL) fresh cracked black pepper

½ teaspoon (2 mL) ground nutmeg

1 cup (250 mL) heirloom tomatoes, sliced (about 2 medium tomatoes)

¼ cup (60 mL) shredded mozzarella cheese

4 ounces (115 g) burrata mozzarella

CRÈME BRÛLÉE PUDDING WITH MACERATED BERRIES

Vanilla bean crème brûlée is a dessert we have been making for years. It's the perfect combination of creamy, slightly sweet custard with a crunchy, caramelized sugar top. The addition of tart, macerated summer berries will ignite all of your flavour senses with each bite. This just may be the perfect dessert. And it's gluten-free, too! In this recipe, we divide the sugar between the eggs and cream. If you boil milk or cream without sugar, you risk burning it, but just a small amount of sugar helps suspend the proteins in the dairy and stops them from settling on the bottom, which means it is less likely to burn. **SERVES 8**

1. Preheat the oven to 300°F (150°C). Arrange eight 6-ounce (170 mL) ramekins in a roasting pan.

2. MAKE THE VANILLA CUSTARD In a medium saucepan over medium heat, combine the vanilla, heavy cream, half and half, and ¼ cup (60 mL) of the sugar. Bring to a boil. Remove the saucepan from the heat immediately and set aside to allow the vanilla to infuse the cream.

3. In a medium bowl, whisk the remaining ¼ cup (60 mL) of sugar, the egg yolks, and salt until light and fluffy.

4. Whisking the egg mixture continuously, add a small amount of the warm cream mixture to start tempering the eggs. Continue adding the cream, ½ cup (125 mL) at a time, until all of the cream mixture is combined with the egg mixture. Using a fine-mesh sieve, strain the custard into a pitcher.

5. Divide the custard evenly among the 8 ramekins. Fill the roasting pan with hot water so that it comes three-quarters of the way up the sides of the ramekins. Cover the pan with foil. Bake for 50 to 60 minutes, until the custard is just set. Using tongs, carefully remove the ramekins from the water bath. Cover each ramekin with plastic wrap and transfer to the fridge to chill for at least 2 hours or overnight.

6. MAKE THE MACERATED BERRIES Place the mixed berries in a bowl. Add the sugar and toss to coat evenly. Let rest at room temperature for at least 1 hour.

VANILLA CUSTARD

1 vanilla bean, split and seeds scraped

2 cups (500 mL) heavy (35%) cream

2 cups (500 mL) half and half (10%) cream

½ cup (125 mL) granulated sugar, divided

8 large egg yolks

½ teaspoon (2 mL) kosher salt

MACERATED BERRIES

2 cups (500 mL) chopped fresh mixed berries (we like strawberries, raspberries, blueberries, and blackberries)

½ cup (125 mL) granulated sugar

FOR SERVING

8 tablespoons (120 mL) granulated sugar, divided

recipe continues

7. Before serving, sprinkle each ramekin of custard with 1 tablespoon (15 mL) of granulated sugar. Use a kitchen torch to caramelize the sugar. This takes a little bit of practice, but if you spin the ramekin in your fingers as you heat the sugar, the tops should come out evenly caramelized and crisp. Top each ramekin with 2 to 3 tablespoons (30 to 45 mL) macerated berries. Serve cold.

8. This custard is an excellent dessert to make ahead. Store in the ramekins, wrapped tightly with plastic wrap, in the fridge for up to 5 days. Do not add the sugar topping or fruit until you are ready to serve. Custard that has been brûléed does not store well, as the crunchy sugar will soften in the fridge.

RICOTTA CHEESECAKE WITH SHORTBREAD CRUST AND STEWED STRAWBERRIES

Ricotta lends a light and airy texture to this cheesecake recipe, which is a perfect summer dessert. Use good-quality, full-fat ricotta for the best flavour and texture. Ricotta pairs nicely with all kinds of fruit, but seasonal strawberries are such a treat, we couldn't resist matching them up in this cheesecake recipe. **MAKES FOUR 4-INCH (10 CM) CHEESECAKES OR ONE 9-INCH (23 CM) CHEESECAKE**

1. Preheat the oven to 350°F (180°C). Lightly grease four 4-inch (10 cm) springform pans or one 9-inch (2.5 L) springform pan.

2. **MAKE THE SHORTBREAD CRUST** In a stand mixer fitted with the paddle attachment, beat the butter and sugar on medium speed until soft and fluffy, about 3 minutes. Add the flour and salt. Beat until combined and a soft, crumbly dough forms. Press the mixture into the bottom of the prepared pan(s). Refrigerate until chilled, about 10 minutes. Bake for 12 minutes, until firm and golden.

3. **MAKE THE RICOTTA FILLING** In a stand mixer fitted with the paddle attachment, beat the ricotta, sugar, half and half, flour, lemon zest and juice, and salt on medium speed until smooth, about 2 minutes. Add the eggs and beat on low speed until combined.

4. Transfer the filling to the pan(s) with the crust. If baking a 9-inch (23 cm) cheesecake, bake for 50 minutes, until the centre is just set. If baking 4-inch (10 cm) cheesecakes, bake for 35 minutes, until the centre of each cake is just set. Let cool for 15 minutes. Leave the oven on.

5. **MAKE THE SOUR CREAM GLAZE** In a stand mixer fitted with the paddle attachment, beat the sour cream, sugar, and vanilla until smooth. Spoon and spread the filling overtop the cheesecake(s), leaving a ½-inch (1 cm) border around the edge. Bake for an additional 10 minutes. Remove the cheesecake(s) from the oven. Run a knife around the edge of the pan(s) to loosen the sides of the cake(s). Let cool for 60 minutes. Cover the cake(s) with plastic wrap and transfer to the fridge to chill for at least 3 hours or overnight.

SHORTBREAD CRUST

½ cup (125 mL) unsalted butter, softened

¼ cup (60 mL) granulated sugar

1 cup (250 mL) all-purpose flour

½ teaspoon (2 mL) kosher salt

RICOTTA FILLING

2 pounds (900 g) full-fat ricotta cheese

¾ cup (175 mL) granulated sugar

½ cup (125 mL) half and half (10%) cream

2 tablespoons (30 mL) all-purpose flour

1 teaspoon (5 mL) finely grated fresh lemon zest

1 tablespoon (15 mL) fresh lemon juice

¼ teaspoon (1 mL) kosher salt

2 large eggs, room temperature, lightly beaten

SOUR CREAM GLAZE

¾ cup (175 mL) full-fat sour cream

2 tablespoons (30 mL) granulated sugar

1 teaspoon (5 mL) pure vanilla extract

recipe continues

STEWED STRAWBERRIES

2¾ cups (675 g) fresh strawberries, washed, hulled, and cut into quarters

2 tablespoons (30 mL) granulated sugar

¼ cup (60 mL) toasted pistachios, chopped

Fresh mint leaves, for garnish

6. **MAKE THE STEWED STRAWBERRIES** In a small saucepan, add the strawberries and sugar and stir to coat. Cook over medium heat, stirring occasionally to prevent scorching. Within 4 to 5 minutes, the berries will start to release their juices. Once this happens, continue cooking for another 6 to 8 minutes, until the strawberry juice has thickened and is bubbling. Let cool. Store in an airtight container in the fridge for up to 1 week.

7. To serve, spoon the stewed strawberries over the cheesecake(s). Sprinkle with the chopped pistachios and freshly picked mint leaves, if desired.

8. Store leftover cheesecake, with or without toppings, in an airtight container in the fridge for up to 1 week.

KITCHEN TIP

• Stewed strawberries are also great spooned over pancakes or ice cream.

FALL

TURKEY AND HERB THANKSGIVING CROISSANTS

This recipe is an ingenious way to use up turkey leftovers to create yummy lunches and is a nice change from boring leftover turkey sandwiches. Here, turkey and cranberry sauce are rolled up into buttery, herby croissants. Dip them in warm gravy if you have some of that leftover, too! **MAKES 18 CROISSANTS**

1. **MAKE THE CRANBERRY SAUCE** In a small saucepan over low heat, cook the cranberries, sugar, and orange juice until the cranberries burst and the juices have thickened slightly, about 10 minutes. Remove from the heat and let cool completely. Cranberry sauce can be covered and stored in the fridge for up to 1 week.

2. **MAKE THE THANKSGIVING CROISSANTS** Follow steps 1 to 6 of the recipe for Plain Croissants, making sure to add the thyme, black pepper, and sage to the mixing bowl along with the flour.

3. Place a triangle in front of you so that the base of the triangle is near your left hand and the pointed end is near your right hand. Use one hand to hold the triangle down at the base end, about 2 inches (5 cm) from the edge, and use your other hand to very gently stretch out the point of the triangle to make it about 1 inch (2.5 cm) longer than it was to start. Rotate the triangle so that the base is closest to you and the pointed end is pointing away from you. Using a pastry brush, brush about 1 tablespoon (15 mL) of the cranberry sauce onto the triangle. Arrange about ¼ cup (60 mL) of the turkey meat at the base of the croissant. Starting at the base end, roll up the croissant. Place it on the prepared baking sheet with the tip of the triangle on the bottom to help seal it shut. Repeat with the remaining dough triangles. If baking immediately, cover the croissants loosely with plastic wrap and let proof in a warm spot for 30 to 40 minutes, until the croissants are puffy and jiggly when you gently tap the baking sheet. If baking at a later date, place the baking sheet in the freezer immediately after rolling the croissants. Once they are frozen, transfer them to a zip-top bag. Croissants can be stored in the freezer for up to 1 week. Simply thaw in the fridge overnight and proceed with the recipe after covering the croissants loosely with plastic wrap and letting them proof in a warm spot for 30 to 40 minutes.

CRANBERRY SAUCE

2 cups (500 mL) fresh or frozen cranberries

½ cup (125 mL) granulated sugar

½ cup (125 mL) orange juice

THANKSGIVING CROISSANTS

1 batch Plain Croissants (page 275, steps 1 to 6)

2 tablespoons (30 mL) chopped fresh thyme

½ teaspoon (2 mL) fresh cracked black pepper

1 teaspoon (5 mL) dried sage

4 cups (1 L) shredded roasted turkey meat

4 large egg yolks

½ cup (125 mL) heavy (35%) cream

Flaky sea salt (we use Maldon), for sprinkling

recipe continues

4. Preheat the oven to 375°F (190°C).

5. Prepare an egg wash. In a small bowl, whisk the egg yolks and cream. Using a pastry brush, gently brush each croissant with the egg wash, making sure to cover the whole surface in a thin layer. This will ensure a golden brown colour and a shiny top. Sprinkle each croissant with a pinch of sea salt. Bake for 15 to 18 minutes, or until the croissants turn a deep caramel brown.

6. Croissants are best served on the day they are made but can be stored in an airtight container at room temperature for up to 2 days.

ROASTED BUTTERNUT SQUASH QUICHE WITH SWISS CHARD AND CHEDDAR

Butternut squash and sage are quintessential fall flavours, but don't feel that you *must* use butternut squash to make this recipe. With the exception of spaghetti squash, any other fall squash will substitute easily; you can use your favourite and follow the same roasting instructions. We like this quiche with acorn, delicata, or pumpkin squash. By switching up the squash, you will change the flavour profile of this recipe a bit, and you might just land on a new favourite—have fun with it! **SERVES 6**

1. Preheat the oven to 375°F (190°C). Line a baking sheet with parchment paper.

2. On a lightly floured work surface, roll the Savoury Pie Dough into a 14-inch (35 cm) circle. Roll the dough around the rolling pin and unroll it over a 10-inch (25 cm) tart pan with a removable bottom. Gently press the dough into the bottom and sides of the pan and remove any excess dough with a paring knife. Transfer to the fridge to chill for at least 30 minutes.

3. Place the butternut squash on the prepared baking sheet and drizzle with 1 tablespoon (15 mL) of the canola oil. Sprinkle with 1 teaspoon (5 mL) of the salt and ¼ teaspoon (1 mL) of the pepper. Toss to coat the squash evenly, then spread it in a single layer. Place the garlic cloves on a piece of aluminum foil. Drizzle with ½ tablespoon (7 mL) of the canola oil and sprinkle with 1 teaspoon (5 mL) of the salt and the remaining ¼ teaspoon (1 mL) of pepper. Wrap up the garlic and place the foil packet on the baking sheet. Bake until the squash is soft and starting to brown, about 30 minutes. Remove the squash and garlic from the oven and reduce the temperature to 350°F (180°C).

4. In a medium skillet over medium heat, add ¼ cup (60 mL) of the canola oil. Add the onions and chard. Cook until the onion is soft and translucent, about 5 minutes. Let cool.

5. In a large bowl, whisk the eggs, sour cream, milk, flour, and the remaining 1 teaspoon (5 mL) of salt.

½ batch Savory Pie Dough (page 271)

2 cups (500 mL) butternut squash, peeled, seeded, and cut into ¼-inch (5 mm) cubes

1½ tablespoons (22 mL) + ½ cup (125 mL) canola oil, divided

1 tablespoon (15 mL) kosher salt, divided

½ teaspoon (2 mL) black pepper, divided

6 cloves garlic, peeled

½ medium yellow onion, chopped

1 cup (250 mL) finely chopped Swiss chard leaves

4 large eggs

½ cup (125 mL) full-fat sour cream

½ cup (125 mL) whole (3.25%) milk

1 tablespoon (15 mL) all-purpose flour

1 cup (250 mL) shredded old cheddar cheese, divided

8 leaves fresh sage

recipe continues

6.   Arrange the squash, onion, chard, whole roasted garlic, and ¾ cup (175 mL) of the cheddar in the bottom of the tart pan. Pour the egg mixture on top, then sprinkle the remaining ¼ cup (60 mL) of cheese overtop. Bake for 40 minutes, until the filling is just set and jiggles only slightly in the middle when you move the pan. Let cool for at least 15 minutes before serving.

7.   Line a small plate with paper towels. In a small skillet over medium heat, heat the remaining ¼ cup (60 mL) of vegetable oil. Add the sage leaves and fry until crisp, about 2 to 3 seconds. Using a fork, transfer the sage to the lined plate to drain.

8.   Top the quiche with the fried sage. Serve warm or at room temperature.

9.   Store any leftovers in an airtight container in the fridge for up to 2 days. Before serving leftovers, reheat in a 350°F (180°C) oven for 10 minutes.

PUMPKIN PUDDING JARS

Pumpkin pudding is basically a "no-crust" pumpkin pie—which also means it's gluten-free. Here, we make up for the lack of crust by garnishing the pudding with a salty-sweet pumpkin seed brittle. When buying pumpkin purée, make sure to purchase pure pumpkin purée and not pumpkin pie filling. You might think it would be best to roast your own pumpkin and make the purée yourself, but this recipe requires a particular amount of moisture to ensure that the pudding sets, and roasting your own pumpkin may yield inconsistent results. Use a canned purée to ensure success. If you have time, try making this pudding on the day before you plan to serve it. Giving it additional time to set will improve the flavour of the spices and the consistency of the pudding. **SERVES 8**

1. Line a baking sheet with parchment paper.

2. **MAKE THE PUMPKIN SEED BRITTLE** In a medium saucepan over high heat, combine the sugar, water, corn syrup, and butter. Bring to a boil and let cook over high heat, without stirring. After about 10 minutes, the mixture should start to turn a light amber colour. You'll know the mixture is ready to come off the heat when it turns almost reddish in colour, around the 20-minute mark. Stir to ensure consistent colour. Remove the saucepan from the heat and use a heatproof spatula to stir in the salt, pumpkin seeds, and baking soda. Working quickly to ensure that the sugar does not start to set, use the spatula to spread the mixture onto the prepared baking sheet—the mixture will be very hot, so be careful! Let cool to room temperature. Break into 2-inch (5 cm) pieces. Store in an airtight container at room temperature for up to 2 weeks. The brittle is a delicious snacking food all on its own.

3. **MAKE THE PUMPKIN PUDDING** In a medium saucepan, whisk 3 cups (750 mL) of the milk, the pumpkin purée, cinnamon, ginger, allspice, and cloves. Place the saucepan over medium heat and bring to a simmer.

4. While the milk mixture is heating, in a medium bowl, whisk the sugar, cornstarch, and salt. Whisk in the egg yolks and the remaining 1 cup (250 mL) of milk.

PUMPKIN SEED BRITTLE

2 cups (500 mL) granulated sugar
½ cup (125 mL) water
¼ cup (60 mL) corn syrup
¼ cup (60 mL) unsalted butter
1½ tablespoons (7 mL) kosher salt
1½ cups (375 mL) dry roasted
  pumpkin seeds
½ teaspoon (2 mL) baking soda

PUMPKIN PUDDING

4 cups (1 L) whole (3.25%) milk,
  divided
1½ cups (375 mL) pure pumpkin
  purée
1 teaspoon (5 mL) ground cinnamon
½ teaspoon (2 mL) ground ginger
¼ teaspoon (1 mL) ground allspice
¼ teaspoon (1 mL) ground cloves
1¼ cup (300 mL) granulated sugar
⅓ cup (75 mL) cornstarch
1 teaspoon (5 mL) kosher salt
5 large egg yolks
2 tablespoons (30 mL) unsalted butter
1 teaspoon (5 mL) pure vanilla extract

recipe continues

5. Once the milk mixture has reached a simmer, slowly whisk half of it into the egg mixture, until smooth. Pour everything back into the saucepan. Cook over medium heat, stirring constantly, until the mixture comes to a boil. Immediately remove the saucepan from the heat. Stir in the butter and vanilla, until the butter is melted and the mixture is well combined.

6. Divide the pudding among eight 8-ounce (250 mL) jars. Cover the jars with plastic wrap and transfer to the fridge to chill for at least 3 hours or overnight. Garnish each pudding with pumpkin seed brittle before serving.

7. Store leftover pudding, covered tightly with plastic wrap, in the fridge for up to 3 days.

KITCHEN TIP

- If you want to switch up the garnish, try substituting an equal amount of your favourite nut (we love peanuts or pecans!) for the pumpkin seeds in the recipe for the Pumpkin Seed Brittle.

ACORN SQUASH CHEESECAKE WITH ALMOND SABLÉ COOKIE CRUST AND CANDIED PECANS

In this recipe, we use acorn squash as a nice change from the regular pumpkin. It creates a soft purée because it roasts so easily, and it pairs perfectly with warm fall spices in this cheesecake. For the crust, we use our Toasted Almond Sablé Cookies (page 31), and the candied pecan garnish has a thick, gooey sauce that will leave you wanting more. **MAKES ONE 9-INCH (23 CM) CHEESECAKE**

1. **MAKE THE ALMOND SABLÉ COOKIE CRUST** Pulse the Toasted Almond Sablé Cookies in a food processor to create fine crumbs. In a medium bowl, combine the cookie crumbs, brown sugar, cinnamon, and salt. Add the butter and stir with a wooden spoon until the butter is fully incorporated.

2. **MAKE THE CREAM CHEESE FILLING** Preheat the oven to 475°F (240°C). Line a baking sheet with parchment paper.

3. Wrap each squash half loosely in aluminum foil and place them, cut side up, on the prepared baking sheet. Roast for 40 to 50 minutes, until the flesh can be easily pierced with a fork. Let cool. Reduce the oven temperature to 350°F (180°C). Once the squash is cool enough to handle, remove the skin and discard. Place the squash in a small bowl and mash with a fork.

4. In a stand mixer fitted with the paddle attachment, beat the cream cheese, sugar, cinnamon, ginger, and cardamom on medium speed until well combined. Add the eggs one at a time, mixing until combined. Add 1⅔ cups (400 mL) of the mashed squash, the flour, and sour cream and mix until smooth.

5. Lightly grease the sides of a 9-inch (2.5 L) springform pan. Firmly and evenly press the crust into the bottom of the pan. Pour the filling over the crust. Bake for 30 to 35 minutes, until the edges are firm and the centre jiggles only slightly when you move the pan. Let cool for 10 minutes. Cover the cheesecake in plastic wrap and transfer to the fridge to chill for at least 6 hours or overnight.

ALMOND SABLÉ COOKIE CRUST

2 cups (500 mL) Toasted Almond Sablé Cookies (page 31)

½ cup (125 mL) lightly packed brown sugar

1 teaspoon (5 mL) ground cinnamon

1 teaspoon (5 mL) kosher salt

½ cup (125 mL) unsalted butter, melted

CREAM CHEESE FILLING

2 acorn squashes, halved and seeds scraped

1⅔ cups (400 mL) plain cream cheese

1⅓ cups (325 mL) granulated sugar

1 teaspoon (5 mL) ground cinnamon

1 teaspoon (5 mL) ground ginger

½ teaspoon (2 mL) ground cardamom

3 large eggs

2 tablespoons (30 mL) all-purpose flour

1 cup (250 mL) full-fat sour cream

recipe continues

CANDIED PECANS

4 tablespoons (60 mL) unsalted
  butter
½ cup (125 mL) lightly packed brown
  sugar
½ teaspoon (2 mL) ground cinnamon
¼ cup (60 mL) heavy (35%) cream
1¾ cups (425 mL) pecan halves
½ teaspoon (2 mL) kosher salt

6. **MAKE THE CANDIED PECANS** In a non-stick skillet over low heat, melt the butter. Stir in the brown sugar. Cook over low heat until bubbly, about 5 minutes. Add the cinnamon, cream, pecans, and salt. Stir until evenly coated. Remove the skillet from the heat and let cool to room temperature. Keep the pecans at room temperature until ready to serve.

7. Spoon the candied pecans over the chilled cheesecake. Cut it into slices and divide it among plates.

8. Store leftover cheesecake, with the topping, in an airtight container in the fridge for up to 4 days.

WINTER

DOUBLE BAKED ALMOND CROISSANTS

This is an excellent way to use up day-old Plain Croissants (page 275), and after you bake them with almond cream, no one will suspect they aren't at peak freshness. **MAKES 4 CROISSANTS**

1. Preheat the oven to 350°F (180°C). Line a baking sheet with parchment paper.

2. **MAKE THE ALMOND CREAM** Add the flour, sugar, butter, and salt to a stand mixer fitted with the paddle attachment. Beat on medium speed until well combined, about 2 minutes. Add the eggs and almond extract. Beat for 1 minute, until combined. Cover the almond cream with plastic wrap and place it in the fridge to chill.

3. Cut the croissants in half, as if making a sandwich, and arrange them on the prepared baking sheet, cut sides up. As much as possible, keep the two halves of the same croissant together. Bake for 20 minutes, or until the croissants are a deep golden brown. The browner the croissants are, the more simple syrup they will soak up. Remove the croissants from the oven but leave the oven on.

4. **MAKE THE VANILLA SIMPLE SYRUP** In a small saucepan, combine the sugar, water, and vanilla. Bring to a boil, stir, and reduce the heat to low for 2 to 3 minutes, until the sugar is dissolved. Remove from the heat and let cool slightly. Transfer the syrup to a wide, shallow bowl.

5. Dunk a croissant half in the simple syrup, cut side down, and hold it there for a few seconds. Return it to the baking sheet, cut side up. Repeat with the remaining croissant halves. Spoon the almond cream into a pastry bag and cut off the tip. Pipe a zigzag of cream on the bottom half of each croissant. Top with the matching croissant top. Pipe another zigzag of almond cream on top of each croissant. Sprinkle each with about 2 tablespoons (30 mL) of the sliced raw almonds.

6. Bake for 15 to 20 minutes, until the almonds are golden brown. Let cool slightly. Dust with icing sugar before serving. These croissants, already being leftovers, should be enjoyed on the day they are made and do not keep well overnight.

ALMOND CREAM

1 cup (250 mL) almond flour
½ cup (125 mL) granulated sugar
7 tablespoons (105 mL) unsalted butter, softened
½ teaspoon (2 mL) kosher salt
2 large eggs, room temperature
⅛ teaspoon (0.5 mL) pure almond extract

VANILLA SIMPLE SYRUP

½ cup (125 mL) granulated sugar
½ cup (125 mL) water
½ vanilla bean, split and seeds scraped

4 day-old Plain Croissants (page 275)
½ cup (125 mL) sliced raw almonds
Icing sugar, for dusting

BEET AND FETA QUICHE

Beets are an amazing winter vegetable. They're hearty, they keep well through the long winter months, and they offer a welcome blast of colour when the weather outside feels endlessly grey. Featuring both red and yellow beets, this tart might even be bright enough to convince you it's the middle of summer while you're eating it. **SERVES 6**

2 medium yellow beets

2 medium red beets

½ batch Savoury Pie Dough (page 271)

1½ cups (375 mL) crumbled feta cheese, divided

1 cup (250 mL) heavy (35%) cream

½ cup (125 mL) whole (3.25%) milk

2 large eggs

2 tablespoons (30 mL) chopped fresh thyme

1 teaspoon (5 mL) kosher salt

½ teaspoon (2 mL) ground cumin

¼ teaspoon (1 mL) fresh cracked black pepper

Microgreens, for garnish (optional)

1. Preheat the oven to 400°F (200°C).

2. Wrap each beet in aluminum foil and place them directly on the rack in the oven. Bake for 75 minutes, or until the beets are tender when pierced with a knife. Let cool to room temperature. Using a clean kitchen rag, rub the skins off the beets and discard. Cut the beets into ¼-inch (5 mm) slices and set aside. Reduce the oven temperature to 350°F (180°C).

3. On a lightly floured work surface, roll the Savoury Pie Dough into a 14-inch (35 cm) circle. Roll the dough around the rolling pin and unroll it over a 9-inch (23 cm) tart pan with a removable bottom. Gently press the dough into the bottom and sides of the pan and remove any excess dough with a paring knife. Transfer to the fridge to chill for at least 30 minutes.

4. In a medium bowl, combine 1 cup (250 mL) of the feta, the cream, milk, eggs, thyme, salt, cumin, and pepper.

5. Arrange the beets in a ring in the bottom of the tart pan so that one beet overlaps the next by about half and the colours alternate. Pour the egg mixture on top. Sprinkle the remaining ½ cup (125 mL) of feta overtop. Bake for 45 minutes, or until the filling is set and jiggles only slightly when you move the pan. Let stand for 10 minutes before serving. Garnish with microgreens, if desired.

6. Store any leftovers in an airtight container in the fridge for up to 2 days. Before serving leftovers, reheat in a 350°F (180°C) oven for 10 minutes.

CHOCOLATE MOCHA PUDDING

Chocolate and coffee are two flavours that go together so well because they often mimic each other. Chocolate, especially dark chocolate, can have coffee undertones, and coffee often has notes of chocolate. This is flavour-pairing excellence! Top this pudding with some Chantilly Cream (page 281) and you'll have a twist on a café mocha for dessert. The recipe is also inherently gluten-free, so keep it handy for when you want to accommodate dietary restrictions. **SERVES 6 TO 8**

1. In a 4-cup (1 L) liquid measuring cup, combine the milk and espresso powder. Stir until the espresso is dissolved.

2. In a medium saucepan, whisk the sugar, cocoa powder, cornstarch, and salt. Slowly add the espresso milk, about 1 cup (250 mL) at a time, whisking vigorously after each addition until all of the espresso milk has been added and the mixture is perfectly smooth.

3. Place the saucepan with the pudding mixture over medium heat and bring to a boil. Cook, stirring continuously, until the mixture starts to thicken, about 10 minutes. Remove from the heat and immediately stir in the chocolate and butter. Continue stirring until the chocolate and butter are melted and fully incorporated.

4. Transfer to a large bowl and cover, placing plastic wrap directly on the surface of the pudding to prevent a skin forming. Chill in the fridge for at least 6 hours.

5. Serve the pudding family-style or divide it among individual serving bowls. Finish with a dollop of Chantilly Cream, if desired, and some chocolate-covered espresso beans.

6. Store leftover pudding, without the toppings, in an airtight container in the fridge for up to 5 days.

3 cups (750 mL) whole (3.25%) milk

4 teaspoons (20 mL) instant espresso powder

½ cup (125 mL) granulated sugar

¼ cup (60 mL) cocoa powder

¼ cup (60 mL) cornstarch

1 teaspoon (5 mL) kosher salt

1 cup (250 mL) chopped good-quality dark chocolate

2 tablespoons (30 mL) unsalted butter, softened

1 batch Chantilly Cream (page 281) (optional)

Chocolate-covered espresso beans, for garnish

CHOCOLATE AND VANILLA BRÛLÉE CHEESECAKE

Why have chocolate *or* vanilla cheesecake when you can have both? This two-toned stunner offers the best of both cheesecake worlds. The crust is made from the Chocolate Cookie Wafers used in our Chocolate Peppermint Sandwich (page 35). A small kitchen torch can be used for more than just crème brûlée. Try using yours to brûlée the top of this cheesecake before you serve it. The satisfying *crack* when your fork goes through the top is unmatched. **MAKES ONE 8-INCH (20 CM) CHEESECAKE**

1. Preheat the oven to 300°F (150°C). Lightly grease an 8-inch (2 L) springform pan.

2. **MAKE THE CHOCOLATE COOKIE CRUST** Pulse the Chocolate Cookie Wafers in a food processor until they turn to fine crumbs. Place the crumbs, sugar, and butter in a small bowl and stir to combine. Press the crust into the bottom of the prepared pan and up the sides to reach the rim. Use the bottom of a measuring cup to keep the inside edge nice and square. Transfer to the fridge to chill for 30 minutes, until firm.

3. **MAKE THE CREAM CHEESE FILLING** Place the cream cheese, ricotta, and 1 cup (250 mL) of the sugar in the bowl of a food processor. Process for 2 to 3 minutes, until smooth. Scrape down the sides of the bowl. Add the eggs and 1 teaspoon (5 mL) of the vanilla and process until smooth. Transfer two-thirds of the mixture to a medium bowl and set aside. Add the melted chocolate to the remaining mixture in the food processor and process until well combined. Pour the chocolate filling over the chilled cookie crust.

4. In a small bowl, combine the remaining 1 teaspoon (5 mL) of vanilla and the cornstarch. Add the mixture to the reserved filling and stir with a spatula until combined. Gently spoon the vanilla filling over the chocolate filling in the pan. Use the back of a spoon to smooth it into an even layer.

5. Bake for about 55 minutes, until the edges are set and the centre jiggles only slightly when you move the pan. Turn off the oven. Let the cheesecake rest inside the hot oven, with the door closed, for 20 minutes to set completely. Remove from the oven

CHOCOLATE COOKIE CRUST

14 ounces (400 g) Chocolate Cookie Wafers (page 35)

6 tablespoons (90 mL) granulated sugar

¾ cup (175 mL) unsalted butter, melted

CREAM CHEESE FILLING

2 cups (500 mL) plain cream cheese, softened

12 ounces (340 g) full-fat ricotta cheese

1 cup (250 mL) + 3 tablespoons (45 mL) granulated sugar, divided

4 large eggs

2 teaspoons (10 mL) pure vanilla extract, divided

7 ounces (200 g) good quality semisweet chocolate, melted

2 teaspoons (10 mL) cornstarch

recipe continues

and let stand at room temperature for 30 minutes. Cover the cheesecake in plastic wrap and transfer to the fridge to chill for at least 3 hours.

6. To brûlée the top of the cheesecake, evenly sprinkle the remaining 3 tablespoons (45 mL) of sugar overtop. Just before serving, use a small kitchen torch to scorch the sugar, making sure to brown all of it so that no patches of granulated sugar remain.

7. Store leftover cheesecake in an airtight container in the fridge for up to 3 days.

KITCHEN TIP

• It is best to brûlée the cheesecake right before serving because the brûléed sugar will soften the longer it sits, and you will not get the characteristic brûlée *crack* when you cut into it with your fork.

STAPLES

SWEET PIE DOUGH

We use this recipe in a number of different ways in this book. It goes against everything we learned as pastry chefs—never overmix and keep everything cold or you will not have a flaky dough. This dough is light, flaky, and delicious, and you cannot overmix it. **MAKES TWO 10-INCH (25 CM) SHELLS**

2 cups (500 mL) all-purpose flour
1 tablespoon (15 mL) granulated sugar
1 teaspoon (5 mL) kosher salt
1 cup (250 mL) vegetable shortening
⅓ cup (75 mL) cold water

1. In a stand mixer fitted with the paddle attachment, combine the flour, sugar, and salt. With the mixer on low speed, add the shortening 1 tablespoon (15 mL) at a time, until all of the shortening has been added and the mixture is crumbly. Add the water and continue mixing on low speed until the dough comes together and is smooth, almost like a paste.

2. Transfer the dough to a lightly floured work surface. Lightly knead the dough, about 1 minute, until it pulls away from the floured surface. Divide the dough into 2 equal portions. Shape the dough into 2 discs and wrap each tightly in plastic wrap. If making a half batch of dough, shape the dough into a single disc and wrap tightly in plastic wrap. Place the dough in the fridge to chill for at least 1 hour.

3. Store in the fridge for up to 1 week or in the freezer for up to 3 weeks. If using from frozen, thaw the dough in the fridge overnight before using it.

SAVOURY PIE DOUGH

Our savoury pie dough is another one of our cooking hacks. By eliminating sugar and adding a small amount of black pepper, you get an equally flaky, delightful pie crust that pairs better with savoury pies.

MAKES TWO 10-INCH (25 CM) SHELLS

2 cups (500 mL) all-purpose flour

1 teaspoon (5 mL) fresh cracked black pepper

1 teaspoon (5 mL) kosher salt

1 cup (250 mL) vegetable shortening

⅓ cup (75 mL) cold water

1. In a stand mixer fitted with the paddle attachment, combine the flour, pepper, and salt. With the mixer on low speed, add the shortening 1 tablespoon (15 mL) at a time, until all of the shortening has been added and the mixture is crumbly. Add the water and continue mixing on low speed until the dough comes together and is smooth, almost like a paste.

2. Transfer the dough to a lightly floured work surface. Lightly knead the dough, about 1 minute, until it pulls away from the floured surface. Divide it into 2 equal portions. Shape the dough into 2 discs and wrap each tightly in plastic wrap. If making a half batch of dough, shape the dough into a single disc and wrap tightly in plastic wrap. Place the dough in the fridge to chill for at least 1 hour.

3. Store in the fridge for up to 1 week or in the freezer for up to 3 weeks. If using from frozen, thaw the dough in the fridge overnight before using it.

BLITZ PUFF PASTRY

We know that convenience is king—and it is super easy to purchase puff pastry—but if you have the time and patience, this recipe is not too difficult and the result is so much better than anything you can buy at the store. Making puff pastry requires you to "turn" the dough. Turning is a process of folding the butter and flour to produce the many layers that ultimately laminate the dough and create this pastry's characteristic puff. This technique does take some time, but we promise that it's not very challenging! **MAKES 3 POUNDS (1.4 KG)**

4 cups (1 L) all-purpose flour
2 teaspoons (10 mL) kosher salt
1 pound (450 g) cold unsalted butter, cut into 1-inch (2.5 cm) cubes
2 cups (500 mL) heavy (35%) cream

1. In a stand mixer fitted with the paddle attachment, mix the flour and salt on low speed to combine. Add the butter a few cubes at a time, until all of the cubes are combined but still look roughly like cubes. Turn off the mixer. You will be working this dough quite a bit, so you don't want to overmix it at this point. Add the cream. Mix on the lowest speed just until the flour is moistened but the mixture is still very shaggy.

2. Turn the dough out onto a clean work surface. At this point, it may be a bit difficult to work with, but it gets easier with every turn of the dough. This recipe requires 6 single turns. A single turn consists of folding the dough in thirds. Using a rolling pin and your hands, as needed, shape the dough into a 6- × 18-inch (15 × 45 cm) rectangle. Use a ruler to make sure the measurements are accurate. Fold the dough into thirds, as you would a letter before placing it in an envelope: fold one of the short edges toward the middle and the opposite edge toward the middle to rest on top. Wrap the dough tightly in plastic wrap and write the number 1 on the plastic wrap to help you remember how many turns you've completed. Place the dough in the fridge to chill for 30 minutes. Repeat the process of rolling out and folding the dough 5 more times, making sure to add a number to the plastic wrap with each turn. Once you've completed 6 turns, the dough is ready.

3. Divide the dough into 3 equal portions. Each portion will be about 1 pound (450 g). Wrap each portion tightly in plastic wrap and store it in the fridge until ready to use, up to 1 week. The dough can also be stored in the freezer for up to 6 months when wrapped tightly in plastic or placed in a zip-top freezer bag. If using from frozen, thaw the dough in the fridge overnight before using it.

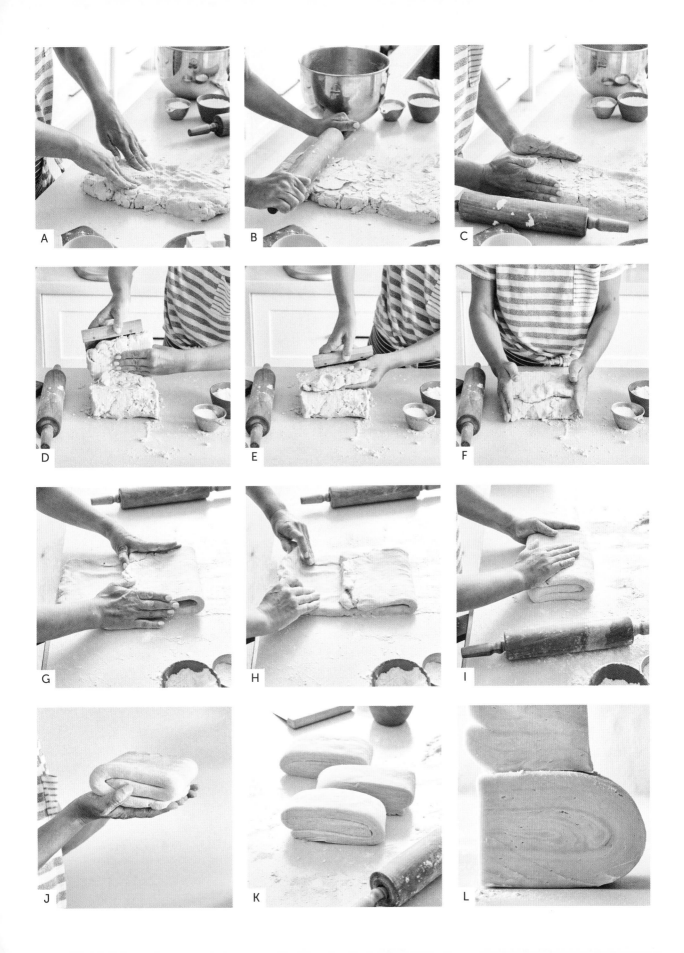

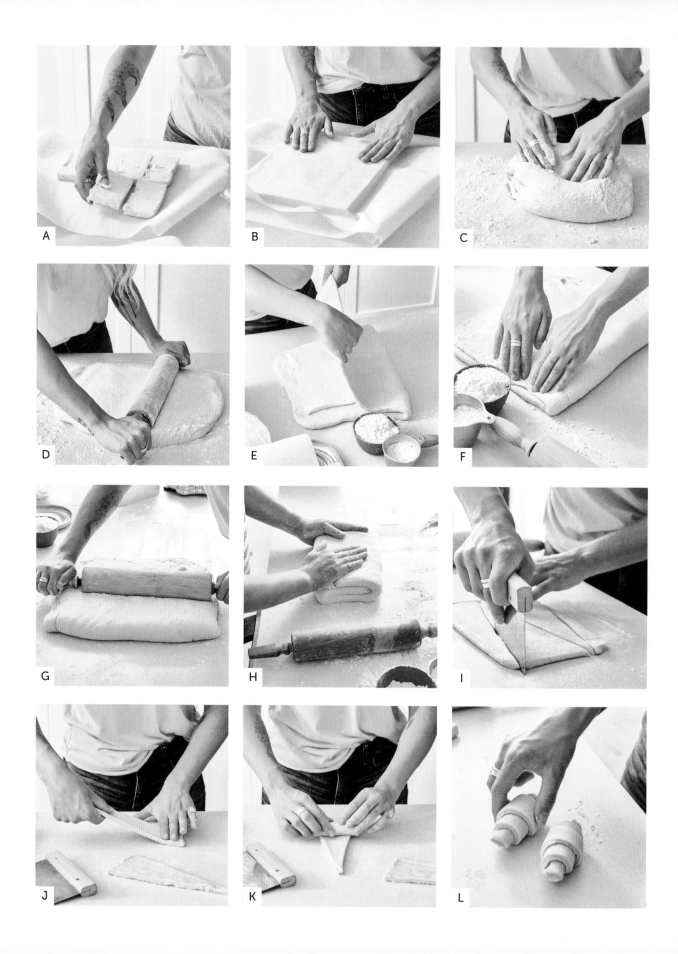

PLAIN CROISSANTS

The idea of making croissants can be intimidating, but they are well worth the time and effort. If you pay close attention to the method and follow our step-by-step photos, you'll wind up with a tray of perfectly buttery and flaky pastries for you and your family to savour. They key here is patience. Croissants do not like to be rushed, so take your time—you've got this! **MAKES ABOUT 18 CROISSANTS**

1. Line a baking sheet with parchment paper.

2. MAKE THE CROISSANT DOUGH In a stand mixer fitted with the dough hook, mix the flour, salt, yeast, sugar, honey, butter, milk, and water on low speed for 1 minute. Increase the speed to medium and mix for 3 minutes, until combined.

3. Tip the dough out onto a clean work surface. Using a rolling pin and your hands, as needed, shape the dough into a 6- × 10-inch (15 × 25 cm) rectangle. Transfer the dough to the prepared baking sheet. Chill in the fridge for 1 hour.

4. PREPARE THE ROLL-IN BUTTER Cut the butter lengthwise into 4 equal portions and arrange them next to each other (make sure they are touching) on a piece of parchment paper to create a rectangle. Sprinkle the butter with 1 tablespoon (15 mL) of the flour and place another piece of parchment paper on top. The butter should be sandwiched between 2 pieces of parchment paper. Flip the sandwich over. Remove the piece of parchment paper on top, but do not discard it. Sprinkle the butter evenly with 1 tablespoon (15 mL) of the flour. Using a rolling pin, pound the butter until it is pliable but not soft. Place the parchment paper back on top and flip everything over, pounding the butter with the pin on the other side until the butter forms a 6- × 10-inch (15 × 25 cm) rectangle. Wrap the butter in plastic wrap and keep at room temperature, about 70°F (21°C). You want the croissant dough and the roll-in butter to have the same pliability.

5. LAMINATE THE DOUGH Remove the dough from the fridge, place it on a lightly floured work surface, and roll it into a 12- × 20-inch (30 × 50 cm) rectangle. Place the roll-in butter on half of the dough, leaving about a ½-inch (1 cm) border of dough

CROISSANT DOUGH

6 cups (1.5 L) + 2 tablespoons (30 mL) bread flour

8 teaspoons (40 mL) kosher salt

2 tablespoons (30 mL) instant yeast

3 tablespoons (45 mL) granulated sugar

2 teaspoons (10 mL) pure liquid honey

3½ tablespoons (52 mL) unsalted butter, room temperature

⅔ cup (150 mL) + 1 tablespoon (15 mL) whole (3.25%) milk

1⅓ cups (325 mL) cold water

ROLL-IN BUTTER

1 pound (450 g) cold unsalted butter

2 tablespoons (30 mL) bread flour, divided

EGG WASH

4 large egg yolks

½ cup (125 mL) heavy (35%) cream

recipe continues

around the edges. Fold the other half of the dough over the butter and pinch gently around the edges to seal it. Roll the whole thing out into an 8- × 12-inch (20 × 30 cm) rectangle. Fold the dough in thirds as you would a letter before placing it in an envelope: fold one of the short edges toward the middle and the opposite edge toward the middle to rest on top. This is a single fold. Cover tightly with plastic wrap and chill in the fridge for 20 minutes. Repeat 2 more times, chilling for 20 minutes after each fold and rotating the dough 90 degrees so that the layered ends of the previous fold become the short ends of the new rectangle.

6.   On a well-floured work surface, roll the dough into a 9- × 20-inch (23 × 50 cm) rectangle, about ¼-inch (5 mm) thick. Gently lift the dough to make sure it is not stuck to the surface and to encourage it to shrink if it needs to. If you notice considerable shrinkage, let it rest for 1 to 2 minutes, then gently roll it out again. Repeat until the rectangle is the right size. Using a sharp knife, cut the dough into isosceles triangles that are 9 inches (23 cm) from the tip of the triangle to the base and 4 inches (10 cm) wide at the base.

7.   Place a triangle in front of you so that the base of the triangle is near your left hand and the pointed end is near your right hand. Use one hand to hold the triangle down at the base end, about 2 inches (5 cm) from the edge, and use your other hand to very gently stretch out the point of the triangle to make it about 1 inch (2.5 cm) longer than it was to start. Rotate the triangle so that the base is closest to you and the pointed end is pointing away from you. Starting at the base end, roll up the croissant. Place it on the prepared baking sheet with the tip of the triangle on the bottom to help seal it shut. Repeat with the remaining dough triangles. If baking immediately, cover the croissants loosely with plastic wrap and let proof in a warm spot for 30 to 40 minutes, until the croissants are puffy and jiggly when you gently tap the baking sheet. If baking at a later date, place the baking sheet in the freezer immediately after rolling the croissants. Once they are frozen, transfer them to a zip-top bag.

Croissants can be stored in the freezer for up to 1 week. Simply thaw them in the fridge overnight and proceed with the recipe after covering the croissants loosely with plastic wrap and letting them proof in a warm spot for 30 to 40 minutes.

8.   Preheat the oven to 375°F (190°C).

9.   PREPARE THE EGG WASH In a small bowl, whisk the egg yolks and cream. Using a pastry brush, gently brush each croissant with the egg wash, making sure to cover the whole surface in a thin layer. This will ensure a golden brown colour and a shiny top.

10. Bake for 15 to 18 minutes, or until the croissants turn a deep caramel brown.

11. Croissants are best served on the day they are made but can be stored in an airtight container at room temperature for up to 3 days.

BRIOCHE

If you're eating it on its own, brioche is best consumed when it is still warm, right after baking, but some recipes in this book call for day-old brioche. So, plan ahead and make this brioche one or two days before you will need it. **MAKES 1 LOAF**

1 tablespoon (15 mL) instant yeast

3 tablespoons (45 mL) granulated sugar

2⅓ cups (575 mL) all-purpose flour

2 large eggs

1 large egg yolk

½ cup (125 mL) warm water

2 teaspoons (10 mL) kosher salt

1 cup (250 mL) unsalted butter, room temperature, cut into cubes

1. Lightly oil a 9- × 5-inch (2 L) loaf pan.

2. In a stand mixer fitted with the paddle attachment, combine the yeast, sugar, and flour.

3. In a medium bowl, gently whisk the eggs, egg yolk, water, and salt.

4. With the mixer on low speed, add the egg mixture to the flour mixture. Mix until well combined. Add the butter, one cube at a time, mixing until all of the butter is combined and the dough is smooth.

5. Transfer the dough (which will seem more like batter at this point) to the prepared loaf pan. Cover with a moist tea towel or loosely with plastic wrap and place on the counter. Let rise until the dough has doubled in size and the brioche slightly peaks over the sides of the loaf pan, up to 3 hours.

6. Preheat the oven to 360°F (185°C).

7. Bake for 50 to 60 minutes, until the top is dark golden brown. Let stand for about 10 minutes. Wrap tightly in plastic wrap and store in the fridge until needed. Brioche will keep in the fridge for up to 2 days or in the freezer for up to 3 months.

CREAM CHEESE FROSTING

It's not surprising that cream cheese frosting seems to have a cult following. It's sort of like spreadable cheesecake that you can slather onto a variety of desserts. In addition to providing a recipe for the classic, we also offer suggestions for flavouring your cream cheese frosting when you want to change it up a bit. **MAKES ABOUT 3 CUPS (750 ML)**

8 ounces (225 g) full-fat plain cream cheese, room temperature

½ cup (125 mL) unsalted butter, room temperature

3¼ cups (810 mL) icing sugar

1 teaspoon (5 mL) pure vanilla extract

¼ teaspoon (1 mL) kosher salt

1. In a stand mixer fitted with the paddle attachment, beat the cream cheese and butter on high speed until smooth and creamy. Add the icing sugar, vanilla, and salt. Beat on low speed until smooth and well combined. Increase the speed to high and beat for an additional 2 minutes.

2. Use immediately or store in an airtight container in the fridge for up to 5 days or in the freezer for up to 3 months. Thaw frozen frosting in the fridge and beat it in a stand mixer fitted with the paddle attachment for a few seconds before using.

KITCHEN TIPS

- Refrigerating cream cheese frosting before piping will help it hold its shape. However, cream cheese frosting is not as sturdy as buttercream, so be sure to complete any intricate piping details you want to add with Swiss Meringue Buttercream (page 280).
- Cream cheese frosting can be flavoured to suit its application. Try creating one of the following flavours by beating an additional ingredient into the cream cheese and butter.
  LEMON: Add 2 teaspoons (10 mL) fresh lemon juice.
  PUMPKIN SPICE: Add ½ teaspoon (2 mL) pumpkin spice blend.
  CARAMEL: Add 2 teaspoons (10 mL) Caramel Sauce (page 284) or Dulce de Leche (page 193)

SWISS MERINGUE BUTTERCREAM

This buttercream is silky smooth and not too sweet. It also keeps incredibly well in the fridge or freezer. **MAKES ABOUT 8 CUPS (2 L), ENOUGH TO FILL AND FROST AN 8-INCH (20 CM) CAKE**

16 large egg whites
2 cups (500 mL) granulated sugar
2 cups (500 mL) icing sugar
1 teaspoon (5 mL) kosher salt
1 teaspoon (5 mL) pure vanilla extract
6 cups (1.5 L) unsalted butter, softened

KITCHEN TIP

• To make a chocolate version of this buttercream, add ¼ cup (60 mL) cocoa powder alongside the icing sugar.

1. Place the egg whites and granulated sugar in the bowl of a stand mixer. Set the bowl over a small saucepan of simmering water over medium heat, making sure the bowl does not touch the water, to create a double boiler. Whisk until the sugar is dissolved and the mixture is well combined. Remove from the heat.

2. Fit the stand mixer with the whisk attachment and place the bowl on the stand. Whip the egg white and sugar mixture on high speed until stiff peaks form, about 4 minutes. Add the icing sugar and whip on low speed until fully incorporated. Add the salt and vanilla and whip on low speed until fully incorporated.

3. With the mixer on medium speed, drop the butter into the bowl 1 tablespoon (15 mL) at a time, allowing each tablespoon to be incorporated before adding the next. The buttercream may look split at this point, but it will come back together. Once you have added all of the butter, increase the speed to high and whip until very light and fluffy, about 8 to 10 minutes. To produce the fluffiest, silkiest buttercream, use a small kitchen torch to gently heat the outside of the mixer bowl while whisking.

4. To frost a cake or fill cookie sandwiches, use immediately. The softer and fluffier the buttercream, the easier it is to work with. However, you can make it ahead or store leftovers for later, if desired. Store buttercream in an airtight container in the fridge for up to 2 weeks or in the freezer for up to 6 months. If using from frozen, thaw the buttercream overnight at room temperature. In a stand mixer fitted with the whisk attachment, whip the buttercream on medium-high speed. It may split, but it will come back together. Gently heat the outside of the mixer bowl with a small kitchen torch to get soft, fluffy buttercream.

CHANTILLY CREAM

The difference between whipped cream and Chantilly cream is in the amount of sweetener used: Chantilly cream is sweeter than whipped cream. Here, we use icing sugar and vanilla as our sweeteners of choice. These additions may be subtle, but everything is in the details.

MAKES ABOUT 2 CUPS (500 ML), ENOUGH TO TOP ONE 9-INCH (23 CM) PIE

2 cups (500 mL) cold heavy (35%) cream
¼ cup (60 mL) icing sugar
1 teaspoon (5 mL) pure vanilla extract

1. Chill the bowl and whisk attachment of a stand mixer in the fridge for about 10 minutes.

2. Fit the bowl and whisk attachment to the stand mixer and whisk the cream, icing sugar, and vanilla until soft peaks form. Use immediately.

KITCHEN TIP

- The colder the cream, the better. Do not try to whip cream when it is at room temperature! You will end up with split cream and butter instead of fluffy whipped cream.

STABILIZED CHANTILLY CREAM

If Chantilly cream is added to a recipe as an ingredient, and not just as a topping, it is a good idea to add a little gelatin to stabilize the cream so that it does not turn back into a liquid.

MAKES ABOUT 2 CUPS (500 ML)

¼ cup (60 mL) cold water
1 tablespoon (15 mL) gelatin powder
2 cups (500 mL) cold heavy (35%) cream
¼ cup (60 mL) icing sugar
1 teaspoon (5 mL) pure vanilla extract

1. Chill the bowl and whisk attachment of a stand mixer in the fridge for about 10 minutes. Place the water in a small heatproof bowl and sprinkle the gelatin powder over the surface. Stir once. Let bloom for about 10 minutes.

2. Heat the gelatin in a microwave oven for 10 to 20 seconds to dissolve it. Let cool.

3. Fit the bowl and whisk attachment to the stand mixer. Whisk the cream on medium-high speed and pour in the dissolved gelatin. Add the icing sugar and vanilla. Continue whisking until stiff peaks form, about 4 minutes.

4. Use immediately or store in an airtight container in the fridge until ready to use, up to 2 days.

WHIPPED CLOTTED CREAM

Clotted cream is essentially baked cream. The result is an ultra-rich, slightly nutty spread for English Muffins (page 161), Crumpets (page 165), scones (pages 73, 74, 77, 78), or anything else you want to finish with this delicious topping. We promise, it will be the most decadent topping you have ever tasted. And it's so easy to make. This recipe requires only one ingredient, but you have to find the *right* ingredient. To make clotted cream, you need to use organic cream without any stabilizers or fillers. The only thing listed on the product label should be cream. Apart from that, you just need some time and a bit of patience. **MAKES 1½ CUPS (375 ML)**

2 cups (500 mL) organic heavy (35%) cream

1. Preheat the oven to 180°F (85°C).

2. Pour the cream into a 9-inch (2.5 L) square baking dish. Bake for 12 to 18 hours, until the cream develops a light brown crust and a thick cover.

3. Transfer the cream to the fridge to chill, uncovered, for 6 hours.

4. Carefully spoon off all of the solid cream, including the light brown crust—this is the clotted cream—and transfer it to a small bowl. Discard the rest. Place the clotted cream in the fridge to chill overnight.

5. Remove from the fridge and let stand on the counter to bring it to room temperature, or heat in a microwave oven for 10 seconds.

6. In a stand mixer fitted with the whisk attachment, whisk the clotted cream for 30 seconds or up to 1 minute.

7. Use immediately or store in an airtight container in the fridge for up to 2 weeks.

KITCHEN TIP

• Clotted cream has similar properties to butter: when it's cold, it's not spreadable. Warm clotted cream in a microwave oven for 10 seconds to make it spreadable once again.

HOMEMADE BUTTER

Making butter at home sounds like it should be terribly difficult, when in fact it is not. It only takes two ingredients, a stand mixer, and a fine-mesh sieve. The nice thing about making your own butter is that you get to control the amount of salt. If you find this recipe too salty, simply decrease or omit the salt. We don't suggest using homemade butter in baking. It's pretty tricky to get all of the moisture out to the same extent as commercial butter, but homemade butter is so much better than commercial for your spreading needs. **MAKES 1 CUP (250 ML)**

2 cups (500 mL) heavy (35%) cream
½ teaspoon (2 mL) kosher salt

1. In a stand mixer fitted with the whisk attachment, whisk the cream on high speed for 8 to 10 minutes, or until the cream splits into solids and a liquid. The butter will be yellow, and the liquid will be white.

2. Drain the mixture through a fine-mesh sieve. Discard the liquid. Rinse the solids thoroughly with cold water and squeeze out any remaining liquid.

3. Return the butter to the bowl of the stand mixer. Fit the mixer with the paddle attachment. Add the salt and mix on medium speed to combine.

4. Use immediately or store in an airtight container in the fridge for up to 2 weeks.

CARAMEL SAUCE

We serve this rich, creamy sauce with a few recipes in this book. It is also fun to use in the fall months as a dip for apples. The darker the colour, the richer the caramel flavour, so it is important to let it cook until it is a golden amber colour. Adding fresh lemon juice to the sugar at the beginning of the recipe will stop crystals from forming; this trick will save you from having to brush down the sides of the pan with water. **MAKES 2 CUPS (500 ML)**

2 cups (500 mL) granulated sugar
1½ cups (375 mL) water
1 teaspoon (5 mL) fresh lemon juice
1 cup (250 mL) heavy (35%) cream
¼ cup (60 mL) unsalted butter, cubed

1. In a medium saucepan over high heat, bring the sugar, water, and lemon juice to a rolling boil. Cook, without stirring, until the mixture turns a deep reddish brown, about 20 minutes. Remove from the heat.

2. Slowly and carefully stir in the cream and butter until combined. The mixture will bubble up quite a bit. Let cool completely before using, about 1 hour. The sauce will thicken as it cools, but 1 minute in a microwave oven on medium heat will make it pourable again.

3. Store in an airtight container in the fridge for up to 2 weeks.

CRUMBLE TOPPING

We refer to this recipe a lot throughout the book. We use it to top Peach Melba Crumble Squares (page 55), Peaches and Cream Pie (page 201), Lemon Olive Oil Crumble Cake (page 122), and Bourbon Peach Crumble Scones (page 74). It is so versatile and keeps very well. If you make a big batch and store it in the freezer, you can just pull it out whenever you need it. This recipe makes a little more than you will need for a full pie. If you have some leftover crumble, you can toast it on a baking sheet in a 350°F (180°C) oven for 10 minutes and sprinkle it over ice cream or yogurt. **MAKES 3 CUPS (750 ML)**

1 cup (250 mL) all-purpose flour
½ cup (125 mL) lightly packed brown sugar
½ teaspoon (2 mL) kosher salt
½ cup (125 mL) unsalted butter
¾ cup (175 mL) rolled oats

1. In a large bowl, whisk the flour, brown sugar, and salt. Add the butter. Use your hands to work the butter into the dry mixture until pea-size lumps form. Add the oats and use your hands to mix until clumps form.

2. Use immediately or store in an airtight container in the fridge for up to 1 week or in the freezer for up to 3 months.

RASPBERRY JAM

This is the easiest raspberry jam recipe you'll ever make. Bettina is extremely lucky to have a raspberry bush in her backyard, and although she's sure she doesn't cultivate it properly, she does get enough fresh, organic raspberries from it every year to make about 12 cups (3 L) of jam. Pectin isn't required to make this fruity spread. The only trick is to cook it to a precise temperature, so make sure you have a candy thermometer handy! **MAKES ABOUT 6 CUPS (1.5 L)**

12 cups (3 L) fresh or frozen
    raspberries
6 cups (1.5 L) granulated sugar
¼ cup (60 mL) fresh lemon juice

1. Sterilize the jars. For this recipe, we use 6 canning jars that each hold about 1 cup (250 mL) of jam, but you can use whatever size you like. To sterilize the jars, place them in a canner pot or a deep saucepan and cover with hot water. Bring the water to a boil over high heat and let boil for 15 minutes. Turn off the heat and let the jars stand in the hot water for 10 minutes.

2. Lay out a clean kitchen towel. Using tongs or a jar lifter, remove the jars and place them upside down on the towel. Bring the water back to a boil, then place the lids and bands in boiling water for 5 minutes to sterilize them as well.

3. To make the jam, combine all of the ingredients in a large heavy-bottomed saucepan over medium heat. Bring to a simmer, stirring frequently. Let simmer over medium heat until a candy thermometer reads 219°F (104°C). Remove from the heat.

4. Fill the jars with the jam, leaving ½ inch (1 cm) of headspace. Place the sterilized lids on the jars and screw on the sterilized bands until tight. Let cool to room temperature. The bubble on the lid of each jar will pop down when the jam is ready to refrigerate.

5. Store in the fridge for up to 6 months.

ACKNOWLEDGEMENTS

After writing a book, the authors' names appear on its cover, and they often get all of the glory. We both know that this book would not be possible without the help and support of many other people.

First, we want to thank our families. We dedicated this book to our parents, and they deserve all kinds of thanks, but a lot of other people helped out along the way.

Erin: Thank you to my brother and sister, Drew and Carolyn, for your constant support and for taking the time to meet up with me for a coffee or just a break. To my dogs, Cricket and Cairo, you were patient when book writing took precedence over dog walks.

Bettina: Thank you to my partner, Tom, for listening to me read the things I wasn't sure made sense out loud while writing this book. To my daughter, Eleanor, for your future understanding that when I said, "Sorry, sweetie, I have to get some work done," I was actually talking about this cookbook. To my dog, Bruce, when deadlines are close, dog walks get shorter; you may never understand why, but you were always easygoing. I also personally need to thank Erin. Erin has become my best friend, my sounding board, and my support, and I am so happy that she wanted to be a pastry chef sixteen years ago.

Thank you to those we work with at all three Bread Bar locations: in Hamilton on Locke St. and James St. and in Guelph. To Mike Spitzig, GM and Head Chef at Bread Bar Locke; Maria Guarnieri, GM at Bread Bar James; and Ben Regatlie, GM at Bread Bar Guelph. To Brendan Naven, Head Chef at Bread Bar James, and Cameron Bell, Head Chef at Bread Bar Guelph. You are all extremely talented and impressively dedicated and were extremely patient when we had to take time away to write or take care of the beautiful photography. Many thanks, also, to the three-women backbone of the baking department at Bread Bar James: Rosie Westrik, Malika Vododokhova, and Denise Frenette. If it were not for you, this book would not have been possible. You stepped up when Erin was away writing or working on the photography. You are all amazing bakers and pastry chefs, and we are so proud that you are a part of the Bread Bar team.

Perhaps the most enjoyable part of writing this cookbook for us was when we were in the photo studio. It gave us a chance to be creative outside the kitchen, and we were honoured to work with the most gifted photography team. Thank you to our food stylist, Claire Stubbs; our photographer, Maya Visnyei; and our prop stylist, Catherine Doherty. Thanks, also, to Maya's two lovely assistants, Jasmine deBoer and Rachel Cicoria. We had such an amazing time working with this mastermind team—each session was a breath of fresh air.

We also want to thank our Bread Bar business partners, Jeff Crump and Aaron Ciancone. Jeff, thank you for your determined vision, wicked guidance, and complete support. Aaron, thank you for your controlled leadership, grand concepts, and longtime friendship. Building the Bread Bar locations has been a complete joy, and we are so proud of what we have accomplished together. Thank you.

Also, to Andrea Magyar and Laura Dosky at Penguin Random House. As chefs, our words are always raw and unformed. If it were not for the talent of publishers and editors, the words in this book would read like a child wrote them. Thank you for turning our words into something we are very honoured to publish.

Finally, we feel it is important to note that we finished writing this book in June 2020—in the middle of an international pandemic, COVID-19. It has been a very interesting, and sometimes unsettling, time. We want to thank all of the front-line and essential workers, including those in health care, grocery stores, and restaurants. Restaurants had to pivot quickly to survive this pandemic, and many were not able to. That fills us with sadness, but hopefully those who did have to close will be able to return post pandemic. To those restaurants who did survive, congratulations! We will be in to dine soon!

INDEX